Electoral Practice and the Election Commission of India

This book offers an insight into the contribution of the Election Commission of India (EC) to the Indian democratic process through its regulatory role in conducting elections between 1990 and 2019. It elaborates upon the EC's interactions with pivotal state institutions – the parliament, the Supreme Court and political parties – to streamline democratic procedures during the aforementioned period. It demonstrates a comparison between important electoral procedures in India and those in other liberal democracies (Canada, the United States, the United Kingdom and South Africa, among others) to highlight the role of electoral institutions in democratisation. It also studies the sociopolitical situatedness of the EC as a body that moulds the political culture in India.

Manjari Katju is Professor of Political Science at the University of Hyderabad, where she teaches courses on Indian and comparative politics. She has researched and written on various facets of Hindu nationalism as well as state institutions in India. She has authored the books *Vishva Hindu Parishad and Indian Politics* (2003) and *Hinduising Democracy: The Vishva Hindu Parishad in Contemporary India* (2017). Her research writings can also be found in journals like the *Economic and Political Weekly, Studies in Indian Politics* and *Contemporary South Asia*.

Electoral Practice and the Election Commission of India

POLITICS, INSTITUTIONS AND DEMOCRACY

Manjari Katju

Shaftesbury Road, Cambridge CB2 8EA, United Kingdom

One Liberty Plaza, 20th Floor, New York, NY 10006, USA

477 Williamstown Road, Port Melbourne, VIC 3207, Australia

314–321, 3rd Floor, Plot 3, Splendor Forum, Jasola District Centre, New Delhi – 110025, India

103 Penang Road, #05–06/07, Visioncrest Commercial, Singapore 238467

Cambridge University Press is part of Cambridge University Press & Assessment, a department of the University of Cambridge.

We share the University's mission to contribute to society through the pursuit of education, learning and research at the highest international levels of excellence.

www.cambridge.org
Information on this title: www.cambridge.org/9781009346863

First published 2023

Printed in India by Avantika Printers Pvt. Ltd.

A catalogue record for this publication is available from the British Library

ISBN 978-1-009-34686-3 Hardback

Contents

Tables

Acknowledgements

The research on which this book is based began in 2005 for a paper, 'The Election Commission and Politics in India', presented at a conference titled 'Structure and Dynamics of Indian Politics', in January 2006, at my alma mater, the Department of Political Science, Maharaja Sayajirao University of Baroda. I am indebted to the department for inviting me to the conference, where the idea of further research on this theme germinated. This conference paper was followed by a few publications, which eventually led to this full-length book on the subject. The Senior Research Fellowship (2016–18) from the Indian Council for Social Science Research (ICSSR) provided me an opportunity to do further research on the Election Commission of India (EC) and its functioning. I am thankful to the ICSSR for this fellowship and, specially, to Upendra Chowdhary (former director, ICSSR, and currently professor at Aligarh Muslim University), who facilitated the official work associated with this fellowship. Thanks are also due to Dr S. M. Verma and Dr Geetanjali of the ICSSR for helping me with the necessary procedures. The fellowship led to this monograph.

I am deeply indebted to S. Y. Quraishi, Nasim Zaidi, V. S. Sampath and T. S. Krishnamurthy, former chief election commissioners (CECs), who made time to converse with me in person, over email or the phone and patiently answered my questions about the working of the EC. Former CEC J. M. Lyngdoh's *Chronicle of an Impossible Election* (2004), T. S. Krishnamurthy's *The Miracle of Democracy: India's Amazing Journey* (2008) and S. Y. Quraishi's *An Undocumented Wonder: The Making of the Great Indian Election* (2014) provided an educative and informative insider's view of the working, achievements and tribulations of the EC. I also want to thank Rajarshi Bhattacharya, a former deputy election commissioner, for being kind enough to talk to me about his experiences as part of the EC.

These interviews and writings improved my understanding of the functioning of the EC and also of the other state institutions of India. I am also grateful to Trilochan Sastry (founder member of the Association for Democratic Reforms and professor at the Indian Institute of Management, Bengaluru) and P. G. Bhat (an active member of civil society and keen observer of electoral procedures), who have worked for the realisation of voters' rights in India, for talking to me about different aspects of elections and electoral procedures in India.

I am indebted to the Nehru Memorial Museum and Library, New Delhi, and the Indira Gandhi Memorial Library, University of Hyderabad, for sources that make this book. I relied on reports in several newspapers and news magazines, which form one of the major sources of discussions and elaborations in the book. I want to acknowledge the reports and writings of the correspondents and commentators of *The Hindu*, the *Indian Express*, the *Times of India*, the *Hindustan Times*, *Outlook* and *Scroll.in*, among many other news publications and portals, which provided me with the building blocks to produce this work. I am thankful to the *Economic and Political Weekly*, *Studies in Indian Politics*, the *India Forum* and *Contemporary South Asia* for publishing my research on the EC and thus helping me expand the study around these published research articles. I am also thankful to these journals for granting me permission to use parts of the published articles in this book. I want to thank Professor Lajwanti Chatani of the Department of Political Science, Maharaja Sayajirao University of Baroda, for organising my lecture on the theme of state institutions in December 2020 as a part of the 'Professor A. H. Somjee and Dr Geeta Somji Colloquium' series. The feedback received here clarified a number of issues about the working of state institutions in democracies.

I am grateful to Shefeeque V. and Bushra Hussain, former scholars of the Department of Political Science, University of Hyderabad, who helped me collect material for the study in its initial stages. I am indebted to the personnel there for easing my procedural and academic work during the time I was doing this research. I want to thank the anonymous reviewers for their helpful suggestions to improve the book. I am also indebted to Qudsiya Ahmed, Anwesha Rana, Priyanka Das and the rest of the Cambridge University Press team for their effort in bringing the manuscript to its current shape. Thanks are due to my parents, brother, friends and students who have always been with me through my academic and non-academic journeys. Aniket, Sara, Rewa – I cannot do without you!

Last but not least, errors in this book are my own.

Hyderabad, 2023   Manjari Katju

Abbreviations

AAP	Aam Aadmi Party
ADR	Association for Democratic Reforms
ATM	automated teller machine
BJP	Bharatiya Janata Party
BLO	block-level officer
BSP	Bahujan Samaj Party
CA	Constituent Assembly
CADs	Constituent Assembly Debates
CAPF	Central Armed Police Force
CEC	chief election commissioner
CEO	chief electoral officer
CIC	Central Information Commission
CPI	Communist Party of India
CPI(M)	Communist Party of India (Marxist)
DEC	deputy election commissioner
DoPT	Department of Personnel and Training
EC	Election Commission of India
ECr	election commissioner
EPIC	elector's photo identity card
EVM	electronic voting machine

FCRA	Foreign Contribution (Regulation) Act
FS	flying squads
GDP	gross domestic product
GoI	Government of India
IAC	India against Corruption
INC	Indian National Congress
J&K	Jammu and Kashmir
MCC	Model Code of Conduct
MLA	member of legislative assembly
MLC	member of legislative council
MP	member of parliament
NCP	Nationalist Congress Party
NCRWC	National Commission to Review the Working of the Constitution
NDA	National Democratic Alliance
NEW	National Election Watch
NGO	non-governmental organisation
NOTA	none of the above
OBCs	Other Backward Classes
ORGI&CCI	Office of the Registrar General and Census Commissioner of India
PAC	Public Affairs Centre
PIB	Press Information Bureau
PIL	public interest litigation
PTI	Press Trust of India
PUCL	People's Union for Civil Liberties
RPA	Representation of the People Act
RTI	Right to Information
SP	Samajwadi Party
SVEEP	Systematic Voters' Education and Electoral Participation
UK	United Kingdom

UPA	United Progressive Alliance
US	United States
UT	union territory
VVPAT	voter verifiable paper audit trail

1

Introduction

The Election Commission of India (henceforth, the EC), shouldering the responsibility of conducting parliamentary and state elections in India, operates the colossal electoral machinery and also works towards social mobilisation that is aimed at deepening democracy. This constitutional institution works all year round, holding elections asynchronously at dual levels. This book looks at the EC and electoral practice in India in a time period spanning between 1990 (the year just before the 10th parliamentary elections of 1991) and 2019 (the year of the 17th parliamentary elections). It analyses the EC's relations and interactions with pivotal state institutions – namely the parliament, the Supreme Court (which along with the EC are constitutional institutions in India) and political parties – to modernise the electoral machinery and streamline democratic procedures. The book primarily puts forth the argument that besides the citizen voters, political parties, social groups and civil society, a crucial role is also played by the EC in consolidating the project of democracy through its work of supervising and conducting elections. In other words, through its regulatory role, the EC is as much involved in the project of democratisation as other institutions or individuals. The book also attempts a comparison between some aspects of the electoral machinery in India and those of a few other liberal democracies (through examples of electoral practice and administration from the United States [US], the United Kingdom [UK], South Africa, Japan and Canada) to highlight the role electoral institutions play in democratisation. This contrast also brings the EC's position and working in India into sharper relief and clarifies its sociopolitical situatedness in India.

Time Location

The year 1990 has been chosen as the starting point of the book because it precedes the 10th general elections, and it was around this time that the party system in India saw unprecedented fragmentation leading to an intense electoral competition. One saw a more actively participating EC that had to mediate the rising inter-party differences and squabbles. As I have argued earlier (Katju, 2006), it was at this time that the EC emerged as the fourth important institutional arrangement in the separation-of-powers model of the Indian political system, alongside the executive, the parliament and the judiciary that oversaw participatory politics. It became an institution which firmed up rules of the game and streamlined electoral procedures that contributed to democratisation. The book concludes its narrative around the year 2019 – the year of the 17th general elections – which saw the EC multifunctionally active as never before and accused of partisanship as never before. The EC had its hands full not only in conducting elections for over 900 million people but also in managing election disputes and several instances of violation of acceptable electoral conduct.

It was between 1990 and 1996 that T. N. Seshan served as the chief election commissioner (CEC) of India. During his tenure, the EC zealously took up the task of streamlining and 'cleansing' the electoral system and making it more rule-bound. This often brought forth allegations of unilateral and arbitrary conduct and put it at loggerheads with political parties and governments. Seshan's 'stern', often obstinate, ways also put him at odds with the other members of the EC when it expanded to include two more members. But undeniably, from his term onwards, the EC grew into a more involved institution, a more 'vocal' referee and a more visible entity; its 'activism' received both admiration and criticism from political participants. Its functioning at this time projected the interconnections between larger structural transformations underway, where formal institutions played an important catalyst role and themselves underwent alterations. The EC moved in directions in which the Indian polity itself moved but also brought about a more procedurally streamlined electoral behaviour.

The role of the EC in successfully conducting elections in 2002 in Jammu and Kashmir (J&K) and Gujarat – rocked by violence at that point in time – was lauded. It received admiration for conducting elections in J&K – a first-hand account of which has been chronicled by the then CEC,

J. M. Lyngdoh himself (Lyngdoh, 2004). The EC also was able to conduct elections successfully in Gujarat – torn by majoritarian violence at that time. What is noteworthy is that the EC in these elections stood by those affected by violence and took steps that enabled them to vote freely and fearlessly. Thereafter, the electoral system came under much focus for its refereeing and regulatory role. Towards the latter end – that is, the year 2019 – the EC faced a barrage of criticisms of going soft on the ruling party, the Bharatiya Janata Party (BJP), and the prime minister, Narendra Modi, for violations of the electoral conduct. It was seen as being indifferent to the ruling party's excesses while being unduly harsh towards the opposition parties, inviting criticism that it had become a mouthpiece of those holding state office.

This time period of about 30 years gives one a fair idea about the issues and problems associated with democratic procedures and practice. It covers the EC's work in 8 general elections and 189 state assembly elections. It examines whether or not the EC and other state institutions in India transformed the understanding of 'appropriateness' (March and Olsen, 1984) in institutional life – reflecting the decisional choices for given situations and thus transforming the exchange between the institution and its environment.

The period from 1990 to 2019 saw 14 CECs in office, namely T. N. Seshan (1990–96), M. S. Gill (1996–2001), J. M. Lyngdoh (2001–04), T. S. Krishnamurthy (2004–05), B. B. Tandon (2005–06), N. Gopalswami (2006–09), Navin Chawla (2009–10), S. Y. Quraishi (2010–12), V. S. Sampath (2012–15), Harishankar Brahma (2015–15), Nasim Zaidi (2015–17), Achal Kumar Jyoti (2017–18), Om Prakash Rawat (2018–18) and Sunil Arora (2018–21).[1] They were drawn mainly from the civil services of India where they served long careers. The book highlights the working of the EC during the tenure of these CECs, but the focus is more on the institution and its metamorphosis rather than the individuals heading it. Useful reforms to the electoral machinery in India were enacted at this time through an emphasis on streamlining and modernising the electoral process and making it more voter-friendly. The reform process was accelerated in 2000–09, and hence the book cites more instances from this period. The working of the EC during this period also brought into spotlight its relation with the government and hence the question of the extent of its autonomy within a parliamentary system.

---

[1] The dates mentioned in parentheses stand for their tenure in office as CECs.

This period saw profound changes in both the electorate and state institutions in India. The country saw different governments in power in this duration – minority governments, big coalitional governments and absolute majority governments. These successive parliamentary regimes were led by the following leaders: Chandra Shekhar (leader of a breakaway faction of the Janata Dal), P. V. Narasimha Rao (Indian National Congress [INC]), Atal Bihari Vajpayee (BJP; became prime minister thrice), H. D. Deve Gowda (Janata Dal), Inder Kumar Gujral (Janata Dal), Manmohan Singh (INC; became prime minister twice) and the current prime minister, Narendra Modi (BJP; became prime minister twice at the time of writing). While the minority and coalition governments brought forth the tugs and pulls of balancing interests, both cultural and political, the absolute majority governments of the BJP saw a centralisation of governmental power and an ideology-centric regime performance. The work of the EC in these different types of regimes (minority, coalitional and absolute majority) displayed its myriad sides and innovative identity. The voting population as well as political parties grew in number and carried with them the influences of a growing formal education and new media technologies. Burgeoning urbanisation meant higher rates of rural-to-urban migrations. More states were carved out in the Indian union, and thus more state assemblies were added. All this meant a phenomenal expansion of the EC's work. The book, while engaging with these transformations, focuses on the interpretation, enforcement and reforming of election procedures by the EC in the vibrant setting of Indian politics.

A look at the relationship between formal institutions and mass politics is important to highlight how a democracy institutionalises itself in a context of growing politicisation and political articulations. The intensifying political competition and heightening political aspirations in India are visible in the rise in the number of voters, electoral candidates and political parties. It is also visible in the growing protests on diverse social and economic issues and the perceptive demands for social recognition and distributive justice in India. Meanwhile, the political pendulum has swung from a one-party dominant system to a coalitional system and back to a one-party dominant orientation, signifying the shifting political preferences between centred and decentred politics. The EC has conducted elections in this rough and tumble of politics, attempting in this tug of war to ensure a rule-bound polity which works in an accountable way. It is procedurally oriented to safeguard democratic norms amidst pressures to conform and become pliant to the executive power.

State Institutions and the Study of Indian Politics

In India, state institutions and laws represent both continuity with the colonial past and a radical departure from it. This continuity, for instance, is reflected in the design of the administrative and police structures and procedures. Some of the punitive and penal laws that were framed in the 19th century by the colonial state are intact even after several years of gaining independence from British rule. A marked break from the colonial past, on the other hand, is displayed in the principles incorporated in the preamble to the Constitution independent India. Individual rights delineated in part three of the Constitution are another example of repudiation of the colonial laws and paving a way for a new beginning. The EC also represents a break from the colonial past in the sense of representing an elaborate administrative machinery to actualise universal adult franchise in the vast Indian political arena.

Studies on the EC filled up the lacuna within institutional studies that gained from a look at institutions which were neither law-making nor judicial but occupied a space that was regulatory and procedural (more on these studies later in this section). Governmental structures and constitutional provisions – that is, the institutional field – found a prominent place in the scholarship on Indian politics in the 1960s. Institutional studies, however, were replaced by research on social and cultural aspects of politics from the 1970s. Movements, demands, strife, social stratification, interests and public opinion were thereafter regarded as the real forces that shaped politics and thus as the real objects of study. Focus moved from institutions to these social forces as it is here that the transformative potential of a polity wrought by social rigidities was seen to lie, and the study of these was considered important to understand Indian politics.

From the early 2000s, however, there was a renewed interest in state institutions in India, leading to valuable insights on their nature and normative standing. The rich corpus of literature highlighted the significance of institutional structures and institutional design in shaping Indian politics and democracy. It was gradually recognised that politics was influenced by an institutional ecosystem, the legal–procedural framework and inter-institutional tussles, and that there was a need to understand institutions in deeper ways than merely as pieces of lifeless machinery set up to accomplish neatly cut-out tasks.

Institutions thus re-entered the ambit of research. The Constitution of India, the presidency, the parliament, the EC, the Supreme Court, the bureaucracy and the financial institutions underwent scholarly probes (for instance, in the works of Rudolph and Rudolph, 2001; Mathur, 2001; Mehra and Kueck, 2003; Hasan, Sridharan and Sudarshan, 2004; Kirpal et al., 2004; Manor, 2005). These evaluative studies highlighted the institutional dynamics at work not only in the functioning and shaping of democracy in India but also in the fulfilment of developmental needs of a struggling economy. They assessed the working of state institutions and their role in fortifying democracy and showcased the institutional experience amidst the intricate web of colonial legacies, politics, laws and executive power. They probed whether institutions fulfilled popular expectations of institutional functioning. This academic attention continued in the second half of the 2000s (Katju, 2006, 2009; Kapur and Mehta, 2007; R. Bhargava, 2008; Shankar, 2009) and extended to the next decade (Shankar and Rodrigues, 2011; Quraishi, 2014; Katju, 2016; Kapur, Mehta and Vaishnav, 2017; De, 2018; Singh and Roy, 2019; Pai, 2020, and so on). Institutional inputs to and disjunctions from democratic functioning and egalitarian visions eventually became a significant part of scholarly attention. The literature drove home the point that '… a neglect of institutions in their own right seriously impedes a proper understanding of Indian society and politics' (Kapur and Mehta, 2007: 3). The studies focused on the nature of and moral vision driving state institutions as well as their capacity to adapt to the socio-economic transformations that India witnessed. The literature also looked at the different aspects of institutional restructuring and change. Exploration of institutional performance in India for over two decades brought forth conclusions that public institutions had not matched with social transformations and there were 'strong headwinds of deep institutional malaise' (Kapur, Mehta and Vaishnav, 2017: 1) that were stalling 'the quality-of-life gains of growth' (Kapur, Mehta and Vaishnav, 2017: 3).

This re-look at state institutions was facilitated to a large extent by debates in the late 1980s and 1990s on the design of the institutional structure best suited to the Indian polity and doubts raised mainly by the political right wing about the validity of certain constitutional values and tenets forming the core of the Indian state. Questions were raised about the authenticity of these foundational ideas. This political contestation led to questions, for instance, about constitutional principles like secularism, religious freedom and individual liberties, which were seen by some to be superfluous in a society beset with values of 'eternal tolerance' that resided in the majority community. Some also expressed opinions that extolled the virtues and soundness of the presidential system and its advantages over a parliamentary system in a country beset with diversity. The presidential system with its supposed 'efficient', 'quick' and 'decisive' qualities was and continues to be seen by many as a more effective system of rule as compared to the parliamentary system with its supposed quality of taking 'everybody along' at all times and going back and forth between institutions for arriving at decisions and thus demonstrating its supposed innate lethargy.

At the turn of the century, there existed a political opinion led by the first National Democratic Alliance (NDA) government under prime minister Atal Bihari Vajpayee that favoured a 'review' of the Constitution of India. Those who opposed this argued that it was not the Constitution which needed an overhauling but those who steered it needed to be more sensitive to constitutional values – that it was the lawmakers who needed a reorientation rather than the document. There was a divergence of views which was clearly visible – for instance, between the party, the BJP, that led the NDA government (1999–2004) and the then president of India, K. R. Narayanan – over the issue of review of the Constitution (see Muralidharan and Venkatesan, 2000). President Narayanan said, '[T]oday when there is so much talk about revising the Constitution or even writing a new Constitution, we have to consider whether it is the Constitution that has failed us or whether it is we who have failed the Constitution' (Murlidharan and Venkatesan, 2000).

These debates were reminiscent of the 'basic structure' debate in the 1960s that discussed whether or not there were certain values of the Constitution that were sacrosanct to democracy and could not be changed or expunged by the parliament in the interest of the people. Studies on the Constitution that were published subsequently (Hasan, Sridharan and Sudarshan, 2004; R. Bhargava, 2008) addressed some of the issues and emphasised the necessity of having Constitutions to restrict the excessive power of modern states that could turn tyrannical (R. Bhargava, 2008). Studies also brought out the way the Constitution, from the very beginning, played a role in transforming lives of ordinary people and thus was firmly rooted in the popular ethos (De,

2018). This was the resurgence of institutional studies within the discipline of political science in India.

Published studies on the EC by academics, judicial practitioners and former CECs enhanced the analytical corpus of institutional studies. While adding to a previously neglected area of research, these studies stressed the importance of the EC within the institutional ecosystem and as a differential structural facet of the state. Scholars highlighted the location of the EC as a depository of rules and regulations which made democratic participation possible and within which democratic assertions took place (Rudolph and Rudolph, 2001; U. K. Singh, 2004). Through its regulatory function, the EC defined democracy. Its presence and interventions were viewed as vital to the smooth running of the democratic project at a time when trust in legislative institutions had ebbed considerably (Rudolph and Rudolph, 2001; U. K. Singh, 2004). Similarly, it was argued that while politics was deepening in India, the need for institutional safeguards for democratic norms had assumed a crucial importance (Katju, 2006). Among political parties, the Communist Party of India (Marxist) (CPI[M]) asked for a thorough accountability of the EC that could lead to a more transparent and objective conduct (CPI[M], 2006). It was stressed that the EC as a referee must be above suspicion and its appointment procedure itself needs to be reformed (Panchu, 2009; Katju, 2009).

Former CEC J. M. Lyngdoh (2004), through a bird's-eye view of the 2002 J&K elections, underscored the crucial position of the EC as an impartial referee. Former CECs T. S. Krishnamurthy (2008) and S. Y. Quraishi (2014) highlighted the design and working of the electoral machinery with its strengths and flaws. They documented the importance of an election and the electoral procedure to the functioning of democracy in India (Murthy, 2008) and gave a glimpse into the finer points of the working of the electoral apparatus (Quraishi, 2014). What came on board was a previously neglected area of electoral management and administration (Quraishi, 2014). This knowledge base grew with studies highlighting reformatory laws, field experience, voters' perspectives, citizenship perceptions and normative standing of the EC in a democratic set-up (Damore et al., 2012; R. Sen, 2012; A. Roy, 2012; Katju, 2013, 2016; Singh and Roy, 2019; Quraishi, 2019). Scholars highlighted the 'paradoxical location' of the EC in the institutional field – its placement in the 'domain of the state' but functioning 'by the logic of democracy' (Singh and Roy, 2019: 7). This book continues the engagement with questions of institutional structures and politics by focusing on the EC's influence on political behaviour. It locates the EC both in the institutional grid of Indian democracy as well as in the larger political field of a multi-party competitive system, and thus attempts to draw out the causality that characterises these relationships.

The Frame and Methodology

The book is located in the realm of new institutionalism. Specifically, it comes within 'normative institutionalism' that foregrounds the need to look afresh at the relationship between formal institutions and political behaviour as it contends that institutional design plays a crucial role in shaping political preferences and not just the other way round. It foregrounds the agency of institutions and steps away from viewing institutions as mere derivatives of social action. Resisting the behavioural pull towards determinateness of social phenomena, it contends that explorations of the political need to recognise the agenda-setting potential of the state and state institutions to come up with a better understanding of how politics is going to unfold in the future. It argues against the claim that individuals always act autonomously, set the menu of political choices and make institutions move in preset directions.

Social science scholars James March and Johan Olsen point out that political theories largely saw '... causal links between society and polity as running from the former to the latter, rather than the other way round' (March and Olsen, 1984: 735). It was assumed that 'class, geography, climate, ethnicity, language, culture, economic conditions, demography, technology, ideology, and religion all affect politics but are not significantly affected by politics' (March and Olsen, 1984: 735). However, the unease with the finality of socio-economic causal explanations as also the method-fetish brought about a dissatisfaction with the behaviouralist perspectives. Ignoring the state as the builder of a normative purpose and setting the course of history was also considered as presenting an incomplete picture of politics.

In the 1980s, a re-look at the state or state institutions to understand political life was emphasised by March and Olsen (1984, 1989) and Evans, Rueschemeyer and Skocpol (1985), among others. March and Olsen (1984: 738; 1989: 17) argued that political democracy is a function of not only the economic and social conditions but also the design of political institutions. Evans, Rueschemeyer and Skocpol (1985: 5) argued that various changes after World War II, like the growing macroeconomic management by national governments and the birth of several new nations which wanted to follow their own political destiny rather than replicating the Western liberal democratic pattern, brought states into the picture, and they began to be seen as 'society-shaping institutional structures'. These scholars underscored the importance of the state and state institutions as laying down legal imperatives that constituted social phenomena. They viewed the state and state institutions as political actors that paved the course of history and transformed societal values through a stable and predictable procedural repertoire. The compendium of the standard operating procedures in the state and state institutions gives them a futuristic character that moulded behaviour.

This 'returning' to institutions in the US was brought about in part by the 'Vietnam and Watergate experiences, each involving arguable abuses of executive authority' (Blumstein 1981: 130). There were other instances of centralisation of authority and threats to individual liberty, which necessitated a look at institutions (Blumstein 1981: 130). March and Olsen (1984: 738) called the renewed interest in institutions (which even came up in economics and sociology) 'the new institutionalism' which blended 'elements of an old institutionalism into the non-institutionalist styles in recent theories of politics'. According to them, the new institutionalism insisted on a more autonomous role for political institutions but without rejecting the importance of social factors and individual motives to political action (March and Olsen 1984: 738). The attempts of 'neoinstitutionalists' to build a sounder theoretical foundation for institutional studies brought to it the analysis of informal structures. Social norms, values and beliefs as reflected in individual and group behaviour came within the institutional research radar. What came to be accepted was that political institutions shaped society and were shaped by society; that institutions constrain behaviour that made the attainment of collective goals possible but also worked within the universe of social norms and values. The neo-institutional scholarship emphasised that institutions were regularly interacting with their social environments that produced and reproduced politics of a certain kind.

The overarching presence and role of the state in post-colonial and struggling economies, which was much evident in the unfolding contemporary histories, brought forth the realisation that to understand politics, the state and institutional perspectives cannot be totally expunged. The post-colonial societies looked upon the state for chalking out developmental paths and even rights issues. The state operated with not only coercive power but also enormous resources at its command and a wide unparalleled social reach. Though the state began to withdraw from many areas with the onset of globalisation and economic reforms, like in India in the 1990s, its importance 'as the chief regulator, facilitator, arbiter, and even allocator of resources for society as a whole by no means diminished' (P. Chatterjee, 2011: 13). Its commanding position made it decisive for ways to work out social change. As such, it was not only influencing but also shaping people's lives and relationships. In such a situation, the state and its institutions had to be brought centre stage to explain social processes. Their causal power had to be recognised and probed to understand social structures and change. As portrayers of value and power, institutions advanced a set of social concerns which moulded societies at particular junctures.

The book situates itself here and, while not discounting the causality of socio-economic conditions, emphasises institutional influences on social behaviour. It underscores the causal influences of institutional structures on social conditioning. Institutions 'behave' in a certain way, and their decisions have long-term implications for political culture; they chalk out the path of political functioning over the long term. They lay out the pathways of 'appropriateness' which defines the way individuals and groups act. Institutions in this way can be categorised as 'political actors in their own right' (March and Olsen, 1984: 738) just like individuals or groups. As such, they have a claim over coherence and autonomy, which means that they take coherent decisions and 'affect the flow of history' (March and Olsen 1984: 739). Political institutions might be affected by external events and forces and also represent some collective interest or intention, but they influence how one looks at policies and decisions (March and Olsen 1984: 739). March and Olsen (2005: 8) argue that political actors conduct themselves in accordance with rules and practices that are 'socially constructed, publicly known, anticipated and accepted'. Institutions are not static, and institutionalisation is not a unidirectional or irreversible process; however, institutions cannot be changed arbitrarily (March and Olsen, 2005: 9).

This book builds on the thesis of March and Olsen (1984, 1989, 2005) mentioned earlier and tries to understand the interplay of state institutions and Indian politics through the conceptual frame provided by them. It looks at the electoral administration as a builder of a more informed and choice-oriented citizen voter. It argues that institutions are repositories of political experience, memories, conventions and power play, and they influence political behaviour in significant ways. It views state institutions as political actors that are constructs of history but also affect how events of history unfold. The layering of diverse experiences in state institutions gives them a binding force that impacts political praxis. In India, constitutional institutions were designed to usher in an era of modernisation and secularisation where the government ruled by law and set procedures. They aimed to integrate and uplift a diverse polity and imbue it with ideas of citizenship enveloped in plurality and individual freedoms.

By giving the EC the responsibility of conducting elections, the book tries to argue that the makers of the Constitution of India attempted to institutionalise equality of participation and a deeper involvement of people in state politics. The idea was to create an institution that would universalise free and fair choice, make the system participatory and carry forward the project of democracy while also consolidating it. The EC in this role was visualised as an equaliser with the responsibility of strengthening a participatory democracy, advancing the values of 'citizen involvement', 'political choice', 'procedural compliance' and 'rule conformity' in a county beset with socio-economic inequalities and development deficit.

The book focuses on formal state institutions, inter-institutional linkage and interactions between institutions and political actors over streamlining the election process as well as interpreting and enforcing rules of electoral competition. It looks at the impact of institutions on political practice and at the endeavours of political actors and regimes to influence institutional functioning in the direction that favours them. In this endeavour, it specifically focuses on the EC and its interactions with the parliament, the Supreme Court and political parties – the institutions which constitute the Indian state and also restrain the government of the day from acting arbitrarily. It argues that by making efforts towards social mobilisation, a more regulated electoral system, electoral transparency and participation, and a more responsive electoral administration, the EC has been an institution that has contributed in its specific ways to the making of a more participatory political culture. Also, in its interaction with the law-making, law-adjudicating and representative institutions, the EC determines the nature of participatory politics through its presence in the institutional ecosystem and its steering of the electoral administration.

The arguments and analysis in this book are based on diverse written and oral sources. For an insight into the constitutional nature of the EC, the book bases itself on the Constituent Assembly Debates (CADs), constitutional provisions, reports of official and unofficial committees, parliamentary decisions and published studies on the EC. To understand the EC's ground-level work, the book draws on published accounts of former CECs, news reports on elections, interviews with some former CECs or election commissioners (ECrs) and electorally active members of civil society. These accounts and commentaries of first-hand experience form an informative resource to understand the colossal machinery that the EC operates. To comprehend the legal trajectory of electoral praxis in India, the book focuses on the Constitution, parliamentary legislation, court judgements and the EC's orders. For information on the changes in the electoral procedures and institutional make-up, the book relies on official reports, interviews (of those mentioned earlier in this paragraph), books, journals and press commentaries.

Interviews for this study were carried out between 2017 and 2020. COVID-19 compulsions meant that some interviews had to be carried out on the phone and via email. The website of the EC was an extremely helpful source as were the online portals and websites of leading national and international dailies together with some judicial law websites. To discuss the international experience on elections, the official websites of electoral commissions of a few countries were referred to as were also news reports regarding changes in electoral law there. The political context of this research has been the overwhelming popularity of Hindu nationalism in India and the BJP's parliamentary victories of 2014 and 2019. These BJP regimes have been unapologetic about their Hindu majoritarian make-up and promotion of an ethnicised politics that is antithetical to the secular and civic nature of Indian democracy. Contemporary India under these regimes has become a place where the notion of citizenship is being redefined around Hindu-centric ideas of nationalism.

In these particular contextual and methodological frames, the book attempts to showcase the EC's agency (with close interaction with the parliament, the Supreme Court and civil society) to bring about a more citizen-oriented and rule-bound electoral competition. It highlights how the EC itself has metamorphosed to respond to transformations in the Indian political terrain. Differences between state institutions have often arisen, which is an innate part of democratic functioning, and this has influenced administrative action and government decisions. Executive and authoritarian pressures that occasionally come up alter the course of action and redraw institutional boundaries, which disturb inter-institutional equilibrium and the separation-of-powers formula of democracies. In contemporary India, the rise of a much more centralised government has had an effect on institutional autonomy, including that of the EC. A powerful executive usually attempts to extend its sphere of influence and contract the space for institutional self-direction. The EC has been affected by this. The book aims to focus on these themes to underscore the impact of this interaction on democratic practice in the time period between 1990 and the parliamentary elections of 2019.

The Election Commission's Growing Tasks

The EC's work over the years has considerably expanded. In a parliamentary system, elections to the parliament and state assemblies are asynchronous, and bypolls (elections for seats which have fallen vacant due to the death, resignation or disqualification of a legislator) have to be conducted too, which keeps the country in election mode all the time. This keeps the EC occupied for most times of the year. As stated earlier, the expansion of political awareness and a greater involvement in politics of Indians have raised the number of parties, contestants and voters, which has added to the work. In this ever-increasing competitive political arena, safeguarding democracy and maintaining rule of law is a serious responsibility which can both establish or enfeeble the legitimacy of and trust in the EC. The EC's work of mobilising voters, conducting a safe election, handling election violence, reducing ruling parties' excesses and curbing money and muscle power are daunting tasks that need to be conducted with a hands-on approach.

The EC and the Supreme Court stand for rule enforcement and arbitration, while the parliament, through elected political representatives and parties, represents rule-making through popular will. The first two stand, at least in theory, above partisanship and prejudice and represent ideological neutrality, while the third represents the partisan or sectional point of view or is set in an ideological mould which can be both singular or competing. Besides dispensing their own functions, these three constitutional institutions are designed to check each other and the executive from abusing power and trampling upon the constitutional rights of citizens. A separation of powers and responsibilities defines their relationship.

A study of the EC's functioning, as also its interactions with other constitutional institutions, assumes importance at such a juncture when India's experiment with democratic praxis has been viewed as largely successful but carrying with it some worrisome trends like ethno-majoritarianism, populist-authoritarianism, curbs on freedom of speech and expression often in the name of 'nationalism', and continued instances of anti-minority, caste and gender violence. The procedural successes of Indian democracy have gone together with muscular nationalism and militant majoritarianism that have laid the groundwork for religion-based ideas of citizenship. These happenings are bothersome and put a question mark on the 'great' Indian democratic experiment. Concerns have been expressed on the erosion of civic ideas of citizenship and all-encompassing nationalism over the last two parliamentary election cycles. In this context, one needs to ask: Has the institutional design advanced democratic practices? Given the social inequalities, how even-handed or non-partisan has institutional conduct in India been? How do institutions deal with the authoritarian impulses of the regime? How inclusive are the institutions when it comes to policy formulation? What is the tendency among elected representatives towards institutional norms? And how do institutions regulate democratic functioning? Questions about the substantive aspect include: How have the underprivileged fared in the Indian democratic state? How well have the goals of equality and justice been handled by the democratic regime? Has the state been able to contain majoritarian violence on the underprivileged and religious minorities? And how far have the fundamental freedoms of citizens been effective and been able to meaningfully safeguard democratic practice?

Answers to these questions reveal the extent of institutionalisation of democracy itself. While democracy reflects popular struggles and demands, it is also about institutional design, norms and rules. The latter have to be probed to understand the directions Indian democracy has traversed. A firmly institutionalised democracy is able to handle political arbitrariness and domination with deftness and curb it on time so that democratic norms are not trampled upon and voices of opposition not silenced by the incumbent regime and the socially dominant sections of society. This book focuses on the procedural side of democracy and tries to answer some questions stated previously about institutions. It deals with formal institutions, their functioning in their institutional fields and their interaction with mass politics in contemporary times.

Chapter Themes

Elections in India have been crucial to shaping the democratic project. Popular participation in elections at the central, state and local levels demonstrates that this participatory exercise is celebratory and has been nurtured by the Indian polity over the years. Political parties interact most closely with the electorate during elections. This is the time when promises are made, demands articulated, *yatras* (tours by an official or members of a political party, movement, and so on) done and roadshows held. People choose their representatives by exercising their franchise in multiparty elections, and their participation rests on a well-run electoral administration. The book, as stated earlier, looks at the EC and its impact on the nature and processes of democratisation in India through its 10 chapters.

The following (second) chapter looks at the main theorisation on institutions and the processes of institutionalisation to locate this study of the EC in the larger framework of institutional studies. It discusses the different standpoints on how institutions have emerged and evolved and their role in sculpting a political system. The scholarship on institutions foregrounds the role they play in moulding political attitudes in decisive ways and how they are themselves influenced by the cross-currents of social value systems. The chapter, through a discussion on the theorisation on institutions, tries to grapple with the question of the place of institutions and institutionalisation in a liberal democracy.

The third chapter discusses the context in which the EC functions. The growing politicisation manifest in the expansion of voter participation and party fragmentation has prepared a ground for the EC to become an active regulatory body in the political landscape of India. This expanded role of the EC often leads to differences between itself and the executive and the legislature. Here civil society and the judiciary make their own interventions, and this dynamic shapes the character of the institutional ecosystem. In pursuit of populist politics, the ruling parties at times infringe laws that bring about action from the EC. The rise in violation of the electoral consensus and election procedures, which has popularly been conceptualised as 'criminalisation' of politics, has brought forth calls for electoral reform. In the last few decades, the political culture of the country has seen the moral image of political leadership at an unprecedented low, which has strengthened the hands of adjudicatory and regulatory institutions as never before.

The fourth chapter looks at the functioning of the EC from the early 1990s. It also discusses the working and changes the EC underwent during the tenure of various ECrs. The EC's relations with the parliament and the Supreme Court are also discussed in relation to its changing nature. Some decisive reform measures taken by the EC under CECs T. N. Seshan, M. S. Gill, J. M. Lyngdoh, T. S. Krishnamurthy, S. Y. Qurashi, V. S. Sampath and Nasim Zaidi, among others, form the focus of this chapter. The fifth chapter focuses on the actual event of elections to highlight the management techniques used by the EC. An election in real time brings up several crucial issues of institutional performance. In India, the working of the electoral rules and laws displays the level of institutionalisation of rule-bound democratic practice. In this context, the interface between the EC and the political parties during the polls forms the subject matter of this chapter.

The sixth chapter looks at voters' rights (disclosures by candidates, none of the above [NOTA], right to recall, lowering of voting age) and interventions by the Supreme Court, the EC and the parliament to strengthen them. Pressures from voters to streamline political behaviour has been an important aspect of electoral practice in India in recent years. This feedback prompted the judiciary and the EC to take decisive steps to strengthen voters' interests. The seventh chapter discusses the issue of election violence and the way it has been conceptualised in research literature. It gives a brief historical sketch of this violence and its changing nature in India. The EC played an important role to curb this violence through legal means. It carried out the modernisation of the election machinery and used technology to reduce violence. The chapter discusses some of these reforms.

The eighth chapter discusses the matters of election campaign finance and spending and also underlines the debates on the same. It elaborates the relation between resources and winnability in an Indian election. The role of the EC, the Supreme Court and the parliament to streamline election finance and the challenges they have faced are highlighted here. The role of civil society to bring about reforms regarding campaign funding is also discussed in this chapter.

The ninth chapter discusses the crucial work of the EC for voter awareness and popular mobilisation. It discusses the multifarious efforts of the EC to generate an enthusiasm among people about voting. From updating the electoral rolls to easing the registration processes and spreading knowledge about elections, the EC has worked on initiatives to expand the number of voters visiting the polling booths and casting their vote. The chapter looks at some of these issues and assesses the successes of the EC in carrying out these tasks.

The final (tenth) chapter sums up the book by highlighting the relationship between state institutions and democracy. From the early 1990s, the regulatory role of the EC changed the way political actors conducted themselves in the electoral arena. The electoral space itself became more rule-bound. The EC streamlined and contributed to the making of political behaviour, which shaped India's political culture. The infusion of procedural clarity and steadfastness, the enthusiasm to modernise and update, the efforts to expand choices and bring about transparency were the crucial ways in which this constitutional institution attempted to reconfigure and rationalise behaviour in the electoral field. Despite aberrations like the role of big money, overwhelming executive authority, downscaling of institutional autonomy and populist politics, a way was paved for a more modernised and information-driven participation in Indian electoral democracy.

2

Institutions, Institutionalisation and Politics

As stated in the previous chapter, scholarship on Indian politics returned to institutional studies in a major way in the first two decades of the 21st century by focusing on state institutions and procedural democracy. The field expanded to look at the sculpting of behaviour in the larger field of institutional functioning. It was acknowledged that institutional design and work played a decisive role in shaping politics; institutional structures had agency that acted upon participatory politics and the social environment. The EC contributed to curating and stabilising political practice in the electoral field as did the parliament in the field of law-making and the judiciary in the arena of adjudication. A look at the EC takes us to the larger field of institutional studies in which this study is located. It elucidates why recognising institutional agency becomes vital in a study of politics.

An institution represents defined ways of working as opposed to arbitrary and abrupt modes. It is bigger than an individual and involves groups in a patterned interaction that have a predictability (Peters, 2012: 19). An institution is also an amalgamation of the intrinsic values of society, its collective wisdom and also its power equations, acquiring a definite form through its actions. Together these chalk out a direction for a polity and equip it with a certain mode of accomplishing tasks in routine ways over a long duration. Modernising polities have either replicated institutions of liberal democracy of the industrialised world or crafted their own institutional structures; some of them have even formalised different hybridised institutional arrangements. Specialisation of roles and differentiation of responsibilities characterise modern institutional functioning. The structures vested with specific roles work in an integrated way that brings coherence and stability to the political system. This keeps it in a cycle of orchestrated functionality to accomplish the given tasks. The electoral administration is part of this institutional ecosystem that in tandem with other state institutions actualises democratic citizenship.

Institutional Studies

Institutional theory, as it grew in its neo-institutional phase, emphasised that institutions are entities that impose constraints on actors. Justified and accepted on grounds of stability, order and efficiency, these constraints were seen to maximise gains among collective existence. Organisational theorists Stephen Barley and Pamela Tolbert stress the relation between action and institution and thus call for a 'heuristic' definition of an institution that will help to 'examine the change and reproduction of institutions as general, ongoing, and historically embedded processes' (Barley and Tolbert, 1997: 96). With this in view, they define institutions as 'shared rules and typifications that identify categories of social actors and their appropriate activities or relationships' (Barley and Tolbert 1997: 96). An institution has also been defined as an entity that 'refers not just to manifest political organizations but also to aggregations of norms, values, rules, and practices that shape or constrain political behaviour' (Peters and Pierre, 1998: 565). Institutions are also seen as the 'art of the state because they give it "shape" and "legitimacy"' (Galvin, Shapiro and Skowronek, 2006: 1). It is rightly said that there is no escape from them in the study of politics (Galvin, Shapiro and Skowronek, 2006: 1).

    Political sociologist Claus Offe foregrounds the futuristic aspect of institutional rules (that the rules affect how actors behave in the future) as also the element of legal constraints that institutions beget (Offe, 2006: 10). Institutional studies (neo-institutionalism) are characterised by a heterogeneity that brings into focus multiple aspects of institutional growth and functioning. The various institutionalisms – normative, rational choice, historical and sociological, among others – stand for different explanations that elucidate the emergence, behaviour and endurance of institutions and their interactions with their institutional fields. Even outside these, attempts were made to theorise institutions and their relations with the processes of democratisation. This has fortified the recognition of institutions, whether legislative, electoral or judicial, as agents of both altering and reproducing behaviour.

James March and Johan Olsen (1984, 1989, 2005) look at institutions from the point of view of the 'logic of appropriateness', the right or proper response to a given situation as opposed to a response that is driven by a reasoning of benefits or gains. This has been termed 'normative institutionalism' (Peters, 2012) because of the emphasis it places on the intricate web of norms and values that inform the appropriate response. Institutions, in other words, work within a logic of appropriateness that determine a set of 'appropriate' actions for a particular situation. Looking at the appropriateness of an action is 'a means of understanding how they [institutions] function and how they determine, or at least shape, individual behaviour' (Peters, 2012: 20). Institutions have a normative content – certain dos and don'ts – that are fortified by sanctions. The decisions of state institutions are legally binding. They direct political action along an arranged path and influence what political actors choose to do.

The rational choice perspective, also called rational choice institutionalism, foregrounds the centrality of individual interests in the formation of institutions. It argues that individuals agree to come together and function within institutions to maximise their interests. According to institutional economist Douglass North, who looked at the role of institutions in the performance of economies, they 'are humanely devised constraints that structure political, economic and social interaction' (D. North, 1991: 97). He says, 'Effective institutions raise the benefits of cooperative solutions or the costs of defection, to use game theoretic terms. In transaction cost terms, institutions reduce transaction and production costs per exchange so that the potential gains from trade are realizeable' (D. North, 1991: 98). This view informed rational choice institutionalism within political studies, too, stressing the point that the chances of irreparable differences or clashes are high when individuals act atomistically. This reduces gains for everyone. Institutions constrain egotistical behaviour and create conditions that lead to maximisation of gains for all. The understanding here also is that if institutions are not able to maximise utilities, they can be replaced with a different set of institutions. Practically, however, this is beset with its own set of complications. Anticipation of social trauma and the economic costs of this replacement often act as deterrents to this choice.

Historical institutionalism, on the other hand, underscores that the initial policy choices of a government or an organisation tend to persist over a long course of time (Skocpol, 1992; Pierson and Skocpol, 2002). Their persistence can be attributed to reasons like greater comfort levels in old policies and high costs of operationalising new policies. Also, the political and electoral costs of abandoning the initial policy pathways are a deterring factor in switching to new ones. The past has a critical place in policymaking, and therefore one has to look at time and history to gain a clarity about the unfolding processes of political development (Skocpol, 1992; Pierson, 2000). Policies made at earlier junctures of history tend to survive way ahead into the future or influence future programmes. In other words, there is a path dependency in the way a policy programme works (Pierson, 2000). An organisation at a particular juncture may take a decision to handle a particular situation, and this may continue well into the future, so that issues that come up then are also resolved in similar ways. Institutions persist because of their utility and the practices of society. Historical institutionalists, as some scholars pointed out, have focused more on dramatic shifts rather than subtle and incremental changes which are more common (Peters, Pierre and King, 2005: 1278). Also, they foreground that changes happen within the possibilities outlined in the initial phase of the institution (see Peters, 2012: 73). The contributions of historical institutionalists in expanding the horizons of political enquiry, however, far outweighed the limitations in their analysis. It paved a way for deep probes into evolution of institutions.

Sociological institutionalism, which is close to normative institutionalism, emphasises the embeddedness of institutions – that they are products of their environment. Institutions in this way emerge out of the social frames in which they are situated, and symbols and values play a role in defining an institution (see Peters, 2012: 130–33). This perspective draws attention to the cumulativeness of institutions – the ongoing process of adaptation, 'sedimentation' in institutional formation (Tolbert and Zucker, 1996). The layers of experience and cultural peculiarities give an institution its personality. Members of an institution look at a situation through the structures in which they are placed and bring to it the culture they are a part of. Sociological institutionalists also highlight the processes of institutionalisation and the change that takes place over the years in the life of an organisation (Selznick, 1949). Practices or procedures with the passage of time grow roots; they become socially acceptable and legitimised. They acquire 'value' and 'stability' which indicates their institutionalisation (Huntington, 1968: 12). Also, organisational diversity in the initial stages gives way to homogenisation in the long run – a process described as 'isomorphism' – where one finds that organisations become similar over time (DiMaggio and Powell, 1983). Isomorphism is reflected, for instance, in the government and administrative structures of new democracies that are modelled on institutions that were successful in the industrialised world or have come to resemble them.

Institutions are thus theorised as providing pathways for maximising benefits and reducing obstacles to society which is an amalgam of multiple interests and values. They are crystallisation of work practices and conventions suited to and accepted by a polity. They acquire permanence because they are valued and in turn provide stability to a system – in this case, the political system. This tangibility and certainty help in maintaining continuity in the event of changes in bureaucratic personnel, political actors and even political circumstances. Institutions, it is argued, are embedded in their sociocultural contexts. Much like individual selves, they are situated in their environments which they shape and are shaped by. To take them as autonomous entities disconnected from the spatial and temporal context in which they function would be to misunderstand institutions and their functioning. As stated by March and Olsen (1984: 742), 'Institutions seem to be neither neutral reflections of exogenous environmental forces nor neutral arenas for the performances of individuals driven by exogenous preferences and expectations.' They reflect society's preferences and values at a given time as also the social differentiations or hierarchies prevalent therein. However, once there, institutions play an important role in building social consensus and agreement on values. They provide a structure that acts as a springboard for evolution of ideas, policy options and debates.

For a long time, following the rational choice analysis, institutions were seen as structures of cooperation and voluntary exchange. They were viewed as maximising benefits and solving collective problems in the best possible way. However, as institutional scholarship developed, a need was felt to focus on the 'power' dimension sufficiently. It was emphasised that 'power' is an important factor that needs to be adequately theorised within institutional analysis (Offe, 2006; Moe, 2006). Political scientist Terry M. Moe argues that institutions may be structures of cooperation but they 'may also be structures of power', and thinking of power is essential to understand political institutions (Moe, 2006: 32). He argues that leaving aside predatory rule, even in democratically administered terrains, institutions 'are not cooperative or mutually beneficial for many of the people affected by them' as they involve 'the exercise of power' (Moe, 2006: 38). According to him, the winners gain, and the losers have to 'accept the winners' decisions which may make the losers 'worse off, perhaps by a lot' (Moe, 2006: 38). Offe draws attention to similar issues: how institutions affect the distribution of social power among actors and how they themselves are constituted by the exercise of power need to be looked at (Offe, 2006: 9). According to him, institutions 'endow specific actors with power' (Offe, 2006: 21) who are able to 'take unfair advantage of others' and/or to 'exclude others from the decision making process' (Offe, 2006: 9). As political actors, they project a certain viewpoint which they bring to the political field. According to Offe, institutions operate in a setting of a 'tripolar field of power conflicts' between 'the guardians (enforcers and educators), beneficiaries, and potential challengers' (Offe, 2006: 21).

Institutions do imbibe from the leadership and personnel that operate them, but these add to the procedures outlined and pathways chalked out rather than markedly alter the logic of appropriateness. Inter-institutional exchanges also might affect institutional decisions in multiple ways that might alter modes and responses over the long term. Formal institutions embody a procedural regimen based on the prevailing distribution of power and stratifications at a given historical juncture. At certain moments, with transformations in social power and hierarchies, the logic of appropriateness changes, altering the once defined ways of doing things. Once the new way is set, it consolidates over time. Institutions remain in constant interaction with their institutional fields and the larger social environment. Regime types also throw up impulses that might change the appropriateness meter, but changes in the established pathways of work entail times and costs. Institutions thus endure rather than being dismantled and replaced at frequent intervals. Their endurance affects the form of political behaviour which in turn contributes to the making of political culture of a society.

Emergence, Endurance and Institutionalisation

Path dependency in institutional responses has not prevented closure or change – quite the contrary. Institutions have emerged, evolved, matured, decayed and also been discarded. They are products of processes of negotiation, accommodation, shifts in social power, regime changes and emulation. Delving into institutional biographies is important to adequately understand policy processes and pathways. Some institutions are products of evolutionary changes like the British parliament and the American congress, which reflect the replacement of landed power with the emergent mercantile and industrial interests, leading to the decline of the hold of the monarchy and the rise of the republican state. Years of debate, deliberations, differences and, at times, conflict led to the moulding of these legislative institutions in the form they exist today. Institutions have also emerged out of revolutionary upheavals like in the former Union of Soviet Socialist Republics (USSR) (1917) and post-revolutionary China (1949). Radical political shifts here led to ruptures and institutional overhaul. Political experience and replication have also given rise to institutions in entirely different social environments, like the Indian Constitution which was largely a product of the nationalist struggles against colonialism and adoption of certain best practices of the Constitutions of functioning democracies.

Institutions bring a permanent quality to policy mechanisms. They may seem frozen or static entities because their fixity and predictability display a fixed regimen of rules and dry procedures. However, as institutional theory highlights, institutions are outcomes of ideas, debates, choices and events over time and are constantly evolving. They are 'not as rigid as it sometimes is made to appear' (Peters and Pierre, 1998: 566). Through choice and action, individuals and organisations can bring about changes in institutions and even eliminate them (Barley and Tolbert, 1997: 94). Institutions change 'to meet changing demands and changing personnel; that change is often incremental and undramatic, but it is nonetheless real' (Peters and Pierre, 1998: 566). Their endurance conceals that they are cumulative products of dynamic processes. This process of evolution might not be immediately visible, but it is present – manifest in changes in the structure that govern behaviour. It can be seen in the transformations in internal mechanisms like rules, laws, work culture, problem-solving methods, and so on, which affect policy and political praxis. But typically, with time, the work culture crystallises, leading to maturity and institutionalisation. What this means is that institutions must be studied as entities whose temporal dimension cannot be ignored (Lawrence, Winn and Jennings, 2001). Time is an important factor to understand institutions and their functioning (Lawrence, Winn and Jennings, 2001; Peters and Pierre, 1998: 567; Barley and Tolbert, 1997; Pierson, 2000). The process of institutionalisation in a political system takes time – it can be both short- or long-term. Work practices develop over time and acquire maturity, leading to stable and valued institutions. The passage of time also leads to the discarding of decaying institutions. These are replaced with new ones, which again need time to establish themselves. Political scientists B. Guy Peters and Jon Pierre point out that there are many conceptions of how institutions change in institutional theory, but these explanations are overshadowed by the general emphasis on stability and predictability (Peters and Pierre, 1998: 567).

Both incremental and sweeping changes take place which transform the power and the way of functioning of institutions. There are also instances where the structure exists but is empty of substance – this happens during a sustained erosion of institutional functions and power. There are different factors that bring about changes in institutions. First, there might be changes due to exogenous factors – an institution changes when there is change in the institutional field or the larger social environment. For instance, industry or market pressures bring about changes in political institutions. The influence of civil society also brings about changes. For example, environmental groups have made governments institutionalise environmental concerns, which has made it mandatory for big projects to seek environmental clearances.

Second, an institution changes because of endogenous factors. Internal reform initiatives are significant in institutional change. Amendments to a country's constitutional provisions illustrate how institutions change through internal reforms. In the case of the EC, reform suggestions from its top personnel have led to changes in its regulatory orientation. Third, inter-institutional interactions also change institutions. The agendas and influences that political parties bring to legislatures influence their character, whether these have to do with gender sensitisation, minority rights or electoral and educational reforms. Finally, institutions also see replacement due to tumultuous events. Military coups, armed rebellions, revolutions and civil wars are occasions of tectonic changes in regimes and institutions. The replacement of the institutions of the Kuomintang regime in China by the communist party after 1949, the 1958 coup in France followed by the creation of the Fifth Republic, the 1969 military coup in Libya, the dissolution of former Yugoslavia in 1992 into six successor states following a fierce internecine war – all portray this change. An institutional replacement is followed by a solidification of new institutional formation and practices.

The process of entrenchment of newly introduced procedures or practices through legitimation implies institutionalisation of a practice. Leonard Broom and Philip Selznick call institutionalisation a 'neutral idea' and define it as 'the emergence of orderly, stable, socially integrating patterns out of unstable, loosely organized, or narrowly technical activities' (Broom and Selznick, 1955: 238). Selznick (1996: 271) adds, 'Perhaps the most significant aspect of institutionalization is infusion with value beyond the technical requirements of the task at hand.' Institutionalised activities have also been described as those that stay for long periods of time 'without further justification or elaboration, and are highly resistant to change' (Zucker, 1987: 446). According to Michael Tushman and Elaine Romanelli, 'The process of institutionalization, whereby recruits are rapidly socialized and organizational values and norms are taken for granted, is driven by conformity generating processes throughout the organization' (Tushman and Romanelli, 1985: 193). Institutionalised activities are resistant to change, more specifically rapid or fundamental change. Scholars have drawn attention to the structuration process – the interplay of action and structure (Barley and Tolbert, 1997) – as also discursive practices where actors through their interactions come to accept shared definitions of reality (Phillips, Lawrence and Hardy, 2004) in the process of institutionalisation.

Institutionalisation, however, is far from a linear process of positive achievements. Innovation and stability might not always go together (Ben-Dor, 1975). Maturing and consolidation are intercepted with occasional setbacks. There are possibilities of both institutional breakdown and over-institutionalisation in developing countries (Ben-Dor, 1975: 323). The non-reach of institutional laws, on the one hand, and the intensity of state interventions, on the other, portray such scenarios. All practices do not become equally institutionalised; the diffusion of a practice might not mean its institutionalisation. Similarly, institutional deepening can take place without a practice becoming routine (Tolbert and Zucker, 1996; Barley and Tolbert, 1997; Colyvas and Jonsson, 2011). To respond to the challenges of innovation and modernisation, the institutional structure should be able to do away with organisations which have become dysfunctional and are not able to innovate (Ben-Dor, 1975: 313). In case of the electoral administration in India, a steady modernisation of electoral procedures displays that innovation and stability have combined to produce relatively smooth institutionalisation. The introduction of photo identity cards, computerisation of electoral rolls, digitalisation of registration procedures and mechanisation of the voting system depict the routinisation of modern modes of participation. Biographically speaking, these faced initial hiccups and sometimes serious objections to the point of not being taken on board.

Organisational theorist Christine Oliver draws attention to processes of 'deinstitutionalisation' that follow a phase of successful institutionalisation over a period of time. This is a process of erosion or discontinuing of established practices for a variety of reasons. According to Oliver (1992: 564), deinstitutionalisation is a process 'by which the legitimacy of an established or institutionalized organizational practice erodes or discontinues'. She says that it is a result of 'organizational challenges to or the failure of organizations to reproduce previously legitimated or taken for granted organizational actions' (Oliver, 1992: 564). She identifies political, functional and social mechanisms both within and outside the organisation that lead to deinstitutionalisation (Oliver, 1992: 566). For instance, leader succession (political), intensified competition for scarce resources (functional) and changes in state laws or societal expectations (social) become determinants of deinstitutionalisation (Oliver, 1992: 570, 573, 575).

Fusion of political roles is another determinant of deinstitutionalisation that occurs when a single institution amasses disproportionate power. The boundaries between institutions get blurred and their functions begin to overlap. Disparate institutional structures in such a situation might continue to exist, but their authority decimates. New or weakly institutionalised democracies face such a state of affairs during executive or military takeovers.

Identity and Inputs

The distribution of powers between institutions gives us important clues about politics. This distribution may be vertical or horizontal or a combination of the two. A vertical distribution implies a top-down power flow and delegated authority. This verticality stands for a hierarchy of power and a centralised mode of governmental functioning. On the other hand, a horizontal distribution of power between laterally placed institutions means that there are multiple centres of authority placed at the same level. In practice, countries often design their institutional frameworks combining the two.

The institutional structure and political actors interact in political life which shapes behaviour and the environment. Both are active agents that determine the political culture of a given time. Formal institutional structures in democracies try to streamline and regulate a political process and direct it to appropriate ends. Rather than only reproducing power relations, they have a scope to alter them and create pushbacks to democratic backsliding, thus creating conditions of rewriting the logic of appropriateness using their autonomy. Parties and regimes in power tend to nurture situations where state institutions move in the directions that favour them. For instance, they attempt to direct electoral and judicial institutions on pathways that are agreeable to them. In a social context like India's where community attachments and identity markers are influential factors, clientelism is often at work in politics. Here, a commitment to institutional norms works in interesting ways where violation of rules is often not seen as such but as reciprocal gestures to reward sociopolitical support. The EC has to deal with such pressures while conducting elections. According to March and Olsen (1984: 742), 'Human actions, social contexts, and institutions work upon each other in complicated ways, and these complex, interactive processes of action and the formation of meaning are important to political life.' This also brings into focus the informal institutions and social practices that influence the workings of formal institutions. A case in point is the social hierarchies and dominant interests that are reflected in the building of institutional structures and their performance.

Democracy is an institutional form of government, and democratic consolidation rests on a well-calibrated institutional machinery working through checks and balances and transparency. In democracies, formal institutions check and restrain arbitrary action of the state and other dominant forces. They also imply secularised and non-personal functioning. They are impersonal and do not function on idiosyncrasies of individuals (Sanchez-Cuenca, 2003: 63). In democracies, institutions minimise partisan behaviour of governments and their power-driven actions. Institutional rules 'tame brute power' (Sanchez-Cuenca, 2003: 65).

Since a democracy works through distribution of powers between institutions and is structurally opposed to concentration of powers in a single individual or institution, a study of institutions helps in understanding its peculiar processes. Institutions here become a channel for representative functioning, and through them participatory rule becomes possible. Modern institutional functioning implies specialisation and differentiation of functions, which means governmental tasks are distributed between different institutions, thereby ensuring checks on arbitrary rule. The relation of institutions to politics is substantive. Their presence gives meaning to political practice. They shape politics and are in turn shaped by them. As systems of predictable and patterned behaviour, institutions minimise chaos that might result in a non-rule-based environment. Innovations or changes in institutional rules might mean increased costs in different ways: 'economically (it increases risks), cognitively (it requires more thought) and socially (it

reduces legitimacy and the access to resources that accompany legitimacy)'
(Phillips, Lawrence and Hardy, 2000: 28).[1] Conversely, laws create incentives
that 'men have no interest in subverting the institutional order' (Sanchez-
Cuenca, 2003: 63).

The importance of institutions and institutional norms for successful
democratic praxis has been emphasised in studies in comparative politics and
democracy with regularity (Neumann, 1963; Sanchez-Cuenca, 1998; Maravall
and Przeworski, 2003). Sigmund Neumann, while comparing political
parties, highlighted that that there are two kinds of political leadership –
institutional and personal (Neumann, 1963: 358). The first is largely a feature
of democracies where institutional set-ups might be different – for instance,
parliamentary or presidential systems – but the working of the polity here
happens within institutional norms and rules (Neumann, 1963: 358). On
the contrary, leadership in a dictatorial regime is personal, and the very
rise of modern dictators is an indication of the 'weakening or nonexistence
of political institutions' (Neumann, 1963: 358). New research, however,
points out that dictators prefer retaining institutions to prolong their rule.
Institutions like political parties, legislature and judiciary help the leader in
counterbalancing the opposition and retaining state power. Authoritarian
takeovers rely on institutional structures to neutralise rivals and help allies
(Brownlee, 2007; Gandhi and Lust-Okar, 2009; Ezrow and Frantz, 2011) –
more on this later in the chapter.

Political institutions restrain random, fanciful, individualistic behaviour
and guide the polity along impersonal and universal paths. According to
Ignacio Sanchez-Cuenca, 'Unless some limitations are applied to the capacity
for self-government, democracy may become a highly inefficient system,
unable to cope with the problems of collective weakness of will, lack of
credibility of promises and threats, collective action, and the instability of
collective choice' (Sanchez-Cuenca, 1998: 108). Institutions keep a democracy
anchored. Rules of the game are imperative for responsible political practice.

What about situations when institutions do not restrain arbitrary action
but become tools of a democratically elected regime of the day? There can
be situations when elected regimes resort to arbitrary action or violence and

---

[1] Phillips, Lawrence and Hardy (2000) look at collaborations to argue that institutionalised
rules and resources have a fundamental impact upon the dynamics of organisational
collaborations. Collaborations in turn influence the development of the institutional
field and the direction that is taken by institutionalisation.

break institutional rules themselves. Such violations of rules (constitutional law and established conventions) are usually given populist justifications. Rules are put aside in the name of 'development', 'national interest' or 'people's interests'. Institutions become instruments in the hands of the government to be deployed to curb political opposition and individual freedoms. Institutions then become tools of oppression rather than vehicles of regulated democratic praxis. If they exist, it is so nominally. As has been highlighted, even dictatorships or autocratic power rely on an institutional structure and some notion of the rule of law to rule (Barros, 2003). A stable institutional structure is not incompatible with autocratic rule. Conversely, rule by law or institutions are not exclusive to democracies (Barros, 2003). Political parties and legislatures help dictatorial regimes to distribute spoils, co-opt potential opponents and give party members access to scarce resources and contracts and circumvent government restrictions – the end result is that these regimes, because of their reliance on institutions, last longer (Brownlee, 2007; Gandhi and Lust-Okar, 2009; Ezrow and Frantz, 2011).

Examples of authoritarianism display that the autocrat or oligarch stands above institutions in authoritarian states – that is, political leadership and its supporters are above rules. Once entrenched in power, they let rules fall by the wayside. Retaining some institutions, however, actually helps dictatorial regimes. The difference is that power here flows from the individual leader and not institutions. In other words, in authoritarian regimes, power is vested in the leader, and in democracies power resides in institutions. Democratic rule relies on institutional norms and rules rather than the will and fancies of a few individuals (who hold the top offices of a state). Institutions are assumed to stand their ground in the face of executive pressures. Democratic rule becomes meaningful only when government is based on established institutional functioning that can withstand abuse of power at the hands of the executive. The government is as bound by rules as ordinary citizens and follows the rule of law. In practice, a democratically elected government might challenge this arrangement. Also, institutions have to negotiate more emphatically between regime pressures and institutional autonomy.

Liberal democracy has largely stood for a division of governmental powers. In other words, a separation of powers between different branches of government exists to restrain abuse of power by those steering the state (Maravall and Przeworski, 2003: 10). Divided power means limited power, greater interdependence and thereby limited government. Divided power is the antithesis of complete takeover of the state by the executive and arbitrary rule. However, a separation of powers and a system of checks and balances between different institutions of state is not enough and might not imply a government by rule of law. Even if powers are separated between different branches, a government may not be limited (Maravall and Przeworski, 2003: 11). It might still be able to misuse the power placed at its disposal through a popular mandate.

In other words, separation of powers between the executive, the legislature and the judiciary might not mean a democratic or limited government because these institutions may bend to the government's diktat and against the political opposition. Studies show that the judiciary many a time has acted in line with the ruling party or coalition (Gargarella, 2003: 161). Those who are in charge of state institutions can get together at particular junctures to crush just demands raised by the opposition. What makes separation of powers effective and conducive to moderate rule is when 'institutions have means and incentives to check one another and when their institutional prerogatives are backed by support from organized interests' (Maravall and Przeworski, 2003: 12). For instance, regimes moderate themselves to achieve a catch-all support base because they see in this an incentive to get re-elected. Conversely, the judiciary backed by civil society, opposition parties and media puts certain eligibility conditions on electoral candidates (including those of the ruling parties) for greater transparency in the system. The incentives for courts here are to prevent future erosion of the powers of the judiciary and a greater popular faith in the credibility of the judiciary – the popular vote might replace the incumbent government. The ruling party accepts this as it is in its interest when it is in opposition. Here one sees incentives and organised interests at work in the functioning of institutions.

Roberto Gargarella suggests that 'exogenous' controls like popular interventions and citizen activism might be more effective in protecting the rights of minorities and restraining abuse of power by political representatives. Legislative debates being open to the public might be more successful than relying exclusively on separation of powers with 'endogenous' controls like the judiciary or the executive to control parliamentary power (Gargarella, 2003: 156). The internal checks in themselves might not be enough to maintain rule of law and could need popular involvement or overreach. This arrangement is helped by a more egalitarian economy (Gargarella, 2003: 164).

The importance of internal and external constraints on governmental authority is evident from the distinct role each plays in regulating democratic practice. Internal checks manifest in separation of powers between different state institutions prevent concentration of power and thus make for interdependence and limited influence. Divided power also makes up for institutional lapses when one branch of the state structure compensates for what the other missed. Such work by supplementation of efforts helps in making legislation all-rounded as well as curbing undemocratic endeavours. Moreover, here the aggrieved can seek redressal cross-institutionally if need be. Such separation of powers leads to delay in policy formation which usually proves helpful in the long run, especially if that policy has long-term implications and covers a wide section of the citizenry.

This separation of power might not be sufficient in itself to constrain abuse of power by government if, as pointed out earlier, the other branches of the state stand with the ruling opinion. It is here that external or exogenous constraints help. Opening up key issues to the public might check the ruling authority – which is important to curb autocratic moves by the elected representatives. Public debates on key issues clearly bring both the majority and minority opinions to the front as also transparency in policymaking. Public debate is important, especially to put the representatives back in touch with their constituencies in case the hiatus has grown. The internal and external constraints have to go together to maintain the democratic spirit of representative government. This means that institutions that uphold democracy have to be open to democratic checks themselves.

The study of the EC and electoral practice in this context becomes important as it highlights these very tussles of control versus autonomy, arbitrary action versus institutionalised action, and executive dominance versus free and deliberative decision-making. Inter-institutional relationships, posturings of the political executive, institutional constraints, adherence to the rule of law and popular controls on institutional functioning bring out how resilient or otherwise a democratic set-up is. The implementation of the rule of law and institutional procedures is defied and challenged every now and then, especially by the dominant and the ruling. This study attempts to bring out the dynamics of this process.

The institutions, administration and procedures of elections have received relatively little attention compared to political praxis. While the role of politics in shaping institutions has been a focus of considerable attention, the reverse process has usually fallen on the backburner of research efforts. According to Robert Pastor, '... elections are both the supreme political act and a routine administrative exercise' (Pastor, 1999: 2). In advanced democracies, electoral procedures 'are taken for granted', but in poor and developing countries 'the administration of an election is no simple matter' (Pastor, 1999: 2). In these countries, 'the boundary line separating political manipulation and technical incapacity is rarely surveyed, and elections can fail for one or both reasons' (Pastor, 1999: 2). Elections are a big logistical and expensive exercise involving personnel, resources, technology and coordinated action. Pastor (1999) considers a study of electoral administration necessary to better understand the causes and consequences of democracy and also its effect on democratic transition. With passing time such studies have been undertaken.

Electoral institutions are crucial to democracies and legitimise the path to regime formation. This book with its focus on the EC tries to address some of these issues concerning the role of formal institutions in moulding democratic praxis. It argues that the EC through its distinct agency has institutionalised certain practices that have made political behaviour in India more participatory and choice-oriented besides systematising and streamlining electoral conduct. Despite facing pressures to conform, the EC has worked to ease the voting process for the citizen voters and helped them make informed choices, thus contributing to the institutionalisation of a more organised and modernised democratic praxis.

3

A Transforming India and the Role of the Election Commission

The context in which the EC functions has seen a transformation in more ways than one between 1990 and 2019. The purpose of this chapter is to give a glimpse into these changes to situate the EC within them and highlight how this institution has been an agent of a more predictable and procedural praxis within a socially and politically changing terrain beset by constant activity and restlessness. The 1990s were a time when the overarching presence of the INC weakened as also the numerical dominance of a single party in the parliament, and one saw the rise of minority and coalition governments. This was also a period of economic liberalisation, the rise of Hindutva and the political ascendence of the socially disadvantaged. The decade of the 2000s saw the consolidation of some of these trends in an era of growing accessibility to technology. After 2014, politics in India seemed to have moved again in the one-party dominant direction with a firmer executive control.

A 'Young' and Tech-Savvy India

The India between 1990 and 2019 (the period of this study) has seen many crucial changes. This is an India that has become younger over the years. According to the 2001 census, the age group between 15 and 24 years was 18.4 per cent of India's population (Census of India, 2001). By the 2011 census, this number – that is, of people between the ages of 15 and 24 years – rose to 19.2 per cent (Census of India and United Nations Population Fund [UNFPA], 2014: 7). In 2017, more than half the population was below 25 years of age, and two-thirds less than 35 years (Sharma, 2017). The proportion of 'economically active population (15–59 years) has increased from 53.4 to 56.3 percent during 1971 to 1981 and 57.7 to 62.5 per cent during 1991 to 2011' (Census of India, 2011: 7). With the liberalisation of the economy since 1991, even the middle class has seen a phenomenal growth – from less than 1 per cent of India's population in the 1990s to about 5 per cent in 2004 (A. Roy, 2018: 33). In 2016, scholars highlighted that the estimates of the size of the middle class vary, ranging from 5–6 per cent to 25–30 per cent of India's population (Jodhka and Prakash, 2016: 7). In 2019, using a diverse set of variables, Maryam Aslany demonstrated that the middle class in India was 28.05 per cent of the total Indian population (Aslany, 2019: 11). She highlighted that the most distinctive features of this middle class were over-representation of salaried employment and higher education (university-level education) (Aslany, 2019: 11–12). Considered important for economic, cultural and political reasons, the middle class is seen to propel market-driven growth, set cultural parameters of contemporary times and steer political opinions. Relatedly, cities where much of the middle class resides have gradually expanded to absorb village areas and urbanised the surrounding spaces. Census data (2011) points out that more than 30 per cent of India's population lives in urban areas today – the number could be much higher if one were to look at satellite data and relax the official definition of an urban settlement (Sreevatsan, 2017).

Beginning in the mid-1990s, India also witnessed a leap in media and communication technology. Internet usage grew phenomenally as Table 3.1 indicates.

Mobile phones and internet technology brought about far-reaching changes in the lives of Indians. For millions, these technologies meant 'choices, options, efficiency, privacy' (Agrawal, 2018: 14). These technologies eventually led to the emergence of the smartphone which 'could be India's great equalizer' as it gives people 'access to technologies that were until recently the preserve of a rich elite' (Agrawal, 2018: 5). The active use of new media technologies, especially by those on the margins, transformed the sociopolitical terrain. These new experiences diversified the Indian political culture. The monochromatic political choices gave way to diverse options, language, meanings and symbolisms. Caste and religious identity as the main basis of political choices, however, continued to play their role perhaps more strongly. What one witnessed was a 'fractured and splintered nature of the electorate' (Rangarajan, 2005: 3604), an 'ethnicization of electoral politics' (Jaffrelot and Verniers, 2011: 1105) and the 'rising social cleavages around

Table 3.1   Individuals using the internet in India

Year	Percentage of population
1995	0.026
2000	0.528
2005	2.388
2010	7.5
2015	14.9
2020	43

Source: World Bank, https://data.worldbank.org/indicator/IT.NET.
USER.ZS?locations=IN (accessed on 22 July 2022).

religion and caste' (Palshikar, 2013: 179). The voters in this social milieu entered an information age. The growth of information and knowledge economies contributed to raising consciousness about political rights and the popular expectations from successive governments for welfare benefits. Caste and community cleavages as identity markers, however, continued to play a role.

An increase in voter turnout in elections to some extent was brought about by the spread of media. Globally, traditional or print media is finding it hard to hold its ground and maintain its circulation, but in India it has grown significantly along with its digital variant. According to one estimate, newspaper circulation in India grew from 39.1 million copies in 2006 to 62.8 million copies in 2016 (Zehra, 2017). In 2015, it was estimated that this circulation went up by 12 per cent in India, while in many countries it declined – for instance, by 12 per cent in the UK, 7 per cent in the US and 3 per cent in Germany and France (Zehra, 2017). Rural and regional markets in India are providing an expanded scope to the media that is encouraging media houses to go 'hyperlocal' (S. Bansal, 2016). This focus has led to more vernacular and city or town editions of newspapers. Studies have pointed out that '[d]emographics, ever increasing literacy rates, educational needs, and strong desire to consume news and content in local languages, combined with nascent digital/broadband penetration' increase the spread of media in both its traditional and digital forms (Laghate, 2016). In April 2015, it was reported that the use of social media had grown 100 per cent in rural India (25 million users) and 35 per cent (143 million users) in urban India in the past one year, and that people accessed Internet mainly to use sites like Facebook and Twitter (Y. Bhargava, 2015). It is expected that the number of smartphone users is going to double from 404.1 million in 2017 to 829 million in 2022 (Indo-Asian News Service [IANS], 2018). The growth of the media has led to the dissemination of political news and messages to a wide cross section of the electorate in lesser and lesser time. Research has pointed out that the greater the level of exposure to the media, the higher is the interest in politics (Syal, 2012: 434) and also the level of political awareness among the youth (Attri, 2014: 6). Comparisons across regions point out that rural youth become more politically aware than their urban counterparts when they attain a high level of media exposure (Attri 2014: 6). The level of electoral participation among the younger voters is also positively related to exposure to media, though not as intensely as political awareness (Sampat and Mishra 2014: 37). The unprecedented spread of 'news' and 'fake news' in instant time through 'smart' technology means that voter choices are backed by more information, as also misinformation, about politics and economy than in the past. Technology is influencing politics, and the impact of the digital spread must be recognised (Mehta, 2019). Political parties, too, sensing the spread of digital media, have taken to digital platforms for campaigning and advertising, mainly among younger voters.

There might not be a complete causal symmetry between knowledge and a more assertive polity, but the former definitely plays a role in greater participation of voters in politics. The expansion of social media and the flood of information means new platforms of reporting, expression of political opinions and debate and faster flow of information. Acrimony and hostile exchanges on social media are also a factor that spurs greater political involvement. At higher levels, it means greater participation in political activities, including protest and demonstrations and contesting elections.

Looking at literacy, enrolment and higher education levels, one sees that they have steadily gone up in India. The total enrolment in higher education went up from 0.40 million in 1950–51 to 4.92 million in 1990–91, and rose further to 17.21 million in 2007–08. This increase between 1950–51 and 2007–08 was at a compound annual growth rate of 6.49 per cent (Government of India [GoI], 2011: B-2). The enrolment numbers rose to 38.53 million in 2019–20 (GoI, 2020: 13), which was a growth of 3.04 per cent from the previous year, 2018–19. The highest enrolment was at the undergraduate level (GoI, 2020: 13). Research indicates that education levels have a positive effect not only on the electorate's interest in politics, but also on political participation where participation stands for 'attending election meetings, participation in processions and rallies, door to door canvassing etc' (Syal, 2012: 435). Until the college or graduate level, the rise in education leads to higher political participation (Syal, 2012: 435). This in turn implies a more politically engaged citizenry even if its participation in politics is far from direct such as campaigning or contesting for elections. This increasing politicisation of individuals and groups in India has, on the one hand, led to demands for a more development-oriented, accountable and people-friendly political leadership. On the other hand, this has meant a more identity-driven electorate that votes with a heightened sense of a distinct social location, whether regional, religious or caste-based. These sociopolitical and technological changes over the last several years, especially since the early 1990s, meant that there have been new and politically conscious entrants into politics, and hence a more crucial and extended role for the EC.

Growing Politicisation and Participation

The growing assertions and politicisation of groups on the political margins (the Other Backward Classes [OBCs], Dalits, women and *adivasis*), conceptualised as the 'second democratic upsurge' (Yadav, 1996, 2000, 2004), was a major transformation in Indian politics in the 1990s. Besides this sectional upsurge, there was a regionalisation of politics at the state levels, the rise of Hindu nationalist politics, or Hindutva, and the unfolding of 'globalisation' (Hansen and Jaffrelot, 1999; Menon and Nigam, 2008; Venu, 2013). Politics of regional identity was the assertion of local power structures and that of cultural specificity at the state levels. Region-centric political parties came to power and established their hold over states. The upholders of Hindutva propagated the idea of India as a Hindu nation and argued that over centuries Hindu nationhood had been oppressed by 'alien' ideas and, after independence, by secular civic nationalism. They called for 're-establishing' Hindu political supremacy in India. The Hindu nationalist BJP's political footprint grew in the 1990s, and it provided a formidable opposition to the INC. The BJP steered the NDA coalition government between 1999 and 2004 – that is, for a full five-year term – and its electoral victories made it gradually outspoken about its Hindutva ideological leanings. Its growing countrywide popularity not only indicated anti-incumbency but also reflected the *Hindutva-ised* politicisation and the receptivity of *Hindutva* ideas in India.

Table 3.2   Voter turnout in Lok Sabha elections, 1951–85

Election	Year	Turnout (per cent)
First	1951	45.67
Second	1957	47.76
Third	1962	55.42
Fourth	1967	61.33
Fifth	1971	55.29
Sixth	1977	60.49
Seventh	1980	56.92
Eighth	1984–85	64.01

Source: *Electoral Statistics Pocket Book 2017* (New Delhi: Election Commission of India), 37.

During the same time period, globalisation was on a roll and led to India's economic liberalisation and integration with the global economy. There was a loosening of state controls over the economy, enhancement of private entrepreneurship, rise of foreign manufacturing collaboration and reduction in state-run monopolies. One also saw the diminishing of import licences and tariffs and the entry of private banks, among some other economic policy changes, during the tenure of former prime minister Narsimha Rao and finance minister Manmohan Singh (who later served as the prime minister for two terms between 2004 and 2014).

Alongside, voter participation saw a steady rise in successive elections (Table 3.2) as evident from the serpentine queues outside booths on polling days and also from the protests of those whose names were found missing from electoral rolls. In remote areas, voters were mobilised by their representatives and made their presence felt at the polling booths, turning election day into a vibrant festival. They moved in groups enjoying the 'day out' in each other's company and participated in the collective act of franchise. According to a former deputy election commissioner (DEC), 'In remote areas, political involvement apart from voting is not much. But during elections, each voter feels that he/she is contributing to the victory of their candidate – this makes them feel very proud and they also feel that their vote has value. Voters feel that they are helping their leader win.'[1] The number of voters saw a rise too. Voter participation in India during the first

---

[1] Rajarshi Bhattacharya, personal interview with the author, New Delhi, 5 August 2017.

Table 3.3 Voter turnout in Lok Sabha elections since 1989

Election	Year	Turnout (per cent)
Ninth	1989	61.95
Tenth	1991	56.93
Eleventh	1996	57.94
Twelfth	1998	61.97
Thirteenth	1999	59.99
Fourteenth	2004	57.65
Fifteenth	2009	58.19
Sixteenth	2014	66.4
Seventeenth	2019	67.11

Source: Election Commission of India, http://eci.nic.in/eci_main1/votingprecentage_loksabha. aspx (accessed on 14 July 2016); Election Commission of India, http://eci.nic.in/eci_main1/ SVEEP/VoterTurnoutHighlightsLokSabha2014.pdf (accessed on 4 June 2019).

parliamentary elections in 1952, which was 173 million, rose to 713 million in 2009 and to over 800 million in 2014 (EC, 2014a: 4). This grew further in 2019 as Table 3.3 displays.

The turnout went up to 64 per cent in the eighth general elections held in 1984–85, and it is believed that people thronged to the polling stations in sympathy to vote for Rajiv Gandhi as the INC's prime ministerial candidate after his mother, prime minister Indira Gandhi, was assassinated in October 1984. Voter participation was particularly high in 2014 and went higher in the 2019 elections where voters expressed their overwhelming support for prime minister Narendra Modi.

In percentage figures, this increase in voter turnout looks small, but its real meaning is revealed when seen in actual numbers. In 2009, the number of people who cast their votes in the Lok Sabha elections was 41.7 crore (417 million), according to the EC, and in 2014 this figure rose to 55.38 crore (553.8 million).[2] In the 2019 Lok Sabha elections, this figure jumped to about 61.31 crore (613.1 million) (EC, 2019). The figures when seen in isolation, however, do not reveal a striking aspect of the voter turnout – that 'the social composition of those who vote and take part in political activities has undergone a major change' (Yadav, 2015 [2000]: 120). 'There is a participatory upsurge among the socially underprivileged' (Yadav, 2015 [2000]: 120). As

---

[2] These figures are greater than the total population of the US.

discussed earlier, higher political consciousness mediated by class, caste and religious considerations has enhanced voter participation. The EC has also played a proactive role in portraying elections as a social responsibility and encouraging a positive attitude towards the 'vote'. It has worked hard to make elections a broader participatory exercise. The voting enthusiasm of the underprivileged witnessed over subsequent elections has brought the Indian election closer to the meaning of 'popular participation'. For instance, an encouraging development has been the rise in the number of women voters, bridging the gender gap in voter turnout in India (Kapoor and Ravi, 2014: 63–67; Roy and Sopariwala, 2019: 38–45; A. Bansal, 2019). Kapoor and Ravi (2014: 67) write that there is a 'significant and persistent reduction in gender inequality' in voter turnout 'in all state elections in India, over the past 50 years [1962–2012]'. They point out that the number of women voters to every 1,000 men voters increased from 715 in the 1960s to 883 in the 2000s (Kapoor and Ravi, 2014: 63). As stated earlier, the EC played a hands-on role to raise turnout among sections like women who generally shied away from the polling booth (more details in Chapter 9).

Election Campaigns and Regime Change

The 1990s were a time of minority governments. Election campaigns of different parties – mainly the BJP, the INC and the National Front (an alliance of political parties) – starting from the 1991 elections, centred on issues of construction of the Ram temple at Ayodhya, the Mandal Commission report, OBC reservations, social justice, stability, communal harmony, economic liberalisation and *swadeshi* (home manufacturing and local enterprise) (see Andersen, 1991; Yadav, 1999; S. Kumar, 2004). '*Mandir*, Mandal and market' were relatively new issues but dominated the election scene. The 1999 election battle was between 'videshi' and 'swadeshi' – epithets used for the INC's Sonia Gandhi and the BJP's Atal Bihari Vajpayee. The BJP also brought the successes of the previous Vajpayee government in the Kargil war to the campaign field. More important in deciding voters' choices but which did not gather much media attention were the regional and local political equations and performance of state governments. As Rob Jenkins (2000) points out, it was the 'minute process of localization at work' that became decisive in election results. The NDA coalition, led by the BJP, won the parliamentary elections of 1999.

In 2004, it was noted that while price rise and jobs continued to be influential issues during the elections, the quality of governance also became significant (Virmani, 2004). The quality of governance, which smoothens or toughens the flow of public services to the people, can swing votes one way or the other. In the 2004 elections, the vote went against the incumbent government (Virmani, 2004: 2567). Prime minister Vajpayee's 'India Shinning' campaign, directed mainly at middle-class India, failed to impress the Indian voters (Katju, 2019). In 2009, price rise and inflation were stated by the voters to be the most important electoral issues, and more so by the salaried urban voters (Rai, 2009: 81). However, the incumbent United Progressive Alliance (UPA) still won the elections (Rai, 2009: 82) and with a bigger mandate – confidence in its government was high. After the completion of elections, voters felt that the new government should take up issues like employment, price rise and poverty (Rai, 2009: 82).

During the campaign for the 2014 Lok Sabha elections, the same issues of price rise and 'development' came to the fore together with 'corruption'. The UPA government could not defend itself against the allegations of various scams – coal, the Commonwealth Games, 2G, and so on – it was accused of being involved in. The India against Corruption (IAC) campaign of 2011–12 that targeted the ruling UPA coalition for its alleged corruption scandals saw a surge of support among the urban middle class.[3] The IAC saw a significant involvement of the Rashtriya Swayamsevak Sangh (RSS) and BJP members, which was seen to have helped the latter politically. Inflation, corruption and governance were some major issues that influenced the relation of the citizens with the central and state governments and, consequently, their voting choices. 'Nationalism' and 'national security' also became major issues that stirred the electorate during the parliamentary elections of 2014 and 2019. The invoking of 'national security' and border clashes with Pakistan affected the electoral climate, especially events like the Pulwama attack and the consequent Balakot airstrike in early 2019.

Religious polarisation along the lines of nationalism and Hindu–Muslim relations contributed to influencing the voting choices of people. As it

---

[3] Pavan K. Varma, writing on the Indian middle class, highlights that it has 'singled out one issue above all else for expressing its anger: corruption' (Varma, 2014: 42). He also points out that 'even while expressing the most righteous indignation about corruption in "high" places, a middle-class person will readily become complicit in corruption for personal goals in the privacy of his individual world' (Varma, 2014: 43).

happens, community consciousness heightened, creating a climate for votes to be cast along 'Hindu', 'Muslim' or 'Hindu nationalist' lines. Increasingly, the issues which were usually identified with the middle class – namely masculinist nationalism, ardent patriotism and political religiosity – saw larger popular support. Election data revealed a strong affinity between the BJP and the urban middle classes (which includes a substantial proportion of the privileged and upper castes) and its support for Narendra Modi as the prime minister, which extended to the younger electorate in these classes (Sridharan, 2014: 74–75) during the 2014 elections. This combined with the votes of those who voted like the conventional middle class substantially increased the support for Modi. In fact, this round of elections was seen by some as a 'Modi election' whose campaign was 'American-style' and 'personalized' (Andersen, 2015: 50). The UPA lost the general elections in 2014 to the BJP-led NDA, and Modi became the prime minister. In Delhi, the new Aam Admi Party (AAP, an offshoot of the IAC campaign, formed with an overwhelming base among urban voters on the plank of rooting out graft and 'cleaning' politics) formed the government with INC support in 2013. It won these elections overwhelmingly on its own in 2015.

Besides inflation, corruption and governance issues, people's involvement in protests and demonstrations on issues of land takeovers, religious and caste discriminations, gender-based violence, agrarian crisis, and so on, rose. Unrest in Nandigram and Singur in 2007–08 over land takeovers by the state government in West Bengal for industrialisation is one such case. Protests around the installation of nuclear plants in Kudankulam and Jaitapur in 2010–11 is another example. Popular protests asking the state to be proactive on issues of violence against women after the Nirbhaya gang-rape in 2012–13 and protests against non-implementation of rehabilitation and resettlement measures in 2014 because of displacements caused by the Posco steel project are some other instances that saw people's involvement in big numbers. These popular agitations were successful in denting the popularity of the incumbent governments, especially the central government led by the UPA.

The election year of 2014 brought about major political shifts, one of which was the expansion of Hindu right politics and the ethnicisation of its democracy. One witnessed the growing traction of religio-cultural questions as vote mobilisers surpassed the swing potential of economic distress in the context of unequal development and growing digital literacy. The BJP's towering stature in politics, which began in 2014, strengthened in 2019. State power, overwhelming popular support and considerable financial assets made it an authoritative force in Indian politics, reviving the latter's one-party dominant characteristic (though with a difference in that this time the dominance is much stronger and consolidated). Scholars, however, have emphasised the strong possibility of a two-party framework referring to the BJP and the INC, looking at their countrywide presence and the way parliamentary politics have been coalescing around them. In 1999, it was said that 'it is not absurd to visualise Indian polity in essentially a two-party framework' (P. Ghosh, 1999: 3342). Though the parliamentary presence of the INC has considerably shrunk, it remains a countrywide opposition force both at the parliamentary and state levels.

Party Fragmentation

Talking of the party system in India, it became more diversified and competitive in the 1990s. Political alignments and realignments of smaller parties and individual leaders changed the political terrain and intensified competition. Party splintering and floor crossings became a norm. Voters displayed divergent affiliations – they often voted for different parties in parliamentary and state elections. The divisions within the party system began mainly with the breaking up of the grand old party, namely the INC, due to a variety of reasons that ranged from a centralised control (grip of the 'high command') over the party structure and consequent deinstitutionalisation of work culture, a depleting national consensus on secularism and socialism, growing regional aspirations, de-consolidation of power centres, 'mandalisation of politics', and so on. The party saw a gradual chipping away of its ethos and the emergence of smaller parties that were mainly led by the socially and economically dominant groups in the states, which marked their presence around lingual and regional pride as also caste identity.

The new parties were vocal about their social distinctiveness and showcased it vis-à-vis the INC. According to Eswaran Sridharan and Peter Ronald deSouza, political parties no longer shy away from being ethnically based or extreme in their orientation because these help in getting them elected in their region of origin, and they get a share of power in an 'appropriate coalition' (Sridharan and deSouza, 2006: 26). It was the Lok Sabha elections of 1996 which brought about a new phase of Indian politics as well as a party system (Sheth, 1996; Pai, 1996; Palshikar, 2013). People felt 'more involved' in politics (Sheth, 1996: 44), and elections become 'much more competitive than before' (Palshikar 2013: 170). This political fragmentation was variedly seen as the rise of 'federalization' (Pai, 1996: 1182), 'regionalization of state politics' (Pai, 1998) and 'multiple bi-polarities' at the state level and 'fragmented party system' with partial alliances at the national level (Sridharan, 2010). It was also noted that most parties were new and 'there is no uniform pattern of party competition across the states of India' (Suri, 2013: 210). Possibilities of a two-party framework in times ahead were also expressed as discussed earlier.

Scholars draw attention to the paradox of deficit of inner-party democracy in the larger setting of democratization (P. B. Mehta, 2001; Suri, 2013). In fact, party fragmentation has been explained as the consequence of lack of inner-party democracy. According to Pratap Bhanu Mehta, 'If there are no formal mechanisms to challenge entrenched party hierarchies and regulate conflict within parties, they are more likely to fragment' (P. B. Mehta, 2001). He points out, 'Comparative evidence from Europe and Latin America also suggests that where intraparty democracy is better institutionalized, there is less likely to be fragmentation of the party system' (P. B. Mehta, 2001).

The rise of coalition government was also seen as giving rise to regional parties because the latter saw coalition government as increasing benefits and payoffs like ministerial berths, increased discretionary funds, and so on (Ziegfeld, 2012: 76). It was argued that rather than ethnicity, it is factors like clientelism, coalition government and elite positionings that determine the success of regional parties (Ziegfeld, 2016: 19). Growing politicisation of the electorate has seen a rise in aspirations which the centralised party system has not been able to fulfil adequately. This has led to a drive for self-representation and floating of parties by dissatisfied groups themselves. An alternative framework to explain the proliferation of political parties was presented by Chhibber, Jensenius and Suryanarayan (2014), who demonstrated that the level of party organisation has an impact on party volatility and the number of political parties. They argued that in states where political parties are more organised, there is a lower effective number of parties compared to those where parties are less organised. They argued that in mixed systems, where both less and more organised parties exist, the number of political parties can go even higher.

The rise in the number of political parties in India is an established fact, and what is also recognised is that these parties are largely marked by a lack of inner-party democracy. The party leadership (often a family) keeps a tight hold over the party organisation in a centralised mould. Concerns have been expressed regarding the lack of inner-party democracy (Sridharan and deSouza, 2006: 24). The National Commission to Review the Working of the Constitution (NCRWC) also noted this absence along with some other problems in political parties like lack of women's representation in legislative forums, secrecy in party funding, falling moral standards of political leaders, lack of undertaking of political education by political parties, and so on (NCRWC, 2002b: 425–27). Due to these factors, inner-party democracy remains a far cry in the Indian party system.

Besides facilitating the emergence of new parties, the demise of the 'Congress system' propelled the state as the most significant and effective political unit (Yadav, 2004: 5384; Yadav and Palshikar, 2006: 104). The state became 'the relevant unit at which politics was conducted and was intelligible as well' (Yadav and Palshikar, 2006: 104). New parties making the state their first ground of political battle was a phenomenon that became widespread in the 1990s. A trend which was also noticed during 1989–2004 was that the turnout was often higher in the state assembly elections than at the parliamentary level, strengthening the claim that people related more to the state government than the central one (Palshikar and Kumar, 2004: 5412-13; Roy and Sopariwala, 2019: 57). Though the BJP won the 2014 Lok Sabha elections with an absolute majority, it would be too soon to see this development as a metamorphosis of 'fragmentation into the nationalization of the party system' (Jaffrelot and Verniers, 2015: 28–29). One cannot still dismiss the 'importance of state-based parties and, more broadly, of state politics' (Jaffrelot and Verniers, 2015: 43).

Between the 1950s and 1980s, the vote share of regional parties was around 20–30 per cent before rising significantly in the 1990s and levelling at about 45 per cent (Ziegfeld, 2012: 73). In 2004 this vote share crossed 50 per cent, and in 2009 it was 53 per cent (Vaishnav, 2014). Even in the 2014 elections, when the BJP single-handedly won an absolute majority, the regional parties gathered more than 40 per cent of the vote (Ziegfeld, 2016: 8). The fragmentation is also clear from the rise in the number of independent candidates contesting the Lok Sabha polls – a seven-fold rise. Their number went up from 533 in 1952 to 2,385 in 2004 and 3,691 in 2009. The number of independent candidates came down marginally to 3,235 in the 2014 general elections.

The party system today is much more split than it was even 20 years ago. There are more than 450 political parties in India today. The party system is also less ideologically oriented than earlier. Though there are the BJP and the Shiv Sena on the right and the communist parties on the left of the ideological spectrum, they have often been driven by pragmatic considerations – power compulsions have led to some dilution of ideology. The INC itself has tried to maintain its centrist stance, though with a social–democratic tilt. The increased multiplicity of parties in India has added its own facets to the task of managing the electoral process. In this atmosphere of heightened political involvement, the quantum of work of the EC has increased, and it has acquired a more active role in regulating electoral practice.

Composition of Legislative Forums

Deficiency of democracy, if not a complete absence, has continued to inflict inner-party functioning. While noting the lack of inner-party democracy, Mehta notes, 'The current state of our parties is schooling our politicians in arbitrariness, haphazardness, uncertainty and lack of deliberative purpose' (P. B. Mehta, 2001). Political life is also seen as becoming 'a site for the crook, the criminal and the compromised' in an environment where the Nehruvian consensus about an egalitarian order is seen 'as irrelevant now' (Khare, 2001). In 2003, there were about 700 legislators (members of parliament [MPs], members of legislative assembly [MLAs] and members of legislative council [MLCs]) in the country with criminal records (Samuel and Jagadananda, 2003: xi). Contemporary times have seen an intensified competition in Indian politics with the aim to influence public office. A scenario of personal gain dominating over public good is seen time and again. Political leadership is often perceived as indulging in subversion of democracy through use of force and wealth. Public morality and sacrifice have been seen by many as scarce entities in Indian politics today.

Data gathered by two non-governmental organisations (NGOs), the National Election Watch (NEW) and the Association for Democratic Reforms (ADR), in 2013 revealed that 1,460 (30 per cent) out of 4,807 sitting MPs and MLAs had criminal cases pending against them – of these 14 per cent of MPs and 15 per cent of MLAs had serious criminal charges against them.[4] In the 16th Lok Sabha, formed after the 2014 general elections, there were 34 per cent, or 186, MPs who had criminal charges against them as

---

[4] See the following reports from *The Hindu* and Rediff.com: Ali (2013) and Nanjappa (2013).

was brought out by the ADR by analysing the election affidavits filed before the EC (Rukmini, 2014; Varghese, 2014). Out of these 186 MPS, there were 112 who declared serious charges against them, including murder, attempt to murder, kidnapping and crimes against women (Varghese, 2014). The figures for 2009 and 2004 were 30 per cent and 24 per cent, respectively (Rukmini, 2014). The ADR data also revealed that those candidates who faced criminal charges were more than twice as likely to win as compared to those with a clean record (Rukmini, 2014).

Despite this 'criminal' content, the legislative forums have actually become more representative. Figures gathered by the Social Watch group in 2003 reveal that the first Lok Sabha had 51 per cent members who were lawyers, doctors, journalists and writers (Samuel and Jagadananda, 2003: 3). The lawyers themselves filled up one-third of the seats in the House. The number of these professionals had fallen to 14.65 per cent in the 12th Lok Sabha (1998 elections). Similarly, traders and industrialists who had 12 per cent seats in the first Lok Sabha saw their numbers come down to a low of 2.25 per cent. On the other hand, agriculturists had just 22.5 per cent of the seats in the first Lok Sabha. Their share in political power rose over the years and touched 49 per cent in the 12th Lok Sabha (Samuel and Jagadananda, 2003: 3). According to B. L. Shankar and Valerian Rodrigues, '... the Indian Parliament has not merely coped with the demands made on it, but has facilitated the process of broadening and deepening democracy' (Shankar and Rodrigues, 2011: 8). There has been an 'inclusion of diverse interests, groups and communities in the making of a polity … and the participation of diverse interests in deliberation and discussion to form public policy' (Shankar and Rodrigues, 2011: 8).

In a contrast to the 1950s, the occupational background of the Lok Sabha in the 1990s was quite diverse, with computer engineers, sportsmen, religious missionaries, artists, actors, management consultants, pilots and even poets making up this diversity (Shankar and Rodrigues, 2011: 94). The number of women members in the Lok Sabha rose too. There were 5 per cent, or 22, women members in the first Lok Sabha in 1952. In the 14th Lok Sabha in 2004, this number grew to 8.29 per cent, or 45. This further rose to 11.3 per cent, or 63, in the 16th Lok Sabha in 2014 and 14 per cent, or 78, in the 17th Lok Sabha in 2019.

In an environment of increased diversity, sectional politicisation and also inter-group competition, ensuring non-coercive, non-manipulative electoral conduct has become the prime responsibility of the EC. It has to ensure the continuation of free and fair elections. What this implies is that as democracy is deepening and parties are increasing, the need for institutional safeguards has not declined but, on the other hand, has assumed critical importance. In such a political situation, the EC's role, along with that of the Supreme Court and the parliament, to maintain democracy in inter-party interaction has become significant.

Ironically, these are also the times when the Indian state has moved away from the social sectors of health, education and employment. Budgetary allocations for these have shrunk over the years, and private ownership is being handed a greater share and freer hand to operate these services. While the education budget has stayed around 3–4 per cent of the gross domestic product (GDP) over the last decade (roughly 2006–16), the health allocations have been more dismal, staying around 1–1.5 per cent of the GDP. Private money, motivated by profits, has taken over these two sectors. Quality and affordable education and healthcare have been and continue to be out of reach for a majority of the people. This is so in the case of employment too. The net of government employment is reducing over the years. Cuts in government jobs and state withdrawal from public sector enterprises have meant that the Indian state is refraining from handing jobs by way of direct employment. Organised employment – both state and private – has shrunk, whereas the share of unorganised and insecure employment is close to a stark 90 per cent.

Need Felt to Reform the Electoral System

In this scenario, the idea behind reforming the electoral system was to make it more participatory, free, fair, equal and transparent. Reform of the electoral procedure in fact became a concern right in the late 1960s. It was felt that changes in law will have to be brought about to rectify the weaknesses and anomalies that affected elections. In 1970, the Joint Parliamentary Committee on Amendments to Election Law was formed to look into the question of electoral reform comprehensively, but it was unable to do much because of the dissolution of the Lok Sabha in December 1970 (Reddy and Ram, 1992: 15). These attempts were followed by others. Several recommendations and suggestions came in from diverse sources such as the EC, political parties, the Law Commission, the Supreme Court, governmental committees and private individuals. Electoral reforms thereafter became a subject of much academic and analytical writing. Civil society and concerned individuals felt that to draw out voters, the registration process had to be kept simple, polling facilities accessible and the voters' confidence upbeat. It was felt that to improve the electoral system there was also a need to curb corrupt practices like bribing, intimidation, violence, hate speeches, distribution of money, and so on. Campaign expenditure also needed regulation so that no one got an undue advantage over others. It typically happens in democracies that the bigger and ruling parties have an advantage over smaller and opposition parties as far as resources and power are concerned. This needs a levelling of the playing field where everyone participates relatively equally. Transparency of the election procedure is another issue which is the responsibility of the election administration. The procedure of voting as well as the counting of votes have to be transparent so that the public is satisfied that its votes are not being manipulated at any level. These concerns were expressed in the public domain by many.

The following committees (mostly official) deliberated at length on electoral reform in India and gave their recommendations on improving the system:

- The Tarkunde Committee Report, also called Report of the Committee on Election Expenses (1975)
- Report of the Committee on Election Expenses (1978)
- The Dinesh Goswami Committee on Electoral Reforms (1990)
- The Vohra Committee Report (1993)
- The Indrajit Gupta Committee on State Funding of Elections (1998)
- The Law Commission on Reform of the Electoral Laws (1999)
- The National Commission to Review the Working of the Constitution (2000)
- Election Commission of India's Proposed Electoral Reforms (2004)
- The Second Administrative Reforms Commission (2005)
- The Law Commission Report (no. 255) on Electoral Reforms (2015)

Why are electoral reforms needed in India? Both general and specific concerns were raised for the need of such reforms. More specifically, the influence of wealth and coercion on elections was seen as having had a spoiler effect. The

Dinesh Goswami Committee (1990) expressed an anxiety about elections in the following words:

> [I]t becomes imperative to take stock of the present state of affairs which causes real concern and anxiety because of the existence of the looming danger threatening to cut at the very roots of free and fair elections.
>
> The role of money and muscle powers at elections deflecting seriously the well accepted democratic values and ethos and corrupting the process; rapid criminalisation of politics greatly encouraging evils of booth capturing, rigging, violence etc.; misuse of official machinery, i.e. official media and ministerial; increasing menace of participation of non-serious candidates; form the core of our electoral problems. Urgent corrective measures are the need of the hour lest the system itself should collapse. (GoI, 1990: 2)

The committee felt perturbed by the money and muscle power and malpractices that were corrupting the election process. Reforms were seen by many as essential for continuing free and fair elections, strengthening of parliamentary democracy, halting the erosion of institutions and the decline of the political process, and maintaining the purity and integrity of the electoral process (S. Sen, 1991: 282; Reddy and Ram, 1992: 5; Dube, 1992: 63; Gehlot, 1992: 81). Over the years, the same reasons were given for bringing in reforms like curbing the use of money power, violence and force in elections, preventing proliferation of parties and candidates, and controlling fissiparous tendencies, casteism and communalism (Law Commission of India, 1999; Ahuja, 2000: 38).

In an opinion poll conducted in 1994 by *India Today* (news fortnightly), it was found that 57 per cent of those who resided in urban areas and 48 per cent of those who lived in rural areas felt that poll reforms were necessary (*India Today*, 1994: 56). Twenty-five per cent of urban and 18 per cent of rural residents felt that they were necessary, but nothing would change. Only 8 per cent of urban and 13 per cent of rural Indians felt that reforms were not necessary (*India Today*, 1994: 56). This poll was done when T. N. Seshan was the CEC. His tenure saw a number of streamlining measures introduced in the electoral system which caused quite some friction with the government in power. The *India Today* poll revealed that people rated Seshan's performance as the CEC very highly (*India Today*, 1994: 56). Overall, the 'clean-up' of the system was received well.

The call for reforms continued as time passed. The Second Administrative Reforms Commission, in its fourth report, called *Ethics in Governance* (2007: 8), said:

> India was fortunate that high standards of ethical conduct were an integral part of the freedom struggle. Unfortunately, ethical capital started getting eroded after the transfer of power. Excesses in elections (in campaign-funding, use of illegitimate money, quantum of expenditure, imperfect electoral rolls, impersonation, booth-capturing, violence, inducements and intimidation), floor-crossing after elections to get into power and abuse of power in public office became major afflictions of the political process over the years.

While noting the 'unhealthy role of money power, muscle power, mafia power and corruption, communalism and casteism', the NCRWC, in its report submitted in 2002, mentioned certain specific problems related to elections where reform was needed. These were:

> Increasing cost of elections leading to unethical and illegal practices where even the mafia was involved to finance elections;

> Competing role expectations and conflict of perceptions e.g. the constituents expect even members of the Union Parliament to attend to their purely local problems because the constituents/electors are the same for all elections from the lowest Panchayat level to the Lok Sabha level;

> ... the mismatch between the majoritarian or first-past-the-post system and the multiplicity of parties and large number of independents.

> The question of defections and the Tenth Schedule.[5]

> Inaccurate and flawed electoral rolls and voter identity leading to rigging and denial of voting rights to a large number of citizens.

> Booth capturing and fraudulent voting by rigging and impersonation. (NCRWC, 2002a)

---

[5] The 10th schedule of the Constitution of India contains provisions with regards to defections from political parties. It elaborates the grounds for disqualification of legislators if they defect from their parties.

Besides mentioning these, it also said that the '[i]nvolvement of officials and local administration in subverting the electoral process, engineered mistakes in counting of votes, increasing number of contestants with serious criminal antecedents' were the problems with the electoral system. It noted that the judicial process dealing with election petitions is 'ineffective and slow', which often makes the whole process 'meaningless'. Problems like fake and non-serious candidates to 'subvert the electoral process' and 'incongruities in delimitation of constituencies' were other issues mentioned by the commission. In the end, it felt that elections were plagued by 'loss of systemic legitimacy due to decay in the standards of political morality and decline in the spirit of service and sacrifice in public life'. In its 255th report, the Law Commission (2015: 1) reiterated that the influence of money and criminal elements in politics and the lack of internal democracy and financial transparency in the functioning of political parties had plagued the electoral system. The EC itself has been a major crusader of voter-friendly elections. It has petitioned the existing governments to carry out changes in election procedures and norms, which it has considered important for making polls freer and fairer. The different CECs wrote to the governments of the day to introduce reforms that would streamline elections and make the process less complicated and transparent (discussed in the subsequent chapters).

It has been felt by the advocates of reforms that they are needed to rectify structural and behavioural flaws. Structural matters like first-past-the-post system, delimitation, possibilities of hung assemblies, dummy candidates, and so on, were seen as issues to be mended. On the behavioural side, the conduct of candidates and parties such as matters of finance and force needed to be reformed. Both of these were seen to render representation less meaningful. The undertone that electoral politics is a sullied terrain which needs to be sanitised is not hard to discern in the talk of electoral reform. According to Yogendra Yadav, this discourse on reform, on the one hand, 'expresses a radical democratic yearning for an alternative kind of politics.... On the other hand, it serves, as a medium for the middle class will to power, unmediated by the tedious processes of democracy' (Yadav, 2005: 30). The call to reform electoral practice thus seems to include both impulses – to democratise politics, on the one hand, and to closely manage it, on the other, which might not always be driven by democratic inclinations. For Yadav, electoral reforms are dominated by the managerial bureaucratic perspective which is closely related to the quest for moral regeneration of public life (Yadav, 2005: 30–31).

The discourse of electoral reform, with its language of 'cleansing', 'correcting', 'rectifying' of the electoral process and 'governance' involving 'various stakeholders', has been a part of the civic domain for some time (Public Affairs Centre [PAC], 2006: 1). This discourse has been popularised by civil society organisations. The PAC, the ADR, the People's Union for Civil Liberties (PUCL), the Catalyst Centre, Action for Good Governance and Networking in India (AGNI), and so on, were some active civil society organisations engaged in highlighting the specific areas that needed electoral reforms. Acting as pressure groups on the parliamentary and judicial systems, they put in efforts to 'cleanse' the electoral process to 'enhance transparency, accountability and citizen participation in electoral processes' (PAC, 2006: 1). This included campaigns to enhance informed choices among voters (PAC, 2006: 1). These initiatives stood on the belief that the quality of governance is contingent upon 'improvement in the quality of the elected leadership' (PAC, 2006: 1). These campaigns focused on (a) voters who represent the 'demand side' and (b) election authorities who form the 'supply side' (PAC, 2006: 2), and partnered with the media to intervene in the electoral process with the aim to 'empower' voters. The PAC itself consciously decided to focus on the urban middle class, which had been seen as apathetic to the electoral process due to lack of information and an indifferent bureaucracy (PAC, 2006: 6).

The engagement with questions of electoral reform in the public arena, though, lay outside the direct political terrain. It did not find much active support from most political parties – the electoral contestants. According to Trilochan Sastry, a founder member of the ADR, the organization's work on reforms has not found much support from political parties, even the smaller ones; on the contrary, its efforts were opposed by political parties.[6] However, the support of the media and the public has been immense as also the support of the EC.[7] Thus, there was not much collaborative work between civil society organisations, the media and political parties on electoral reforms, with the latter being conspicuous by their absence. It is from within the urban middle

---

[6] Trilochan Sastry, personal interview with the author, Bengaluru, 14 November 2016. Sastry teaches at the Indian Institute of Management (IIM), Bangalore, and is a founder member and trustee of the ADR, which was formed in 1999 by a group of professors at IIM Ahmedabad, where Sastry was a professor back then. The ADR is an NGO which works in the areas of improvement in governance and of electoral and political reforms.

[7] Trilochan Sastry, personal interview with the author, Bengaluru, 14 November 2016.

class, which makes up the ranks of civil society in India, that the concern and effort to reform came. This, mainly the professional middle class, which constitutes an observer of politics rather than a direct participant, articulated the need for more transparency in the system and an enhancement of voters' rights. The talk of reform was directed towards regional power centres that dominated politics as also developmental resources at the regional levels, and thus had come to acquire 'muscle' as a means of social influence.

The pressure to reform politics which came from the professional middle class reflected the impatience of the class with the newly emergent forces that were trying to find a space for themselves beyond the boundaries of local politics. According to Surinder Jodhka and Aseem Prakash, although a large majority of the middle class 'were happy to embrace modernity, they were not always comfortable with growing demands for inclusion from below through the dynamics of "democracy"' (Jodhka and Prakash, 2016: 94). The discourse of reform focusing on accountability of action, more transparency in procedures, openness about past conduct, strict restraints on the use of coercion, and so on, became the points of contention between reform facilitators and political competitors in state and national politics. The former felt that the latter need to be restrained and educated about norms and also be bound by them. The latter, on the other hand, felt that they did not need reforms and restraints – their victory in elections established their legitimacy.

It is in this context of political cross-currents and competition that the EC conducted elections between 1990 and 2019. Far-reaching political, economic and social changes occurred, and they constituted the shifting terrain in which the electoral administration tried to infuse procedural conformity and structured conduct.

4

The Election Commission

Leading the Electoral Administration

The conduct of elections in India after independence became the responsibility of the EC, which came up as a constitutional institution in 1950. It was visualised as a structure with a definite function – Article 324 of the Constitution of India elaborates its tasks and responsibilities. It had the normative purpose of concretising the process of representation and free choice in government formation as also streamlining democratic praxis. This chapter highlights its nature and role in transforming Indian democracy. The EC, from being a regulatory institution that oversaw elections, also became a path-paver for political practice. It systematised voting and contesting practices and made efforts towards a more transparent and accountable electoral conduct. In other words, it contributed to bolstering procedural democracy. The Supreme Court, with its judgments and directions, strengthened the EC's hands in this endeavour. Voters and parties in course of time expected more from the electoral administration, demanding procedural simplification, work efficiency and more choices (such as the choice to express their disapproval of contestants). The EC worked towards the fulfilment of some of these expectations.

Constitutional Institution

According to Robert Pastor, it is after the Second World War that independent election commissions began to emerge and evolve (1999: 5). These commissions were important in bringing about 'horizontal and vertical accountability' and 'defend[ing] democracy outside the courts' (Pastor, 1999: 5; Kildea,

2020: 469). In India it was from the time of political reforms of 1919 under the colonial state that 'distinct legal structures for elections were codified' (Gilmartin and Moog, 2012: 136–37). Unlike electoral commissions of many democracies such as the UK, the US, Canada, Australia and New Zealand, which were created by legislative statutes, the EC of India was created by the Constitution (the Electoral Commission of South Africa, which came into being much later – that is, in 1996 – is also a constitutional institution). According to David Gilmartin and Robert Moog, the EC of India was conceptualised as standing 'apart' from the government and 'above' everyday politics, and its significance lay in the constitutional effort to link the process of elections to the idea of the 'nation' (Gilmartin and Moog, 2012: 137).

The setting up of an election commission was the subject of an intense debate in the Constituent Assembly (CA). B. R. Ambedkar, the chairperson of the Drafting Committee of the Constitution of India, pointed out during the CADs on 15 June 1949 that there were two options before the Drafting Committee regarding the setting up of an election commission: first, there should be in existence a permanent body of four or five members to continue in office without any break, and, second, a body should be appointed by the president as and when an election was scheduled (for details, see Katju, 2006). The committee took a middle course and proposed to the CA to have permanently in office one person called the CEC so that a 'skeleton machinery would always be available' to handle the in-between work of, say, a by-election or mid-term election in the event of the dissolution of a House before five years and also the revision of the electoral rolls (see Katju, 2006). The proposal was that the president in the event of an election might add other members to the EC subject to the laws made by the parliament in this regard. Much later, the EC became a three-member body – a change brought about by the government and upheld by the Supreme Court.

In India, the electoral machinery is centralised, implying that there is a single EC to manage elections to both the parliament and the state legislatures. There was much discussion in the CA regarding the setting up of a single body to handle elections at the two levels. Some members of the CA saw this as a move towards an uncalled-for centralisation. Ambedkar elaborated the reason for going for a single EC to handle both central and state elections (Katju, 2006). He informed the CA that the central government had received reports from certain provinces claiming that sections that did not racially, culturally or linguistically belong there were being discriminated against and were excluded from being brought into the electoral rolls by the governments of those provinces. Ambedkar noted that it was to prevent this injustice that the Drafting Committee had moved away from the original proposal of separate election commissions for different provinces and opted for the single and centralised EC. Besides this, issues like economic development, unity and integrity of the new nation and border security were weighing on the new state, taking it towards a strong-centre policy (see CADs, 15–16 June 1949, for further details). Hence, the decision for a single, centralised EC was taken.

The EC has been termed as 'the means to the end of a vibrant representative democracy' (deSouza, 1998: 53) and as a 'bulwark for free and fair elections in India' (Rudolph and Rudolph, 2001: 154). The institution of elections has been seen as 'one of the few bridges available for political traffic' amidst an environment where all other mediating institutions have collapsed (Yadav, 1996: 96). It also has been viewed as 'one of the most important and credible institutions' that has contributed to Indian democracy (Murthy, 2008: 199). Gilmartin and Moog (2012: 138) point out, 'To understand fully the role of the EC in election administration, however, it is critical to understand its dynamic relationship to the broader structure of court-adjudicated electoral law.' While 'the EC's authority in some ways lies outside the purview of direct judicial oversight', its position has to be understood 'in relationship to a large body of statutory electoral law that also defines the legal parameters of India's electoral processes largely independently of EC authority' (Gilmartin and Moog, 2012: 138).

A look at the role of the EC in the 1990s suggests that 'the strengthening of its regulatory role has coincided with the period during which confidence in cabinet and Parliament, the instruments of developmental, interventionist state, has eroded' (Rudolph and Rudolph, 2001: 161). One witnessed more popular trust reposed in it than in legislative bodies that represent the body politic. Its constitutional status and people's trust gave it a stature of remarkable substance.

The EC has 'considerable autonomy of action' as it 'derives its authority directly from the Constitution' (U. K. Singh, 2004: 10). But there are ambivalences about its terrain of work. As Ujjwal Kumar Singh points out, '[c]ontending claims of the Parliament and the Election Commission, over the power to govern and the responsibility to govern, respectively' come up (U. K. Singh, 2004: 23). It has an 'authoritative' role, a 'commanding' position in its work sphere where its writ becomes the rule that is binding on all, whether the government, the opposition, the bureaucracy or the voting public, but its power is drawn from its constitutional location and the parliamentary jurisdiction within which it functions. This implies that the EC occupies a unique space and a distinct set of responsibilities, but as an institution it is not autonomous in the institutional structure of democracy. Like the parliament and the Supreme Court, it is a constitutional institution, but in the institutional hierarchy it is preceded by them. The parliamentary laws shape the EC's functioning, and the court judgements clear the grey areas and give the EC direction on the ground. The parliament and the Supreme Court are crucial in strengthening its autonomy. The EC is also not a multitasking organisation as the above two. Its task is to regulate electoral conduct and elections. The parliament and the judiciary, on the other hand, handle a variety of issues related to representation, policy and adjudication – and the parliament, of course, makes laws on all issues pertaining to the state and society.

Within this interconnected institutional field, the Constitution empowers the EC to take decisions fairly independently. To enable the EC to work in a reasonably autonomous manner without undue interference from the government, a provision was incorporated in the Constitution that said that 'the Chief Election Commissioner shall not be removed from his office except in like manner and on the like grounds as a Judge of the Supreme Court', that his conditions of service would not be altered to his disadvantage after he took over as the CEC (Article 324: clause 5). This provision shields the EC from considerable political pressures coming from the government in office.

The EC works on a dual axis – that is, it is placed between the citizen voter and the political parties and also between the citizen voter and the government of the day. Institutions like the EC make sure that citizen voters are not deprived of their right to elect their political representatives freely. The EC safeguards the rights of the citizen voters to choose. This right is the same across classes, manifest in the practice of universal adult franchise. Universal adult franchise is an equaliser, and the EC has the responsibility of safeguarding it. It is said that 'many general elections have been held through out [sic] the country, few cases have reached the Supreme Court. This is a great tribute to the fair and efficient working of the Elections Commission of India' (Reddy, 2010 [2008]: 276).

The EC functions under the law ministry and consists of about 300 officials who work in a hierarchical set-up (EC, 2018c). Its expenses are met with a budget that is decided in consultation with the finance ministry.[1] In its own words, 'The latter generally accepts the recommendations of the Commission for its budgets' (EC, 2018c). The expenses of parliamentary elections are borne by the government at the centre and those of legislative assemblies by the state or union territory concerned. Expenditure for elections that are simultaneous is shared equally by the union and state governments as also the capital equipment expenditure related to the preparation of electoral rolls and the making of electors' identity cards (EC, 2018c).

The EC's senior officials – the CEC, ECrs, DECs and director generals – are drawn from the civil services (administrative, revenue, and so on) and serve the EC on deputation for a limited time period. It follows a functional and territorial distribution of work. In its own words,

> The work is organised in Divisions, Branches and sections; each of the last mentioned units is in charge of a Section Officer. The main functional divisions are Planning, Judicial, Administration, Systematic Voters' Education and Electoral Participation, SVEEP, Information Systems, Media and Secretariat Co-ordination. The territorial work is distributed among separate units responsible for different Zones into which the 35 constituent States and Union Territories of the country are grouped for convenience of management. (EC, 2018c)

The subordinate officials are permanent staff who work for it in a long-term capacity and are appointed by the Department of Personnel and Training (DoPT). It is said that a key reform would be to provide the EC with a permanent and independent secretariat (where, for instance, it does its own appointments and recruitment) to protect its staff from various pulls and pressures coming from the executive (Mohanty, 2019). The Goswami Committee on electoral reforms (1990) had suggested the setting up of a secretariat for the EC on the lines of the Lok Sabha Secretariat (Article 98 [2]), which gives the parliament a regulatory role regarding the recruitment and service conditions of persons appointed as secretarial staff for the Lok Sabha (EC, 2016f: 5). Subsequently, the government introduced the Constitution (Seventieth Amendment) Bill, 1990, in the Rajya Sabha to give

---

[1] The EC has recommended that its budget should not be drawn from the law ministry's budget but from the Consolidated Fund of India to give it more autonomy in its functioning. These suggestions were made as far back as 1998 (*The Telegraph*, 2016).

effect to the recommendation of the Goswami Committee. This Bill was, however, withdrawn because the EC became a multi-member institution from a single-member one. It was not reintroduced thereafter (EC, 2016f: 5). The EC reiterated this position of an independent secretariat in 1998 and again in 2004 (EC, 2016f: 5). The EC felt that 'in order to fully insulate the Commission from political pressure or executive interference, it is essential to set up an independent Secretariat for the independent functioning of the Election Commission' (EC, 2016f: 5).

According to T. S. Krishnamurthy, a former CEC, 'political neutrality' is an essential component of the functioning of the EC and the sanctity of the elections, but there are several instances when this becomes doubtful (Murthy, 2008: 36–47). The personnel who take part in election management many a time face political pressures and come under partisan influences that make a mockery of non-partisan work. Also, 'it is not uncommon for family members of senior civil servants to take an active part in elections; some even contest on party tickets' (Murthy, 2008: 40). Like the administrative services, the EC has to guard against these influences and pressures to avoid turning into an extension of the government and a 'committed bureaucracy'. The dangers of succumbing to political pressures are strong because the appointments, especially the higher ones, are political appointments. The independence of the EC is important, and it 'must also be *perceived* as independent and competent' (Pastor, 1999: 18). As mentioned earlier, most of the ECrs are drawn from the bureaucracy, mainly the Indian Administrative Service (IAS). According to former CEC S. Y. Quraishi, there is a reason for this, which is ground experience. He says, 'Experience of working in varied departments of the government helps in working in the EC.'[2] As the job requires a fair amount of administrative experience, IAS credentials help in handling local situations deftly.

Handling Elections

Organising and managing an election is an enormous task and involves huge resources – human, financial and technical. An infrastructure has to be created and maintained regularly. The importance of electoral administration

---

[2] S. Y. Quraishi, personal interview with the author, Gurugram (Gurgaon), 23 January 2017.

has been underscored by scholars time and again (Jinadu, 1997; Pastor, 1999; Mozaffar and Schedler, 2002; Karp et al., 2017; Clark, 2019; Garnett, 2019; Ham and Garnett, 2019; James et al., 2019). In established democracies of the world, these procedures and processes are taken for granted but in developing countries 'the administration of an election is no simple matter' (Pastor, 1999: 2). Low levels of education, incapacities of the bureaucratic personnel, weak infrastructure and an inexperienced and coercive political domain make it hard for developing countries to hold and manage elections (Pastor, 1999: 10). In a situation of stretched resources and capacities, there exist enormous problems in putting together and managing this machinery. Developing and resource-poor countries often find it difficult to organise elections. They do not have the wherewithal in terms of resources, trained personnel and technology to hold regular elections that are defining features of democratic functioning. A number of problems and weaknesses of electoral administration in several African countries is due to underdevelopment and economic crises (Jinadu, 1997). Violence and internal conflicts add to the difficulties in enfranchisement and registration as in the case of Sierra Leone (Kandeh, 2003: 194). Resource crunch, strife and lack of trained personnel have acted as significant deterrents to conducting elections. Elections also need autonomous electoral commissions in democratic and democratising countries that are free from party and regime biases (Gazibo, 2006). All in all, the capacity and money needed to conduct elections might not be there – it is not merely a matter of intentions.

In India, the election administration and procedures were set up in colonial times. This experience helped much in managing elections after independence, though in free India elections became true to their meaning with the introduction of universal adult franchise and a multiparty system. Over time, the apparatus was strengthened with appropriate laws and machinery. The staff of the 'steel' bureaucracy helped in managing the onerous task of elections. According to a former DEC, the higher officials of the EC are helped and supported by the staff of the EC whose role is important and determines the character of the institution.[3] As Eswaran Sridharan and Milan Vaishnav point out, the successful holding of elections in India after independence 'faced – and, in many ways, still faces today – a host of cumbersome challenges...' (Sridharan and Vaishnav, 2017: 417). In the face of

---

[3] Rajarshi Bhattacharya, former DEC, personal interview with the author, New Delhi, 5 August 2017.

these challenges, the EC 'has proven to be a model of election management...' (Sridharan and Vaishnav, 2017: 417). The EC, besides the Lok Sabha and state assembly elections, also handles the presidential, vice-presidential and Rajya Sabha polls – not to mention by-elections all year round.

Administrative and police personnel are deputed by the central and state governments for the purpose of elections. There is no alternative administrative machinery meant for the purpose, which means that the same bureaucratic personnel conduct elections. These personnel remain on deputation to the EC as returning officers, presiding officers, polling officers, and so on, from the date of the formal notification of elections till the declaration of results. They work for the EC during this period as per Section 28A of the Representation of the People Act, (RPA) 1951. To remove or minimise chances of undue advantage to ruling parties, the EC has the power to post and transfer these officials. This has caused much friction between the EC and political parties (discussed in detail later in the book). The Supreme Court in 1984, in the case of *Election Commission v. State of Haryana*, held that though the state government was the best possible entity to assess the law-and-order situation in a state, it was the EC which had the ultimate authority to decide whether law and order in a place was conducive to holding an election. The EC does a thorough exercise to assess the deployment of police forces in various states before an election. It also assesses whether there is a need for extra forces from outside the state and the time needed to move the central forces from one state to another (see EC, 2009b).

In *Krishna Ballabh Prasad Singh v. Sub-Divisional Officer Hilsa-cum-Returning Officer and Others* (1985), the Supreme Court clarified that the process of election comes to an end only after the returning officer makes the declaration of election results in Form 21C (declaring a candidate elected) and completes the other formalities like issuing the certificate of election in Form 22 to the victorious candidate. Thereafter, the control over the bureaucratic machinery reverts to the central and state governments.

Article 329 of the Constitution restricts the courts from interfering in the electoral process during elections. Article 329 (b) of the Constitution states that

> no election to either House of Parliament or to the House or either House of the Legislature of a State shall be called in question except by an election petition presented to such authority and in such manner as may be provided for by or under any law made by the appropriate Legislature.

The election of a candidate can only be challenged through an election petition filed before the High Court. For presidential and vice-presidential polls, this petition has to be filed before the Supreme Court. Election petitions can be filed by candidates or voters (under Article 329 [b] of the Constitution and Section 80 of the RPA, 1951) if they are convinced that an election to the Lok Sabha or state legislatures was won unfairly – that is, it involved unfair, corrupt or non-statutory practices. An election petition can be filed within 45 days of the declaration of the results for a constituency. If the irregularity or illegality is proven in the court, the election of the returned candidate is declared void and re-election scheduled by the EC.

Speedy trial of these election petitions is emphasised in law. Section 86 (6) of the RPA, 1951, states:

> The trial of an election petition shall, so far as is practicable consistently with the interests of justice in respect of the trial, be continued from day to day until its conclusion, unless the High Court finds the adjournment of the trial beyond the following day to be necessary for reasons to be recorded.

Sub-Section 7 of Section 86 says:

> Every election petition shall be tried as expeditiously as possible and endeavour shall be made to conclude the trial within six months from the date on which the election petition is presented to the High Court for trial.

Section 100 of the RPA, 1951, specifies the grounds on which the high court can declare an election void. These are:

(*a*) [...] on the day of the election a returned candidate was not qualified to contest the election or stood disqualified from the seat,

(*b*) [...] the returned candidate or his/her election agent or any other person with the consent of the former is guilty of a corrupt practice,

(*c*) [...] any nomination has been improperly rejected, and

(*d*) [...] the result of the election has been affected by improper acceptance of any nomination, or corrupt practice, or anomaly of any vote, or any kind of non-compliance with the Constitution of India or the RPA, 1951, or any other election rules.

An appeal against the order of the High Court can be made in the Supreme Court within 30 days from the date of the order. In such a case, the decision of the Supreme Court on the election petition is final. Filing of election petitions challenging results has not been uncommon in India. Elections of presidential candidates have also been challenged. For instance, petitions were filed against the election of the first president of India, Rajendra Prasad, as also against Zakir Hussain, V. V. Giri, Neelam Sanjiva Reddy and Giani Zail Singh (see J. K. Chopra 1989: 149–51). A petition was also filed against former president Pranab Mukherjee by P. A. Sangma who lost the election to Mukherjee. In an interesting case, the Madhya Pradesh High Court in 2013 set aside the election of Paras Saklecha, an independent MLA from the Ratlam city constituency (who had raised the Vyapam scam issue in the state assembly in 2009), for 'corrupt practices' just six months before he completed his five-year term in the Madhya Pradesh assembly. The election petition was filed by Himmat Kothari of the BJP, a former minister and, in this case, the defeated rival candidate. Kothari's contention was that Saklecha had made baseless allegations against him, which had influenced the mind of voters. The High Court disqualified Saklecha as he did not produce documentary evidence of the allegations of financial irregularities he had levelled against Kothari. Saklecha petitioned the Supreme Court against the lower court's verdict. The Supreme Court stayed the High Court judgment and granted him some relief – Saklecha could attend the assembly proceedings but could not vote.

In *B. Sundra Rami Reddy v. Election Commission of India and Others* (1991), the Supreme Court held that the respondents in these petitions can only be those who are mentioned in Section 82 and 86 (4) of the RPA, 1951 – that is, the candidates who had contested elections in that particular election and no other. The EC, it was made clear by the Supreme Court, could not be made a respondent in an election petition by the petitioners. These rulings by the Supreme Court reinforced the EC's position as a referee whenever doubts arose. It clearly became more empowered to guide democratic processes in the face of dominant political forces. It only had to use that strength. The main restraint had to be applied vis-à-vis the ruling parties who had state power at their disposal. This is where the autonomy of mediatory institutions like the EC holds importance as it becomes key to fair and free elections. Inability to restrain ruling parties from electoral malpractices is tantamount to institutional infirmity in the face of the ruling power.

Parties and Voters

As distinct from external checks like civil society, media or people's movements, the EC forms an internal systemic check on the government and political parties. It is part of the formal institutional structure constituting a safeguard which restraints the arbitrary exercise of power during elections that disturbs the electoral equilibrium. It is also a stocktaking and feedback agency to refine the electoral system. Representative politics in modern democracies need regulatory institutions like the EC to ensure that the process of representation moves ahead smoothly. This is especially so in a vast and diverse country like India where the enthusiasm for participating in elections has grown phenomenally over the years. Indian elections have been aptly called 'carnivals of democracy' – celebratory events that stretch out to the entire country and generate oneness. In 2015, the EC stated that 1,866 political parties were registered with it – 56 of these were recognized as registered national and state parties (Press Trust of India [PTI], 2015). In 2014 (March), this number stood at 1,627 (PTI, 2015). However, the number of political parties that actually participate in Lok Sabha elections is fewer as Table 4.1 indicates. In 2019, the number of political parties that contested parliamentary elections was 671 (EC, 2019).

Table 4.1 Number of political parties that participated in Lok Sabha elections

Year	Number	Year	Number
1951	53	1989	113
1957	15	1991–92	154
1962	27	1996	209
1967	25	1998	176
1971	53	1999	169
1977	34	2004	230
1980	36	2009	363
1984–85	42	2014	464

Source: *Electoral Statistics Pocket Book 2017* (New Delhi: Election Commission of India), 39.

The EC plays a role which is both restrictive and facilitative. It attempts to curb political party excesses during elections and reprimands and censures violations of poll code. On the facilitative side, it encourages voters to cast their vote and exercise their democratic right of franchise. Its pedagogical role has been emphasised in its voter mobilizational drives. According to former CEC Nasim Zaidi:

> The EC must educate voters adequately about citizenship and electoral democracy, spread awareness about various facets of their right to vote; voters must be able to use their right to vote in a free and fair manner i.e, they should be able to vote without intimidation and threat and uninfluenced by any form of external inducements.[4]

The efforts of the EC were received well by the voters. According to Zaidi:

> Voter education on ethical voting with many voter friendly innovations launched by ECI was received positively by voters particularly women electors.[5]

It is from the very first elections that the EC has played an educative and persuasive role to mobilise voters to exercise their right of franchise. Historian Ramachandra Guha, writing about the first election in India, says, 'Throughout 1951 the Election Commission used the media of film and radio to educate the public about this novel exercise in democracy' (Guha, 2008: 135). It has gone on mobilisational drives and persuaded people to come to the polling booths. From the term of Quraishi, this role of the EC took on a more enthusiastic turn. The EC has diversified these means of educating the public about elections and used them to enhance voter participation.

The EC has made efforts to draw in more women, young voters and other vote-shy groups into the electoral process and to bring down poll-related violence. It has a say in inter-party activities like use of party symbols, campaigning, mobilising, contesting, and so on, which fall in the public domain. However, it does not have much of a role in intra-party dynamics – say, in selection of party leaders and contestants, writing of manifestos, party policy, and so on, which remain in the so-called 'private' domain of a political

---

[4] Nasim Zaidi, email interview with the author, 4 August 2020.
[5] Nasim Zaidi, email interview with the author, 4 August 2020.

party. The EC has not been able to enter this internal space of political parties, though it tried to intervene here too from the time of CEC T. N. Seshan's tenure. Seshan had urged political parties to elect their office-bearers within a reasonable time frame or face derecognition. The EC, as its authority lies outside the inner-party domain, can only restrain rule deviation in the public arena and regulate inter-party competition.

A paradoxical situation is seen in elections in India. While the EC's presence has grown stronger in the electoral system since the mid-1990s, deviation from rules by political parties has also grown. For instance, cases of violation of the Model Code of Conduct (MCC) and election expenditure limits have gone up. There are increasing cases of hate speech and clientelist behaviour on the part of political parties as well as the violation of spending limits. The permissible spending limits are crossed during elections despite their revision from time to time. Physical acts of violence during elections have come down significantly, but the element of silent intimidation of voters or the distribution of cash and goods to them in violation of poll norms has not been eradicated.

The EC is also powerless in the face of the influence of dominant social forces in an area. This influence can be in a single constituency or spread over several. The EC has not been able to fully root out this influence of the local 'strongman', whose power is localised but immense. This local influence resembles the power of erstwhile feudal lords whose writ ruled in their territories. The voters usually do not vote against the strongman's wishes despite the security offered by the secret ballot, fearing retribution. The EC can prevent outward and visible violence, but this subterranean coercion is difficult to restrain. This is the reason why the EC has recommended the use of 'totalisers' – devices in the electronic voting machines that allow votes from multiple booths to be counted at the same time. This obscures any possible voting patterns from emerging, which in turn protects voters from harassment by local goons once results are declared.[6]

Notwithstanding these problems, the EC has been effective in bringing about a more rule-bound election in recent years. Trilochan Sastry of the ADR, which has been involved for a long time in the work of electoral

---

[6] According to former CEC N. Gopalaswami, totalisers were first recommended after the Uttar Pradesh assembly elections in 2007, when feedback was received that people feared violence from candidates against whom they had voted. Voting figures and caste calculations booth-wise can indicate the voting pattern (*The Telegraph*, 2016).

reforms, corroborates that the EC has been able to bring about far greater compliance to electoral norms than earlier.[7] He says that now there is more 'fear' among political parties about the consequences of violation of rules during elections.[8] About violations of the MCC, Quraishi says:

> Though the penalty for the violation of the code is not more than a reprimand, censure or condemnation (which many people consider toothless!), parties and candidates are extremely cautious not to attract a notice from the EC. Any violation becomes a media headline and attracts condemnation from society in general. (Quraishi, 2015)

According to him, 'The EC is often called toothless and inefficient, but it has been able to ensure a rule bound election where violence is almost nil.'[9]

The EC's visible presence and 'hands-on' approach during the election process has ensured that parties and candidates are more conscious of abiding by the rules than before the early 1990s. This has been supplemented by social pressure and pervasiveness of the media. However, the huge costs of elections and the consequent violation of expenditure limits are still an issue, and law has proved to be less effective – this has been a cause of much concern in civil society. Added to this is the new system of electoral bonds, which obfuscates financial transparency (these issues are taken up in detail in Chapter 7). There is a view that to stamp out unfair practices in elections, 'there is a need to strengthen the hands of the EC and give it more institutional and legal powers', that it must be 'entrusted with powers to punish the errant politicians who transgress and violate the electoral laws' (Kaur, 2008). However, what needs to be foregrounded is that the EC has been able to infuse some normative element into electoral behaviour, because of which voters and parties have acted as checks on each other to make the system more transparent and 'cleaner'.

The EC Consolidates Its Position

The EC's visibility on the political scene came about during the tenure of Seshan as the CEC between 1990 and 1996. During this period, the EC

---

[7] Trilochan Sastry, personal interview with the author, Bengaluru, 14 November 2016.
[8] Trilochan Sastry, personal interview with the author, Bengaluru, 14 November 2016.
[9] S. Y. Quraishi, personal interview with the author, Gurugram (Gurgaon), 23 January 2017.

marked its presence as an unwavering rule-enforcing institution while conducting elections at the national and state levels.[10] This was a phase of its consolidation that is attributable to endogenous factors. According to former CEC J. M. Lyngdoh, it made efforts to equalise and bring the ruling party to the 'level of its competitors' (Lyngdoh, 2004: 70). Krishnamurthy (2008: 58) points out that from this time onwards it 'started asserting its authority by distancing itself from the government of the day'. It asserted itself especially on matters of scheduling of elections and creating a level playing field between the ruling party and the opposition parties (Murthy, 2008: 58). The Kalka (Haryana) and Ranipet (Tamil Nadu) assembly by-polls were cancelled when the respective chief ministers announced new development schemes after the announcement of the elections (Lyngdoh, 2004: 79).

Seshan was varyingly referred to as 'a bull in a china shop' (Sidhu, 1991: 66), a 'dictatorial super government' (Baweja, 1994: 115) and a 'madman' (Baweja, 1994: 115) by political leaders for his steadfastness towards enforcements of EC instructions. J. Jayalalithaa, a former chief minister of Tamil Nadu, called him an 'embodiment of arrogance' (Ramakrishnan, 2019). He warded off criticism by claiming to be 'more popular than Amitabh Bachchan' and an 'endangered species' (Baweja, 1994: 115). It was reported that his involvement in court cases had made the litigation costs of the EC rise from INR 1 lakh (0.1 million) in 1991–92 to INR 22 lakh (2.2 million) in 1993–94 (Mitta, 1994: 75). He remarked that all institutions, including the judiciary, had 'degenerated', at which the Supreme Court warned him to 'keep his mouth shut' (Mitta, 1994: 74). His adamant stance over introduction of voters' identity card brought him into confrontation with governments at the centre and of various states. He announced in 1993 that he would not hold any election after 1 January 1995 in a state if the voters were not provided with identity cards (Mitta, 1994: 75).

The streamlining of election procedures went ahead despite these acerbic exchanges while Seshan was in office. Restraints on spending and display of wealth gathered force during his tenure. It is reported that the November–December 1994 assembly elections, especially in Andhra Pradesh and Karnataka, were 'most lackluster in recent times' (Ansari, 1994: 90). Absent during these elections was the 'vulgar displays of garish posters,

---

[10] J. M. Lyngdoh points out that the first time the EC 'had showed some spine' was in a by-election in 1981 when the EC under S. L. Shakdher did not bow down to the INC's will to postpone the Garhwal parliamentary constituency by-poll (Lyngdoh, 2004: 59).

cutouts and banners'. Also absent were the 'instances of rigging and misuse of government machinery'. Even then prime minister P. V. Narsimha Rao's convoys 'consisted of just a handful of cars' (Ansari, 1994: 90). The EC took a tough stance against candidates who had not filed daily expenditure reports. Election officers stated, 'All along we have heard about free and fair polls. Now Seshan is making it a reality' (Ansari, 1994: 91). In 1995, the state and union ministers were banned from touring from the date of the announcement of the general election schedule (Lyngdoh, 2004: 75).

Seshan won the Ramon Magsaysay award in 1996 'for his resolute actions to bring order, fairness, and integrity to elections in India, the world's largest democracy' (Ramon Magsaysay Award Foundation, 1996). According to the award citation, 'He [Seshan] banned ostentatious campaign displays and noisy rallies and required candidates to clean up walls and building defaced with their slogans.' In a Karnataka village, a voter remarked, 'I have heard the name Seshan. He has put an end to all the ugly posters and blaring loudspeakers. It's the best thing to happen' (Ansari, 1994: 91). The EC thus induced sobriety in election campaigning.

The central government, uneasy with Seshan's firm stance, appointed two additional commissioners to the EC. It also drew out an electoral reform bill in an effort to rein him with a fairly long list of provisions like equating the status of ECrs with the CEC and empowering them to overrule his decisions, legalising the MCC and thus reducing the powers of the commissioners over it, stipulating that the EC cannot issue identity cards without the approval of the government, instructing that the EC hold by-elections within six months of a seat falling vacant, giving statutory status to election observers and thus taking over the authority of the EC over senior government officers and withdrawing the EC's power to countermand elections (Mitta, Agha and Ghimre, 1994: 83). Eventually this reform bill was not tabled by the government for fear of being defeated in the parliament (Baweja, 1994: 114). The moral aura that Seshan had acquired made the government drop the legal move against him.

However, the government continued with its attempts to politically tame the EC. The EC was not always a three-member body. It was a single-member commission till 15 October 1989, with only R. V. S. Peri Sastri, the CEC, as its member. Thereafter, it turned into a three-member body till 1 January 1990. S. S. Dhanoa and V. S. Seigell served as additional ECrs from October 1989 to January 1990. Reportedly, there were problems between Sastri and the then INC government led by Rajiv Gandhi. The result was the appointment of two additional members to the EC on the recommendations of the government. However, from 2 January 1990 to 30 September 1993, it again became a single-member commission because the National Front government removed the two ECrs who had been appointed by the previous INC government.

There was a change again, and from 1 October 1993 the EC turned into a three-member body once more as a result of the alleged tensions between the EC and the central government led by P. V. Narsimha Rao. The CEC during that period was Seshan. As discussed earlier, he was known for his outspokenness and forthrightness with governments. Seshan's straight-talking and abrasiveness had upset the ruling dispensations at the centre and in some states. His way of working might not have had been unique, but it became a source of contention due to its timing. This style obstructed the surge of those on the political margins into the political mainstream and led to stand-offs between him and the elected representatives. Tensions arose between them – an instance of inter-institutional friction – but this interface had an impact on political conduct, pressing upon it the need for greater accountability.

The central government issued an ordinance in 1993 to appoint two additional commissioners. It said, '[T]he business of the Commission shall be transacted by the EC as a whole and if the CEC and other Commissioners differ in opinion on any matter, the matter shall be decided by the opinion of the majority' (see Gadkari, 1996: 22). In 1994, this ordinance was replaced by the Chief Election Commissioner and Other Election Commissioners (Conditions of Service) Amendment Act, 1993, which amended a previous Act of 1991. M. S. Gill and G. V. G. Krishnamurty were appointed as the additional commissioners. The Act was challenged by Seshan along with some others in the Supreme Court. A five-member bench of the Supreme Court, in its judgment of July 1995, dismissed Seshan's petition against the government and unanimously upheld the appointment of two additional commissioners to the EC. On the bitter relations between the CEC and the ECrs, which had been much discussed in the media, the Supreme Court said:

> The CEC and the ECs are high-level functionaries. They have several years of experience as civil servants behind them. All of them have served in responsible positions at different levels. It is a pity they did not try to work as a team. The efforts of Shri Gill to persuade the other two to forget the past and to get going with the job fell on deaf ears. Unfortunately, suspicion and distrust got the better of them. (EC, n.d.5)

The Supreme Court hoped that

> they will forget and forgive, start on a clean state of mutual respect and
> confidence and get going with the task entrusted to them in a sporting
> spirit always bearing in mind the fact that the people of this great
> country are watching them with expectation. For the sake of the people
> and the country we do hope they will eschew their egos and work in a
> spirit of camaraderie. (EC, n.d.5)

The tussle involving the expansion of the EC by appointment of two additional
commissioners saw an inter-institutional engagement – the executive,
legislature and judiciary all became involved to hammer out a constitutional
matter that was decisive for politics in times to come. Eventually all converged
over the desirability of an expanded EC.

Parliamentary unease might be the immediate cause of the addition of
two more members to the EC, but the larger churnings made this expansion
inevitable and desirable. It was a call for depersonalisation or democratisation
of the EC itself. One of the ways to ensure that was through the appointment
of additional commissioners. This was a way of preventing personalisation of
authority and, in fact, was needed to save a constitutional institution from
turning into a mere extension of an individual's whims. It has also indirectly
given more strength to the EC and consolidated its authority to streamline
the electoral process and take on the excesses of power with steadfastness.
The EC has been a three-member body ever since 1993.

About the position of these three members, it should be mentioned that
though the EC works through consensus and majority decisions, the two
ECrs do not enjoy the same constitutional protection as the CEC. While the
latter can only be removed through impeachment, the former can be removed
on the recommendation of the CEC. Suggestions for reforming this feature
of the EC and placing the ECrs on the same position as the CEC have come
up from time to time. The EC under Krishnamurthy proposed some reform
measures just after the 2004 general elections, which included a proposal that
the provision for the removal of the other ECrs should be made the same as
that of the CEC (see Katju, 2009: 10). The proposal document says:

> In order to ensure the independence of the Election Commission and to
> keep it insulated from external pulls and pressures, Clause (5) of Article
> 324 of the Constitution, inter alia, provides that the Chief Election

Commissioner shall not be removed from his office except in like manner and on like grounds as a Judge of the Supreme Court. However, that Clause (5) of Article 324 does not provide similar protection to the Election Commissioners and it merely says that they cannot be removed from office except on the recommendation of the Chief Election Commissioner. The provision, in the opinion of the Election Commission, is inadequate and requires an amendment to provide the very same protection and safeguard in the matter of removability of Election Commissioners from office as is available to the Chief Election Commissioner. (EC, 2004a: 14)

Such a situation arose in 2009 when the incumbent CEC, N. Gopalaswami, made a *suo motu* recommendation to the president for the removal of ECr Navin Chawla on the grounds that the latter had been acting in a partisan manner and was close to the INC, which was then in power. Although the recommendation was rejected by the president, the proposal to bring about a reform to the provision of removal of an ECr gained ground.

Appointment of the EC members

The appointment of the EC members has itself been a subject of debate. At present the CEC and the ECrs are appointed by the president of India on the advice of the government. Suggestions have come that the appointments of the CEC and the other ECrs should be more broad-based so that the question of bias in appointments is eliminated and the EC is viewed as an impartial body by all. The Tarkunde Committee (1975) and the Dinesh Goswami Committee (1990) made their recommendations in this matter (see Katju, 2009: 10). The former recommended that the members of the EC should be appointed by the president on the advice of a committee, consisting of the prime minister, the leader of the opposition (or an MP selected by the opposition) in the Lok Sabha and the chief justice of India. The Goswami Committee on electoral reforms was set up by prime minister V. P. Singh in 1990. It recommended that the CEC should be appointed by the president in consultation with the chief justice and the leader of the opposition, and that the other two ECrs should be appointed in consultation with the chief justice, the leader of the opposition and the CEC. It also said that this consultation process should have statutory backing. Further it recommended that after retirement the CEC and the ECrs should be made ineligible not only for any appointment under the government but also to any office including the post of governor – an issue which is contentious and has come up for debate. For instance, Seshan's and Gill's entry into politics after they completed their CEC tenure stirred up this issue (see Padmanabhan, 2004).

In 1997, former union minister for external affairs Inder Kumar Gujral wrote, 'The Election Commission being an arch stone in the entire democratic system, its impartiality, judiciousness and even mindedness must be ensured' (Gujral, 1997: 3). He suggested that to ensure this, the EC should be a multi-member body 'that should be selected by a panel comprising of the Chief Justice of India, a Senior Judge of the Supreme Court and senior-most Chief Justice of High Courts' (Gujral, 1997: 3).

In fact, during the CADs a suggestion was made by one of the members that the appointment of the CEC should be subject to confirmation by a two-thirds majority in a joint session of both the Houses of the parliament (CAD, 15 June 1949) (Katju, 2009: 10). Finally, it was left to the parliament to make appropriate laws on the matter. In 2006, a suggestion was made by former CEC B. B. Tandon (May 2006) to former president A. P. J. Abdul Kalam (when both were in office) that a seven-member committee headed by the prime minister should choose the CEC and the other ECrs. This committee should include the Lok Sabha speaker, the leader of the opposition in the Lok Sabha, the leader of the opposition in the Rajya Sabha, the law minister, the deputy chairperson of the Rajya Sabha and a judge of the Supreme Court nominated by the chief justice.[11] The CPI(M) had also made a strong case for reform in the EC in 2006 (CPI[M], 2006).[12] S. Y. Qurashi agrees and says, 'Appointment of the EC members should be more broad-based as perception of neutrality is very important. It is important because we are government appointees.'[13]

Growing Responsibilities and Friction

The nature of the EC has seen changes brought about by the transformations in Indian democracy. The growth of competitive politics in the country

---

[11] For details, see *Financial Express* (2006).

[12] For details, see *The Hindu* (2006).

[13] S. Y. Quraishi, personal interview with the author, Gurugram (Gurgaon), 23 January 2017.

enhanced the scope for the EC to take on an activist mantel. The country's transition to coalition and minority governments, emergence of states as multiple nerve centres of politics, duality of voting (where the electorate votes for different parties at the centre and at the state level), influence of social identities on politics and an increased assertion for rights created an environment that enhanced the role of the EC. While this assertive rule-enforcing role was seen by some as happening due to changes in the personnel heading it, one needs to foreground the point that the strong position of the EC was prompted by the larger transformations in Indian politics at that time. Structural changes enhanced the regulatory character of the EC, which in turn put certain mechanisms in place to systematise existing electoral procedures and frame new ones. As Sukumar Muralidharan, a senior journalist, points out, 'In part these changes have been forced by the change in circumstances ... general elections today call forth fierce political contestation' (Muralidharan, 1998). He continues, 'The milieu has become more fragmented with the electoral process being transformed into an arena for the assertion of a bewildering variety of group identities' (Muralidharan, 1998).

Seshan's approach of fast-tracking the process of 'cleaning up' the system, Gill's more 'dialogic' approach in enforcing rules of electoral conduct, Lyngdoh's unwavering stance in the face of majoritarian violence, Quraishi's efforts to raise voter turnouts and Zaidi's emphasis on technological upgradation, among others, were in a large measure prompted by the brisk entry of multiple players in politics and a heightened popular engagement in public life. The EC transformed itself from a quiet institution into an interventionist one. It responded to both internal and external forces and underwent changes because of these responses – moving forward on the trajectory of the logic of appropriateness. The middle class's perception of governments as non-effective and corrupt (Rudolph and Rudolph 2001: 131–32) and its increased articulation on political issues in the post-Mandal phase (Yadav, 2001) encouraged this interventionist role. The growing hiatus between political representatives and the pre-election promises manifest in the glaring gaps between party manifestos and policy initiatives added to this activism. The EC was seen and began seeing itself as a correctional body that had to repair the eroding moral codes in politics.

The friction between the EC, on the one hand, and elected representatives and political parties, on the other, is one instance of the institutional tussles that often take place. These face-offs imply the stretching of institutional boundaries in an assertion of authority. The autonomy of regulatory bodies is often tested when the executive attempts to assert its power over them. Elected governments and political parties would at times like a more malleable civil and security administration and a more pliant EC. The latter has tried to hold its ground and institutionalise compliance of rules. Such friction, for instance, reached a high pitch between Seshan and the central and state governments over the voter identity cards, and then between the EC and the Shiv Sena chief, Bal Thackeray, over an inflammatory speech. The EC barred Thackeray for a period of six years from voting and contesting with effect from 1995. The differences between Lyngdoh and the Gujarat government in 2002 over the scheduling of assembly elections in the state also became serious. In the aftermath of the 2002 anti-Muslim pogrom in Gujarat, Lyngdoh and his team visited the riot-torn cities and relief camps to assess the situation and gauge what problems could arise during elections. This visit was a 'historic decision' taken by the EC (Murthy, 2008: 150). There have been several instances of such differences between the EC and the incumbent government, generally centred around violations of the MCC and the violations of spending limits. The EC tries to enforce rules whenever cases of political parties' excesses are brought before it, often leading to verbal barbs from the ruling parties.

The EC is a public institution, which aims to ensure compliance of procedures to smoothen out the process of contesting and voting. In this way, it tries to fulfil the responsibility of a public institution. Conducting elections is a huge participatory exercise and successfully accomplishing them means actualising citizenship. In the words of Zaidi, 'In the ultimate analysis, ECI belongs to the people; is accountable to the people. Hence all processes right from registration of voters to the act of voting at the polling booth must be simple, easy and voter friendly. This is the voter who should be the central figure in all activities of the ECI. The latter should be in continuous dialogue and communication with electors.'[14] The EC has worked for a voter-centric electoral process but with attempts to systemise it.

During the tenure of Seshan as the CEC, voter identity cards and limits on spending were introduced. The EC under him also began to ensure that the political parties complied seriously with the MCC during elections and

---

[14] Nasim Zaidi, email interview with the author, 4 August 2020. This was also a point incorporated in the 'Vision for ECI' issued by Zaidi in 2015.

did not cross the boundaries of permissible conduct. Krishnamurthy played an active role in introducing electronic voting machines (EVMs) throughout the 2004 general elections.[15] He also wrote a letter to the then prime minister in July 2004, listing all the electoral reforms required.[16]

The EC felt the need to set up a grievance redressal mechanism, and in 2005 it attempted to address the issue (see EC, n.d.1: 23). In a letter to the chief electoral officers (CEOs), it detailed the nature of complaints it usually received. They were of four kinds:

1. complaints which it received from the voters regarding missing names in the voters' list, non-availability of the election photo identity cards, shifting of a name to an inconvenient booth, non-inclusion of names in the electoral rolls during times other than the summary revision or intensive revision, and so on;
2. complaints from political parties and candidates about non-supply of electoral rolls, not consulting them on shifting booths, non-action on their complaints regarding the violation of the MCC, and so on;
3. complaints from government staff regarding using their services for election work but not making the needed arrangements for travel and accommodation, non-payment or delay in payment of travelling allowance (TA) or dearness allowance (DA), vindictiveness towards some staff while favouritism towards others, and so on;
4. complaints from suppliers of election material, transporters and others regarding delays in payments.

The EC in its letter said that these complaints could be taken up at the district and state levels by the local election officers. It also said that proper registers should be maintained which detail the complaints and the action taken on them. It said that the registers must be checked by the CEOs from time to time. It also provided that a time frame of 15 days should be fixed for attending to complaints and giving a reply to the complainant (see EC, n.d.1: 24).

During CEC V. S. Sampath's tenure, NOTA was introduced (under the orders of Supreme Court) covering the entire country in one go, though the

---

[15] T. S. Krishnamurthy, email interview with the author, 7 October 2020.
[16] T. S. Krishnamurthy, email interview with the author, 7 October 2020.

Supreme Court gave flexibility to introduce NOTA in phases.[17] For further transparency in voting, the voter verifiable paper audit trail (VVPAT) facility was introduced to enable voters to see that the EVM correctly registered the vote cast by them. In a small window on the printer unit, the serial number, name and symbol of the party became visible for seven seconds – time enough for the voter to verify that her vote had been registered correctly by the EVM. The VVPAT was first used for the by-election in the Noksen assembly seat in Nagaland in 2013. It was expanded to eight parliamentary constituencies in the 2014 Lok Sabha elections on a trial basis as per the orders of the Supreme Court and then covered polling booths in the entire country during the 2019 elections. The date 9 March 2014 began to be observed as the universal voter verification and enrolment day to provide one more chance to eligible voters to seek enrolment after the announcement of elections to the parliament on 5 March 2014.[18]

The EC during the tenure of Zaidi focused on information technology and encouraged increasing use of technology to make processes of the EC efficient and transparent – be it for online voter registration and related services, electoral roll purification to weed out duplicate voters at all levels, continuous updating of voters' list by deletion of those voters who were no longer residents, improvement of election management practices from stakeholders' viewpoint, real-time monitoring and surveillance of free and fair elections at the booth level by election machinery and use of digital communication to encourage voter participation.[19]

Some reforms have happened and some are pending. They come up for discussion whenever a situation arises that calls for their incorporation. According to Quraishi (2019: 4), there are several issues regarding which 'the ECI has repeatedly written to the government'. However, several issues are long pending 'due to lack of political will or plain lethargy' (Quraishi, 2019: 4). Political will and initiative go a long way in nurturing democratic and deliberative processes of work.

The EC has been a moulder of the political character of our society. It has worked towards boosting voter enthusiasm, electoral transparency and contestant answerability. It has also made efforts to make elections more

---

[17] V. S. Sampath, email interview with the author, 1 August 2020.

[18] V. S. Sampath, email interview with the author, 1 August 2020.

[19] Nasim Zaidi, telephonic interview with the author, 4 August 2020.

information-oriented. While the EC has come a long way in streamlining procedures and infusing more accountability in the electoral process, it has changed too. It works within an institutional field where other organisations also function. Their interactions and deliberations affect all of them and define the political culture. Several issues come up during an actual election – how the EC handles these is the subject of the next chapter.

5

Political Parties, the Event of Elections and the Election Commission

The event of elections is preceded by preparatory tasks by both the EC and political parties. While one is involved with updating and printing of electoral rolls, assessment of problems in the constituencies, calibration of EVMs, voter education, deployment of security personnel, and so on, the other is on the move preparing manifestos, distributing campaign material, doing day-to-day canvassing and making media appearances. As discussed in the last chapter, elections involve enormous resources, personnel, infrastructure, logistics, time and coordination. India's size and numbers make this task even more onerous. The effective working of the electoral administration is of utmost importance to keep the wheels of democracy moving smoothly. The EC has to ensure that voters are able to vote freely, that they do not face intimidation and violence and that elections happen with minimal obstructions within the stipulated time. Accessibility of voting facilities, safety of voters and secrecy of the vote are important responsibilities that can be accomplished only by an efficient, adequately staffed, well-coordinated, sufficiently equipped and sensitive electoral administration.

The 'Big' Indian Elections

The enormity of an Indian election can be gauged from former CEC S. Y. Quraishi's words:

> The EC begins preparing for elections a year before the date of polling. It has to work in real time and prevent fait accompli as its powers end

within a limited time – when an election is complete. The EC meets all political parties before elections to know if they have any fears or needs. This helps us proceed further. The staff which conducts elections for the EC is 11 million strong.[1]

This election machinery of about 11 million people (the enormity of this figure can be gauged by comparing it to the population of Hyderabad, which is about 10 million) conducts a task that begins with the preparation of schedules and sequencing of elections in various states and ends with the declaration of results. The personnel are both directly and indirectly involved in the conduct of the general elections.[2] About 900 million Indians were eligible to vote in 2019, and organising an election for this mammoth number indicates the quantum of responsibility on the shoulders of the EC personnel. Former CEC Nasim Zaidi reiterated the fact about the enormity of responsibility of the electoral administration. He emphasised the hard work put in by the polling officials for months together to plan the one day of polling and make it successful.[3] Elections in India are equivalent to elections in about 90 countries – they need meticulous planning.[4] The personnel work from 180 to 365 days in advance to prepare for an election.[5] Very elaborate planners and calendars of over 100 election activities are prepared and continuously monitored by the EC.[6] Former CEC T. S. Krishnamurthy points out that scheduling elections is a challenging task 'given the diversity in climate and culture' (Murthy, 2008: 121). While fixing the election schedule, the EC takes note of a number of factors. For instance, it keeps in view the dates of school examinations (particularly the central and state board examinations) – this is because schoolteachers are given election duty in polling centres, which are mainly located in school premises, and also the

---

[1] S. Y. Quraishi, personal interview with the author, Gurugram (Gurgaon), 23 January 2017.

[2] V. S. Sampath, email conversation with the author, 1 August 2020.

[3] Nasim Zaidi, telephonic interview with the author, 4 August 2020.

[4] S. Y. Quraishi, personal interview with the author, Gurugram (Gurgaon), 23 January 2017.

[5] S. Y. Quraishi, personal interview with the author, Gurugram (Gurgaon), 23 January 2017.

[6] S. Y. Quraishi, personal interview with the author, Gurugram (Gurgaon), 23 January 2017.

hustle and bustle of elections disturb not only exam schedules but also exam-giving students. Annual exams, entrance exams, and so on, have to be kept in mind when fixing election dates (Murthy, 2008: 121). The EC also takes note of various holidays and festivals during the polling months – as these involve the movement of people between various towns for celebrating festivals with their extended families, which may possibly cause them to move away from their constituencies. The harvest season in various parts of the country is also taken into account as also the monsoon information (see EC, 2009b). According to former CEC V. S. Sampath:

> In some areas there could be pre-monsoon showers. Certain parts of the country are prone to acute summer heat in May. The election schedule takes this into account. Besides from the security point of view, there are regional specific and location specific challenges. There are areas which are relatively more sensitive from the election expenditure point of view. (Sampath, 2014)

The rise in the number of voters in each subsequent election cycle is another fundamental matter that needs to be kept in mind. This implies that the infrastructural capacity of the polling equipment and the number of polling personnel have to be raised for each consecutive election.

Sampath, writing in 2014, made the point clear:

> There has been an increase of about 10 crore [*100 million*] voters between the 2009 and 2014 general elections. It means we need more polling stations. We have added about 100,000 thousands polling stations across the country. This also means an increase in the size of the election machinery and security personnel.
>
> Besides, there is also need to create auxiliary polling stations where the number of electors in a particular polling station is higher. (Sampath, 2014)

By 2014, the EC had to manage the election machinery in about 930,000 polling stations (Quraishi, 2014: 77). Each polling station needs a team of five persons in it to manage polling. Table 5.1 displays the rise in the number of polling stations in India for Lok Sabha elections.

The election personnel 'are allotted polling stations on a random basis to avoid bias, and they are not told till the very last moment the name of the

Table 5.1 Number of polling stations in India

Year of election	Number of polling stations	Year of election	Number of polling stations
1951	196,084	1991–92	591,020
1957	220,478	1996	767,462
1962	238,031	1998	772,681
1967	243,693	1999	774,651
1971	342,918	2004	687,473
1977	373,910	2009	830,866
1980	436,813	2014	927,553
1984–85	506,058	2019	1,035,918
1989	580,798		

Source: *Electoral Statistics Pocket Book 2017* (New Delhi: Election Commission of India), 6, for the figures till 2014; the 2019 figures are in the public domain.

polling station where they have to serve so that they cannot be approached and compromised' (Quraishi, 2014: 78). Complete neutrality is expected of the election personnel, including those posted at the polling stations. Selection and training of personnel involve enormous energy.

The EC streamlined as well as made efforts towards digitalising and mechanising the voting process. The introduction of EVMs, computerisation of electoral rolls and introduction of photo identity cards for voters, among other facilities, are examples of this mechanisation with a view to minimise errors in enumeration and also to ease the voting process.[7] The electoral rolls are normally updated every year to include new voters who have completed 18 years of age by 1 January of the year. Updates are also done on those who have moved from one constituency to another and those who have passed away. The updating of rolls has to be completed before the election dates are finalised. In other words, the updating of rolls of an area comes to an end when the election campaign begins – that is, after the nomination process closes (discussed in Chapter 8). For transporting equipment, material, personnel, and so on, during an election, almost all government vehicles – trucks, buses, cars,

---

[7] It was in 1998 that the EC decided to computerise the electoral rolls of 620 million voters. The computerised rolls are available for sale to the general public, and they are provided free of cost to the national and state parties (see the official website of the EC, http://eci.nic.in/eci/eci.html [accessed on 27 April 2017]).

Table 5.2 Election expenditure by central government (towards states and union territories [UTs] having a legislature) for Lok Sabha elections

Year of election	Expenditure incurred (provisional) (INR)	Year of election	Expenditure incurred (provisional) (INR)
1952	10,45,00,000	1989	154,22,00,000
1957	5,90,00,000	1991–92	359,10,24,679
1962	7,32,00,000	1996	597,34,41,000
1967	10,79,69,000	1998	666,22,16,000
1971	11,60,87,450	2004*	1,016,08,69,000
1977	23,03,68,000	2009†	1,114,38,45,000
1980	54,77,39,000	2014	3,87,034,56,024
1984–85	81,51,34,000		

Source: *Electoral Statistics Pocket Book 2017* (New Delhi: Election Commission of India), 90–91.

Note: This is the expenditure on maintaining electoral offices, preparing and printing electoral rolls, conducting elections and issuing photo identity cards to voters. *The expenditure includes the central government's share paid to the respective state governments by it in connection with the elections to the 14th Lok Sabha. The figure also includes the expenditure incurred on state/UT legislative assembly elections held in 2004 along with the Lok Sabha elections. †Figures relate to the amount demanded by states/UTs for conducting the general elections (2009).

jeeps – available in the districts are requisitioned. If a district does not have the adequate number of vehicles required for elections, they are requisitioned from nearby big cities. In addition, special trains, special coaches in trains, helicopters, boats, steamers, and so on, are also requisitioned.[8] The amount spent by the central government in India on elections highlights the financial capacity needed to conduct a successful election as mentioned in Table 5.2.

Political parties, on their part, work on motivational factors to ensure that large numbers of voters exercise their right on the election day. They spend time, effort and resources to mobilise voters in their favour. Campaigning and mobilisation are moments which bring the EC, voters and political parties in close interaction with each other prior to the elections. Elections themselves are as much social events as political – they represent an exercise of collective action and marking of preferences by voters in acts which are public and at the same time secret. Choosing one's representatives is an important part of democratic functioning, which gives meaning to the collective exercise of power and the idea of citizenship. The conduct of

---

[8] V. S. Sampath, email conversation with the author, 1 August 2020.

political parties during elections is bound by formal procedures – mainly the rules of electoral conduct that political parties have to follow and the EC has to enforce. As stated earlier, the occasion of elections also brings out an important facet of political functioning, which is the interactions between different state institutions. The EC not only interacts with political parties but also with the state administration, the security forces, the government of the day and the judiciary. This interaction is unique as ideally it has to be thoroughly professional and neutral when the elections are planned and occur. The nature of this relationship determines whether an election has been fair or not. Major tensions and rifts that come up during the event of elections are about whether political parties are complying with rules and laws fully, whether the EC is carrying out its work impartially and is not unduly biased towards the ruling parties, whether it is able to enforce the election rules equally for all and whether the state personnel are unbiased towards the ruling state governments during the elections.

Rule-Bound Competition

In India election rules are elaborated in the RPA, 1950 and 1951. These laws were supplemented by the Registration of Electors Rules, 1960, and the Conduct of Election Rules, 1961. The RPA, 1950, contains provisions for the delimitation of constituencies, seat allocation for the Lok Sabha and legislative assemblies, qualifications and eligibility of voters, and the preparation and revision of electoral rolls and photo identity cards for voters. The RPA, 1951, deals with all aspects of the conduct of elections, from deciding whether or not the candidates are qualified to be MPs and state legislatures to making announcements about elections. It also carries provisions regarding the nominations of candidates, counting of votes, by-elections, appeals, electoral disputes, electoral offences and corrupt practices relating to elections.

These laws were amended over the years. One of the changes made was in 1966 whereby the Election Tribunals to adjudicate election disputes were abolished. Thereafter, the High Court was empowered to handle electoral disputes via election petitions. The High Court verdicts, however, could be appealed in the Supreme Court. Matters pertaining to the election of the president and the vice president were directly in the hands of the Supreme Court. Changes were also made in 1988 when it was decided to stop and countermand elections of a polling station if it was seized by criminal elements for fraud voting (popularly called booth capture). In 1996, the post of the observer to monitor elections at the ground level was created. The observer could advise stopping the counting of votes in the event of booth capture at a polling station. In 2002, another fundamental change was incorporated whereby the voters had a right to know about the antecedents of candidates – their educational qualifications, economic assets and offences, if any. Institutional as well as civil society pressures to make the system more transparent and fairer were instrumental in bringing about these changes.

The MCC was also agreed upon in 1960 by political parties through an overarching consensus on what constitutes the domain of acceptable conduct during elections. The purpose was to exercise self-restraint so that electoral laws and limits of 'acceptable' electoral conduct were not transgressed. In 1979, the MCC was further elaborated by placing restrictions on the ruling parties so as to further level the playing field between the ruling and opposition parties (Quraishi, 2014: 240). According to David Gilmartin, '[T]he very idealism behind the Model MCC was widely appealing, and few – even of Seshan's strongest critics – thus challenged the basic idea that there should be a special Model Code for elections in India' (Gilmartin, 2009: 271). The MCC over the years actually became a 'blueprint' on which political participants modelled their conduct.

Through its instructions to political parties and candidates, the MCC attempts to prevent discord between social groups, the criticism and dragging of the private life of individuals onto public platforms, appeals to caste and community feelings for votes, use of religious places for election propaganda, bribery and disruption of the home life of individuals and the political meetings of other political parties. It also explicitly instructs political parties to inform the local police of the meetings and processions they have planned and to follow the rules on them. It directs the ruling party or parties not to use their official position for the purpose of advancing their electoral interests.

In 2013, the Supreme Court directed the EC to frame guidelines in consultation with political parties on the content of election manifestoes. The court's move was towards the possibility of moderation of electoral promises carried in the manifestos of political parties and making them more realistic, especially as they had the potential of influencing voters' choices. The EC thereby, after consulting the parties and in accordance with the apex court's directions, issued these guidelines, which were made part of the MCC. Through these guidelines, it emphasised that manifestos should adhere to the ideals and principles of the Constitution of India as well as the provisions of the MCC; it said that those promises which 'vitiate the purity of the election process' and 'exert undue influence' on voters should be avoided and that rationales for the promises should be mentioned as also their financial requirements and plans (see EC, n.d.7). The EC did admit later that it was not able to ensure that these guidelines are followed. However, what it was able to do was to generate an opinion that there is the need for accountability among political parties in the framing of manifestos (see Anuja and Bhaskar, 2014).

Several instances of violation of the MCC have been witnessed during elections. These have covered almost all aspects listed earlier, but the most marked have been the rise in the reported instances of distribution of cash and goods (including liquor) to voters. This usually happens through the use of resources that are unaccounted for or 'black' money (discussed in Chapter 8). Instances of seizures of bundles of cash by EC officials during the campaign period have revealed the excess amount of money that is poured in by political parties to win an election. This money is beyond the permissible expenditure limits and is discreetly distributed among voters.

The increased invoking of religious and caste identities in campaigning has also been a cause of concern because of its potential for harming community relations. The Supreme Court in its judgment of 2 January 2017 held that asking for votes on the grounds of religion and/or caste of the voters would amount to corrupt practice (see EC, 2017a). The Supreme Court categorically held that since the state was secular in character, it 'will not identify itself with any one of the religions or religious denominations' (EC, 2017a). It said that elections are a secular exercise and the constitutional ethos forbids the mixing of religion and secular functions of the state (EC, 2017a). Subsequently, the EC issued an order that said seeking of votes by political parties and candidates in the name of religion and caste would be seen as violation of the MCC (EC, 2017a).

Over the last few elections, there has been a noteworthy change in the language of public discourse. 'Hate speeches' in India have seen a rise, and there have been growing instances of the political leadership indulging in them. The 2014 elections saw a rise in hate-filled statements and speeches by political leaders in their campaigns for votes that violated the MCC. Hate speeches by political leaders against Hindu or Muslim communities, especially against the Muslim minority, tend to be on a sharp rise on the eve of elections. These speeches not only invoke social identity as a basis of political bonding but also use hate and false propaganda against other communities with the aim of amassing support through social schisms. Harishankar Brahma, a former ECr, remarked that he has been closely observing the elections since 1977 in varied official capacities, and over the course of 2009–14 the standard of political discourse has fallen drastically (R. Chopra, 2014). He further said, 'In my three decades of observing polls, this is probably the lowest discourse has fallen' (cited in Chopra, 2014).

The EC has to curb such transgressions during every election cycle, especially at the time of campaigning by political parties, for reasons of equal participation and minimal friction. Some other democracies too follow certain dos and don'ts of campaigning. A look at these instructions informs us that elections in other democracies too carry elements of discord. In South Africa, political parties are bound by a code of conduct which mentions a list of dos and don'ts for parties and candidates during elections (Electoral Commission of South Africa, 2021). The South African electoral commission calls upon political parties to speak out against violence and threats and help the police in the investigation of election violence and crime. The parties are also urged to inform the authorities of planned rallies and marches. The don'ts list prohibits the use of physical and verbal violence or threats against other parties or supporters of other parties, incitement of violence against other parties, destruction of party material of other parties, disruption of the work of other parties, forcing people to join one's party or donate money, spreading false rumours about other parties, and bribing voters to vote or not vote. Those who break the code invite official action – they can be fined or stopped from working in an area or have their votes in an area or their registration cancelled.

The UK's electoral management body calls upon parliamentary candidates not to 'knowingly make a false statement about the personal character of another candidate' during campaigns (Electoral Commission of UK, 2019: 7). It also impresses upon the candidates to not to pay canvassers where canvassing implies 'trying to persuade an elector to vote for or against a particular candidate or party' (Electoral Commission of UK, 2019: 7). However, it is clearly stated that neither the returning officer nor the commission regulates these offences, and complaints on these matters should be made to the police (Electoral Commission of UK, 2019: 7). The commission acknowledges the pressures on candidates during elections and mentions that at times candidates have been exposed to 'unacceptable levels of harassment and intimidation', especially women candidates (Electoral Commission of UK, 2021: 3). In a document called 'When It Goes Too Far', it advises candidates on the situations they can face and the action they can resort to (Electoral Commission of UK, 2021). It advises candidates to look after their and their friends', families' and colleagues' safety and report intimidation and abuse (Electoral Commission of UK, 2021: 4).

The Australian electoral commission tries to restrict the flow of 'disinformation' (information which can 'either intentionally or unintentionally mislead a voter') during elections (Australian Electoral Commission, 2022). It attempts to ensure that election communication is authorised (to ensure transparency in campaigning), correct any disinformation regarding electoral processes and run a campaign encouraging voters to 'stop and consider' (if there are any doubts about the information that seeks to influence one's vote). The Australian Electoral Commission, as it itself puts it, is not able to determine what is true or false, restrict the placement of communication and regulate the timing of communication (Australian Electoral Commission, 2022).

The code in India, as was discussed earlier, also lists the dos and don'ts of election campaigning. It is based on a contractual understanding and does not have legal backing. Over the years it has assumed the role of a restraining force on party competition. Ujjwal Kumar Singh points out an interesting aspect of the MCC, which is that it 'offers a system of supplementary legality to plug the legal vacuum that existed during election time' (U. K. Singh, 2012: 150). According to J. Venkatesan, the MCC 'is intended to provide a level-playing field for all political parties, to keep the campaign fair and healthy, avoid clashes and conflicts between parties, and ensure peace and order' (J. Venkatesan, 2006). Its main task 'is to ensure that the ruling party, either at the Centre or in the States, does not misuse its official position to gain unfair advantage' (J. Venkatesan, 2006).

According to Sampath, the MCC is a 'unique feature in the conduct of Indian elections'.[9] The MCC comes into force after the EC announces elections. There have been differences over the question of when the MCC comes into effect – from the date of announcement of the election schedule by the EC or from the date of the notification of elections? In its judgment of 1997, the Punjab and Haryana High Court (in the *Harbans Singh Jalal v. Union of India* case) ruled that the MCC comes into effect from the date of announcement of elections. This was challenged by the central government of

---

[9] V. S. Sampath, email interview with the author, 1 August 2020.

the day (led by the then prime minister, Inder Kumar Gujral), which argued that the MCC should come into effect from the date of notification and not from the date of announcement of elections by the EC. But while the appeal was pending before the Supreme Court, the government and the EC came to an understanding that though the MCC would be enforced from the date of announcement of elections, the time gap between the announcement date and the notification date would not ordinarily be more than three weeks (Quraishi, 2014: 242). The MCC is to therefore be followed from the date of announcement of elections by the EC and remains in force till the election results are declared. These rules and codes have been interpreted and fortified every now and then by the EC and the Supreme Court whenever cases of dispute are brought before them.

Demands have been made to legalise the MCC on the grounds that it is toothless and ineffective – legalising it would mean wider compliance, that parties will take it more seriously and think twice before breaking it. Sampath says that it is not correct to regard the MCC as ineffective. According to him:

> In fact during the heat of the moment when election campaign is on, any adverse notice taken by the EC about the conduct of the political party or a candidate will have significant impact on the standing of the party or the candidate. Such action is given wide publicity by the media during the elections and in closely fought contests where the margin of victory could be in few hundreds or thousands of votes; such adverse notice by the EC can even affect the winning chances of a candidate.[10]

Statutory backing of the MCC has not found many backers. This demand for statutory backing has mainly come on grounds that the MCC 'hampers development activities' (Quraishi, 2014: 250). But according to Quraishi (2014: 250), 'No instances have been brought to the notice of the Commission whereby any development activity has been thwarted or abandoned because of the MCC.' Statutory backing, according to Quraishi, is not a good idea as it hampers prompt action on cases of violation of the MCC – statutory status means delays in immediate action as the cases will have to go through bureaucratic and judicial structures.[11] Sampath echoes these views. According

---

[10] V. S. Sampath, email interview with the author, 1 August 2020.

[11] S. Y. Quraishi, personal interview with the author, Gurugram (Gurgaon), 23 January 2017.

to him, 'Delays being inherent in our judicial system, the very object of instantly taking notice and awarding some deterrence by the EC will be lost if the MCC is transferred to the judiciary. Also, transferring this power from the EC will amount to weakening the EC.'[12]

Differences between political parties and the EC over the MCC often occur. Political parties, as the definition goes, aggregate public opinion, articulate popular demands and represent varied social interests within and outside legislative forums. They are multifaceted entities 'deeply rooted and penetrative in civil society or superstructural, highly ideological or purely electoralist, strongly linked to particular sections of society or catchall in character' (Sridharan and deSouza, 2006: 16). They are mass entities which draw their support from ground activism and make their claims on state power from the standpoint of people's backing. Parties in India are specially afflicted with issues like hereditary power structures, familial control, gender imbalances and the absence or near-absence of inner-party democracy, but they work with a sense of greater legitimacy and feel that they stand above procedural norms (Katju, 2016: 81). Popular support over a considerable territorial span imbues them with the sense of a higher moral stature and greater strength. Ruling parties particularly, being the government, feel self-important and become more defiant of rules and regulatory authorities. Being in power amplifies their sense of self-worth, and they claim a greater say in steering political processes (Katju, 2016: 81). Violations of rules are not seen as such by them but as legitimate actions that popular support justifies. Implicit here is an understanding that legislative entities being popularly elected have a stronger voice in making and interpreting rules. Institutional checks are often seen as unnecessary and unjustified controls.

The EC, playing its part of institutional regulation, has often been more literal about the MCC. It has imposed checks and curbs on action which, according to it, transgresses electoral conduct. As a constitutional authority, it stands to ensure that political exercise is based on procedures and that the law is adhered to so that the equalising character of a free and fair election is maintained. In many situations, it has also extended its legal authority and exceeded its constitutional mandate (McMillan, 2012: 199). The EC's unwavering stance on the implementation of the MCC and its insistence on playing its regulatory role to the full have often pulled it into the crosshair of

---

[12] V. S. Sampath, email interview with the author, 1 August 2020.

political parties, drawing their disapproval of its orders and making it a target of their barbs. It has faced criticism from the opposition parties on the grounds that it favours the ruling parties while implementing the MCC (between 2017 and 2019, it faced serious criticism under attack for allegedly favouring the ruling BJP; for instance, the opposition alleged that the ruling party had been favoured by the EC in fixing election schedules and phases) (Dixit, 2019). It has often been seen as leaning towards the ruling party at the centre while playing its regulatory role and lately has appeared rather timid in face of violations of the MCC by the BJP leadership. The EC sees this as an unfair criticism from opposition parties and groups towards its legitimate watchdog responsibilities. However, many a time there is a lot of miscommunication between the administration and the political parties – the EC, for instance, does not stop genuine developmental activities of the government.[13] Nevertheless, this back and forth of arguments between the political parties and the EC over its 'right' conduct has not prevented the middle class and the Indian electorate in general from supporting it for accomplishing its electoral tasks and making the politicians 'fall in line'. It is this support that explains the EC's confidence and tough stance vis-à-vis the political parties regarding the enforcement of electoral procedures, including the MCC, during elections (Katju, 2016: 82). It seems to work with a self-assurance that it can go ahead with its decisions as the entire electorate backs its actions.

When instances of MCC violations by political leaders are brought to its notice, the EC probes the incidents and issues censures, advisories and warnings in the form of show-cause notices to leaders. This can result in barring them from campaigning for a specific period. In case of repeated violations, criminal proceedings can be initiated and police involved, which might lead to an imposition of a fine or a jail term on the violator. Penal and parliamentary laws like the Indian Penal Code (IPC), the Code of Criminal Procedure (CrPC) and the RPA do strengthen the EC's hands, especially when the violations correspond with activities seen as unlawful and criminal in these laws. The EC does not have the power to deregister or derecognise a party if it violates the MCC (though it did temporarily suspend the National People's Party, a recognised state party of Meghalaya in 2015, for not submitting its statement of expenditure within the stipulated time).

---

[13] Trilochan Sastry, ADR, personal interview with the author, Bengaluru, 14 November 2016.

However, its watchfulness has indeed brought about greater rule adherence and moderated behaviour in the electoral arena.

Democratic praxis assumes that institutional regulation and adherence to rules are a vital part of a participatory democratic exercise. Adherence to rules, which are democratically arrived at by a polity, facilitates rather than curbs collective and competitive activity in the public domain. Instruments like the MCC hold significance specifically for the ruling parties to ensure their compliance with the norm of equal restraint. The ruling parties through the advantage of office have greater means to enhance their support. This upsets the playing field and disturbs the electoral equilibrium. Institutions ensure the effectiveness of non-partisan rules as also of a system of checks and balances. The EC's role towards rule compliance comes into play here. It contributes to building a consciousness about rule-boundedness in a democracy for it to become meaningful. Its insistence on compliance with the MCC means that it attempts to nudge political participants to follow designated lines of action, where certain ways of conduct are permissible and acceptable while others are deemed mischievous and provocative and thus nonacceptable.

Such inter-institutional deliberation and bargaining are part of the process of institutionalisation. Occasions of friction over matters of public good are common and typically followed by a search for working solutions along the lines of 'appropriateness'. These solutions find consolidation as guidelines and rules. Irreconcilable differences that might lead to breakdowns necessitate the involvement of mediatory and adjudicating institutions. In this case, the Supreme Court has taken the mediatory role to resolve disputes over law and interpretation or to fill the gaps where law is silent. The parliament has also stepped in during difficult phases.

Recognition and Symbols

An important aspect of electoral procedures is about the initiation and identity of political parties. To enter the electoral arena, the political parties need to be registered with the EC, according to Section 29A of the RPA, 1951. The EC in the first stages of registering a party scrutinises whether there is another party of the same name. It also publishes an advertisement about the party to see if the public has any objections to such an outfit. If the political party comes clear on these two, the EC notifies the party's name in the gazette (for details, see EC, 2004b: 9). The EC is empowered to allot symbols to the parties registered with it. Pictorial symbols give a recognisable identity to the political parties. This system of symbols was chosen so that voters, especially those unlettered, did not have difficulty in recognising the party of their choice in the ballot paper or on the EVMs. Over the years, party symbols have acquired a salience and mobilisational potential of their own. The *haath* (hand symbol) of the INC, the *kamal* (lotus) of the BJP and the hammer and sickle of the left parties have an identity in their own right. They are as important as the names of the parties. The major political parties of India are known by their symbols; with these symbols they enter the electoral field seeking votes.

The Election Symbols (Reservation and Allotment) Order, 1968, gives the EC the power to 'recognise' a party. This recognition enables a party to contest elections. This power of the EC has been challenged and has come under scrutiny more than once in the past, but it has been upheld by the Supreme Court. The EC itself has had to explain and clarify the provisions of the law several times. The clause specifying whether a recognised political party is a state or national party was added to the Order on 1 December 2000. The conditions for a party to be recognised as a national or state party were specified through a notification issued on 14 May 2005 (see EC, 2017c: 5–6). The conditions lay down the specific number of seats and votes a party must have to be recognised as a national or state party.[14] Failure to fulfil these

---

[14] Paragraphs 6, 6A and 6B of the Order say:

> A political party shall be treated as a recognized National party, if, and only if, – either (A) (i) the candidates set up by it, in any 4 or more States, as the last general election to the House of the People, or to the Legislative Assembly of the State concerned, have secured not less than 6 per cent. of the total valid votes polled in their respective States at that general election; and (ii) in addition, it has returned at least 4 members to the House of the People at the aforesaid last general election from any State or States; or (B) (i) its candidates have been elected to the House of the People, at the last general election to that House, from at least 2 per cent of the total number of parliamentary constituencies in India, any fraction exceeding one-half being counted as one; and (ii) the said candidates have been elected to that House from not less than 3 States.
>
> A political party, other than a National party, shall be treated as a recognised State party in a State or States, if, and only if, – either (A) (i) the candidates set up by it, at the last general election to the House of the People, or to the Legislative Assembly

numerical criteria over the next two elections – that is, after every 10 years – leads to the withdrawal of the status of a party as a national or state party as per the amended paragraph 6C of the Elections Symbols (Reservation and Allotment) Order, 1968 (EC, 2016a). Before this amendment, the national or state party status of a party had to be reviewed after every five years – that is, during the upcoming Lok Sabha or assembly elections, as the case may be. However, through a further amendment in 2016, the EC reverted to its earlier position of a five-year review (see EC, 2017c: 6).

In India, there were six national parties (the INC, the BJP, the Communist Party of India [CPI], the CPI[M], the Bahujan Samaj Party [BSP] and the Nationalist Congress Party [NCP]) till September 2016 when the All India Trinamool Congress – having fulfilled the condition of a recognised state party in four states, namely West Bengal, Manipur, Tripura and Arunachal Pradesh – was added to this list. With this addition, the number of national parties in India went up to seven.[15] This recognition means that the election symbols of these national parties are not used by any other party across India. Registered but unrecognised parties have to choose from the 'free' symbols announced by the EC from time to time. The Election Symbols (Reservation and Allotment) Order, 1968, mentions two kinds of symbols – 'reserved' and 'free'. The reserved symbols are reserved for candidates of recognised political parties, and the remaining symbols are called free symbols. A reserved symbol is the same for the candidates of a national party in all states, and it is not given to any other candidate even if no candidate of that particular national party is contesting from a particular constituency. Similarly, a reserved symbol is the same for all the candidates of a recognised state party in a particular state. The same symbol might be allotted to the candidates of another party in a different state.

---

of the State concerned, have secured not less than 6 per cent. of the total valid votes polled in that State at that general election; and (ii) in addition, it has returned at least 2 members to the Legislative Assembly of the State at the last general election to that Assembly; or (B) it wins at least three per cent. of the total number of seats in the Legislative Assembly of the State (any fraction exceeding one-half being counted as one), or at least 3 seats in the Assembly, whichever is more, at the aforesaid general election.

[15] In 2019, the National People's Party also became a national party, taking the tally of national parties to eight.

If a political party loses its recognised status, it can still be allotted the same symbol which belonged to it when it was recognised, provided not more than six years have elapsed from the time it lost its recognised status to the time of notification of the election. The EC has the power to allot, reallot or change symbols of political parties in India. In 2013, it approved the *jhadoo* (broom) symbol for the new Aam Aadmi Party (AAP). From a free symbol, the broom has become a reserved symbol – reserved for the AAP, which is now a recognised state party.

The Election Symbols (Reservation and Allotment) Order, 1968, also empowers the EC to decide which group or faction gets the name and symbol of a party in case of dispute within it. The rise of splinter groups within a political party claiming its ownership necessitates intervention by a neutral entity to settle the dispute and decide which group or faction is 'the party'. The EC has the power to intervene and decide who gets the name and symbol.[16] It has been frequently asked to arbitrate when a party splits (Murthy, 2008: 101). The EC thereby is the arbitrating authority if the dispute within political parties becomes irreconcilable publicly. The EC's decision in such cases is based on majority support to a group in the organisational and legislative wings of the party (at times this becomes a difficult decision, especially when the organisational numbers of the party are unclear). Whichever splinter group has a majority of support is allotted the symbol of the party and hence becomes 'the party'. The EC's decision in such cases is final and binding. In a much-publicised case of split in the Samajwadi Party (SP) between factions led by the then chief minister, Akhilesh Yadav, and his father and SP chief, Mulayam Singh Yadav, just before the Uttar Pradesh assembly elections in 2017, the EC had to decide which group constituted the SP. The bone of contention in this split was also the 'cycle' symbol of the party. Going by the 'majority' criterion, the EC allotted the symbol to the Akhilesh Yadav faction

---

[16] Paragraph 15 of the Election Symbols (Reservation and Allotment) Order, 1968, says:

> When the Commission is satisfied on information in its possession that there are rival sections or groups of a recognised political party each of whom claims to be that party the Commission may, after taking into account all the available facts and circumstances of the case and hearing such representatives of the sections or groups and other persons as desire to be heard decide that one such rival section or group or none of such rival sections or groups is that recognised political party and the decision of the Commission shall be binding on all such rival sections or groups.

who had the majority of SP leaders and office-bearers backing him. Thus, the faction led by Akhilesh Yadav was recognised as the SP.

The Supreme Court has upheld the EC's power to allot symbols and recognition to a party whenever it has been challenged. This happened as early as 1971 in the *Sadiq Ali and Another v. the Election Commission of India* case. The Supreme Court ruled that the 'test of majority and numerical strength' was to decide which splinter group was the party and could be allotted the party symbol. In *Kanhiyalal Omar v. R. K. Trivedi* in 1986, the Supreme Court upheld the EC's authority with regards to the Election Symbols (Reservation and Allotment) Order, 1968. It foregrounded the EC's powers to act where the law was silent. The EC was vested with residuary powers by the Supreme Court to take decisions on its own on issues where the provisions of law were inadequate to handle any electoral matter. The EC in 1997 introduced a rule that a splinter group would not automatically get the status of a national or state party but will have to register itself and contest elections – the status depended on the vote share it got in the elections.

The Delhi High Court passed an order in July 2016, in the *Common Cause v. Bahujan Samaj Party* case, objecting to political parties in power using public funds and places for propagating their election symbols. The court was hearing a plea against the installation of elephant statues (the BSP's electoral symbol) by the BSP all across Uttar Pradesh while in power by allegedly using public money. The High Court called upon the EC to frame guidelines prohibiting political parties in power from using public money for self-propaganda. The court expressed the view that a constitutional functionary like the EC, 'upon finding a wrong or a possibility of wrong in the arena of election', cannot express helplessness that there is no provision in law to take a certain action. The court said that the EC has to devise ways and means to address the wrong 'to maintain purity in the stream of election'. The EC has to be 'continuously evolving' to keep pace with the evolving society and 'ought to have invented the remedy' (see *Common Cause v. Bahujan Samaj Party*, 7 July 2016). The court also said that a political party in power 'cannot use development activities carried out by it and which the government in any case is expected to perform, to propagate its symbol or its leaders so as to come in the way of a free and fair election'. The performance of a political party in governance 'should be allowed to speak for itself'.

The EC in compliance of this court verdict issued an order declaring that utilising public funds or places for promoting party symbols would be treated as violation of the notion of free and fair elections (EC, 2016e). The

EC, in a letter to all political parties, clarified that no political party would be allowed to use public funds or places or government machinery for carrying out any activity that would be an advertisement for that party. It said that propagating its election symbol through the use of public funds or places would be treated as violation of law (EC, 2016e). In present times, when electoral competition has become increasingly intense, the EC's regulatory role has acquired importance, and it has a decisive voice in the way political parties and candidates conduct themselves during elections. The Supreme Court held that three words – 'superintendence, direction and control' – of the Constitution were wide enough to give powers to the EC to conduct free and fair elections so that the will of the people could be expressed. The judiciary thus tried to strengthen the EC's regulatory powers and give it more say in 'its' terrain.

Differing Stances on Derecognition

In 1994, the EC inserted paragraph 16A to the Election Symbols (Reservation and Allotment) Order, 1968, which specified that a party could be derecognised as a national or state party if it failed to observe the MCC or any direction or instruction of the EC. There have been inter-institutional differences over the question of deregistration or derecognition of political parties. In 2000, the Kerala High Court passed a judgment which viewed a 'forcible' *hartal* (a general strike as an act of protest) called by any political party as an 'unconstitutional act'. It called upon the EC to deregister such political parties. The EC on its part took the stand that it did not have the power to deregister political parties – a stand which was overruled by the High Court.

This judgment was given in a case regarding a complaint against the CPI(M) for having called a *hartal* in 1998. The CPI(M) strongly refuted the characterisation of *hartal*s as illegal and unconstitutional (CPI[M], 2000a, 2000b). It saw the move as a 'draconian step' and as 'harmful' for the democratic political system (CPI[M], 2000a, 2000b). It noted that 'the EC took a correct stand in the High Court proceedings that by law it is not empowered to deregister any political party' (CPI[M], 2000a, 2000b). Appeals were filed against this judgment by the INC, the CPI and the CPI(M) in the apex court. The Supreme Court in its judgment partially set aside the High Court verdict. It held that the enforcement of *hartal* by intimidation and coercion by a political party is an unconstitutional act, but also made clear that the EC could not deregister political parties on the grounds of calling a *hartal* by force (P. T. Rao, 2002). It said that the parliament had deliberately not given the EC the power to deregister a political party to ensure the independence of the EC and the free and fair conduct of elections (P. T. Rao, 2002). There were, however, a few exceptions to this. The EC could deregister a political party if it had registered itself through fraudulent means or forgery, or in case it intimated the EC that it had lost faith in the Constitution or the preamble to the Constitution or similar cases not requiring an official enquiry by the EC (P. T. Rao, 2002). What this means is that for all practical purposes the EC does not actually have the power to deregister functioning political parties and can step into the scene only when there is an open-and-shut case of political parties using fraudulent means of registering themselves.

The EC did find that certain parties existed only in name. In December 2016, it delisted 255 parties, thus removing them from the rolls of registered unrecognised parties and taking back their symbols. The EC found that these parties existed only on paper and had not contested any elections, whether parliamentary or for the legislative assembly, since 2005. On verification by the CEOs of the states and union territories (UTs), it was found that these parties were 'no longer in existence or functioning' (EC, 2016b). The EC delisted these parties, through its power of taking back the symbols of these parties, under Section 29A of the RPA, 1951. However, this is not the same as derecognising or deregistering a political party – a power which the EC possesses in a very restricted way.

The EC, however, did try to get itself empowered to deregister or derecognise political parties. In 2018, it said before the Supreme Court that it should be empowered to do so if a party violates the provisions of the Constitution (*Hindustan Times*, 2018). This power, it argued, would discourage fake parties to come up to seek income tax exemptions. There have been recommendations earlier from official bodies like the Ministry of Law and Justice and the Law Commission that the EC should be conferred this power if the parties violate the MCC (*Hindustan Times*, 2018).

Election Campaigns and Limits

In India campaign time is usually of two weeks' duration. According to Section 126 of the RPA, 1951, political parties and candidates have to wrap up their campaigns 48 hours before voting day, and no campaigning is allowed either on the ground or through television or cinematography during this time. These mediums cannot carry any election material or campaign messages. Section 126 also says that election matter during this period cannot be propagated through the holding of a musical concert, a theatrical performance or any other entertainment programme. This 'silence' period is meant for the voters to think and vote peacefully. It ends when polling concludes. Violation of these provisions is punishable by a prison term of up to two years or a fine or both as per the provisions of the Act. The EC adds that during this period leaders and star campaigners should refrain from giving press conferences or interviews to media (see EC, n.d.8). Moreover, Section 130 of the Act categorically prohibits canvassing in or within a distance of 100 metres of a polling station on the date of polling – a provision which is particularly relevant during multiple phases of an election.

The EC has time and again (in 2012, 2015, 2018 and 2019) raised the issue of bringing print media, news portals and social media within the purview of the 48-hour ban on canvassing (B. Jain, 2019; *Firstpost*, 2019) as these are not covered by the silence-period law. In 2019, it wrote to the law ministry seeking an amendment to Section 126 of the RPA, 1951. According to the EC, print media include newspapers, magazines, periodicals, posters, placards, handbills and any other document (B. Jain, 2019). The internet, radio, internet protocol television (IPTV), satellite, terrestrial or cable channels, internet/digital versions of print media, mobile and other media owned by the government or a private party should be included within electronic media (besides television), it said (B. Jain, 2019). However, things are yet to move ahead on these inclusions.

Campaign time limits are considered important in most democracies. For instance, campaigning in Japanese elections is bound by stringent rules (Ferris, 2014; Sim, 2017). The campaign time is only 12 days before the election day. 'Advertising is tightly controlled and heavy shows of signage are not common' (Ferris, 2014). Candidates display signboards in their own allotted and equal-sized spots; they are given free and equal amount of time on public media and also given permission for online campaigning (Ferris, 2014). Door-to-door campaigning is not permitted as also public rallies between 8 p.m. to 8 a.m. (Sim, 2017). In 2013, campaigning on social media was permitted through changes in campaign laws, but the major parties seem to prefer the old ways (Mealey, 2017). Paul Nadeau and Rob Fahey note:

Compared to the hugely expensive, multi-channel extravaganza that voters are subjected to in other advanced democracies, Japan's carefully regulated and very traditional campaigns feel like they come from another era entirely. (Nadeau and Fahey, 2017)

In the UK, campaigns for parliamentary elections usually last for about three weeks (Parliamentary Education Service, n.d.: 6). All broadcasters – radio, television and news websites – have to stop reporting on party campaigning between 12.30 a.m. and 10 p.m. of the election day (these rules do not apply to social media). Broadcasters are allowed to carry the previously posted material. Print media – newspapers and printed posters – are, however, exempt from these rules (see Morrow, 2019). It can continue to carry canvassing material during the voting period. Political parties and candidates are also allowed to campaign during voting time. Political parties come out with their manifestos and other publicity material that specify their policies. The election advertising material and broadcasts for television and radio are prepared by the national headquarter of each party (Parliamentary Education Service, n.d.: 6). The publication of publicity material 'increases dramatically during the election campaign' (Parliamentary Education Service, n.d.: 6). Interestingly,

[d]espite the millions of pounds spent on campaigning, evidence suggests that the majority of voters have decided how they are going to vote before the election campaign begins and few people are influenced by what they read or hear. (Parliamentary Education Service, n.d.: 6)

In Australia the 'silence' or 'blackout' period from the end of Wednesday to the end of the polling day on Saturday applies to television and radio broadcasting. Online services and print media can carry election advertisements during the blackout period (see Australian Communications and Media Authority, n.d.). In Canada, the blackout period includes the day before the elections and the election day. However, certain activities like the following are permitted during the blackouts in Canada: lawn signs and distribution of brochures, personal emails, telephone calls, social media communication, political advertisements on a poster or billboard if they have been posted before the blackout time, among some others (see Elections Ontario, n.d.).

In India, as discussed earlier, rallies, roadshows, television and film canvassing, and so on, have to stop 48 hours before the polling time.

Organising an Election and the Challenges

The EC's work in conducting elections brings up several challenges. According to former CEC Sampath, every election has thrown up unique challenges.[17] The set of challenges has also changed over the years. In the 1980s and 1990s, according to Sampath, 'the main challenge was security'.[18] Also, in the earlier decades, money power was not such a big issue. But in 'the subsequent years, particularly consequent to the creation of wealth in the country after economic reforms in the 1990s, money power came to play a significant role in the conduct of elections'.[19] He also points out that logistical requirements of 'organising a mammoth activity like Indian elections are of gigantic proportions', particularly in the case of a parliamentary election.[20] Problems like infrastructural deficits, lack of personnel and dysfunctional electronic equipment are common and have to be dealt with every election. Setting up properly functioning polling stations in remote and difficult-to-access areas is also a matter that comes up before the EC every election cycle. Former CEC Krishnamurthy also emphasises that challenges before the EC have grown over the years. According to him, challenges have increased particularly in tackling money and muscle power, logistics and number of voters and political parties, as well as in tackling violence and hatred.[21] He says that during the actual event of elections, problems relating to security and law and order, ensuring the accuracy of the voter list and the working of EVMs occupy more time and attention.[22]

With the coming of the internet and social media, fresh challenges, as far as organising an election is concerned, have arisen. Political parties have increasingly taken to new media to canvass and seek support for themselves. Digital campaigning through messages on chatting apps, verbal messages

---

[17] V. S. Sampath, email interview with the author, 1 August 2020.
[18] V. S. Sampath, email interview with the author, 1 August 2020.
[19] V. S. Sampath, email interview with the author, 1 August 2020.
[20] V. S. Sampath, email interview with the author, 1 August 2020.
[21] T. S. Krishnamurthy, email interview with the author, 7 October 2020.
[22] T. S. Krishnamurthy, email interview with the author, 7 October 2020.

on mobile phones, party pages on social media apps, party advertisements on online portals, and so on, are the new norm. Physical political rallies are being gradually replaced with these new techno-campaigns, and the electoral regulatory bodies have to deal with what is an unconventional situation for them. This is a global phenomenon given the technological transformation everywhere. In the UK concerns have been expressed about how in the age of campaigning over social media 'undisclosed "dark money" can influence elections and undermine political equality' (James, 2018).

In India the EC is also confronted with the issue of 'paid news'. The definition of paid news, as provided by the Press Council of India (a statutory media regulatory body), is 'any news or analysis appearing in any media (print and electronic) for a price in cash or kind as consideration'; this definition has been accepted by the EC (see EC, n.d.11). The purpose of paid news is to portray the paying party or candidate in a favourable light. It is an advertisement, a promotional device, but masquerades as news. In a well-known case, a complaint was lodged with the EC against Narottam Mishra of the BJP for allegedly not reporting his election expenses correctly and for paid news. He had won in the 2008 Madhya Pradesh assembly elections from a constituency called Datia. The EC took up the issue and came up with its final report in 2017 where it expressed concern about the 'menace of paid news that has assumed alarming proportions in the electoral landscape' (see Ghatwai, 2017). The EC further noted:

> This phenomenon has been growing increasingly vicious and spreading like cancer. It's a grave electoral malpractice which circumvents election expenditure limits, disturbs the level playing field and militates against the voter's right to accurate information. (See Ghatwai, 2017)

It disqualified Mishra for three years, on 23 June 2017, for not reporting his electoral expenditure correctly, including expenditure for paid news.

The EC had been receiving complaints by political parties and the media on paid news, and the issue was discussed in the parliament as well (EC, n.d.11). The 'frequently asked questions' (FAQ) file of the EC on paid news notes, 'There was consensus among all political parties in their meeting with the Commission on 4th October 2010 and again on 9th March 2011 that stringent measures should be taken against Paid News' (EC, n.d.11). Political parties continued to express concerns over 'paid news' (EC, 2018b). They suggested that to curb 'this menace' it should be made an electoral offence

(EC, 2018b). The EC, on its part, was agreeable to that measure. It appointed a Media Certification and Monitoring Committee (MCMC) at the district and state levels to check for paid news. This committee was vested with the responsibility of scrutinising all newspapers and electronic media 'in order to locate political advertisement in the garb of news coverage and take necessary action against the concerned candidates' (EC, 2018b).

Paid news has adverse implications – a seemingly innocuous and neutral piece of news is actually an item carrying positive publicity of the individual who has paid for it. It carries a potential for duping those who consume news through different media and gives an unfair electoral advantage to those who are portrayed therein. The 'image' creation through news items definitely is a way to influence voters to vote in a particular way.

Preparation for elections, as discussed previously, have thrown up unique and innumerable challenges before the electoral administration. The EC personnel stay on their toes till the declaration of results and the filing of all relevant reports. The triumvirate of political parties, voters and the EC represents the working of democratic praxis. The EC handles the multidimensional logistical operation with the help of the revenue, civil and police administration. It not only has to prepare for the smooth flow of an election schedule that requires coordinated effort, resources and infrastructure, but also has to ensure rule compliance by all political participants, whether political parties, candidates or voters. It is looked up to for direction on free and fair electoral practices and has brought about a predictability on how the electoral process will move ahead.

6

Contestant Information and Voters' Rights

While a proactive and firmer implementation of electoral rules and the MCC happened in the 1990s, the decade of the 2000s was a period of activism on voters' rights which mainly grew out of the activism of urban professionals and media in metropolises like Delhi, Bangalore, Mumbai and Ahmedabad. This civil society activism in the form of campaigns by ordinary citizens, NGOs like the ADR, Lok Prahari and the PUCL made efforts towards greater accountability and transparency in the electoral system, especially regarding the rights of voters to know their representatives better. These organisations campaigned for greater information in the public domain to enable voters to make informed choices at the polling booth. This call for reforms is rooted in the middle class's impatience with political parties and its call to contain corruption and make politics 'cleaner' and 'ethical'. The discourse of voters' rights and accountability of the political class to the people was an endorsement by the middle class of what Surinder Jodhka and Aseem Prakash call a 'new kind of politics which celebrates civil society organizations over political parties and trade unions' (Jodhka and Prakash, 2016: 166).

Right to Know about Prospective Representatives

The middle class in cities frequently voiced concerns over 'corruption' and the use of force and excessive illegal money in elections. It came forward to see that electoral malpractice and complications, which include rigging, difficulties in registering as voters, use of illegal money and coercion, hate speeches based on caste and religion, criminal records of those contesting, and so on, reduce (Sastry, 2004). The role of these ordinary citizens came under much focus as agents of a 'cleaner' politics. Their role was emphasised in reforming the electoral system and ensuring 'cleaner and better candidates and elections' (Sastry, 2004: 1391; Dash, 2004) and their efforts seen as providing the much-needed support to state institutions like the Supreme Court and the EC in improving the system. The logic was that people's power would energise the actions of these institutions in the event of the resistance of political leadership in bringing about the needed political changes – in other words, popular pressure would make institutions decisive and move on the appropriate path.

The reform campaign for more information was voter-rights-centric and focused on personal accomplishments of electoral candidates. It put forth a voter's or citizen's right to 'know' more about candidates they were voting for in terms of the latter's educational and economic status and whether their political careers were 'clean' or tainted by unlawful activities. It also tried to urge the candidates to be more transparent regarding self-information. The campaign was also propelled by the concern for voter awareness – that they make the right choice while casting their votes. This advocacy for informed choice and transparency rode on the inclination to tackle 'criminalisation' of politics. It gradually found support among many quarters, including the media and judiciary. The belief was that more information by way of self-declarations would help bring transparency and curb corrupt practices.

Civil society organisations like the ADR[1] went ahead energetically on the reform path, attempting, on the way, to build public opinion on the matter. They put in determined efforts at expanding voters' rights and creating voter awareness. They filed a public interest litigation (PIL) in 1999 in the Delhi High Court that asked for the disclosure of the criminal, financial and educational background of the candidates contesting elections. Trilochan Sastry of the ADR observed:

---

[1] The ADR was formed in 1999 by a few professors teaching at IIM, Ahmedabad, with the aim 'to improve governance and strengthen democracy by continuous work in the area of Electoral and Political Reforms' (ADR, n.d.). The organisation is involved in 'multiple projects aimed at increasing transparency and accountability in the political and electoral system of the country' (ADR, n.d.).

The work of the ADR regarding electoral reforms and voter awareness was ignored initially, but later we got support from the media, the judiciary and the EC. The ADR worked state by state and with 1,200 NGOs (including the MKSS [Mazdoor Kisan Shakti Sangathan]) to create voter awareness and more transparency on candidates. It contacted eminent personalities like Jt. Venkatachaliah, Jt. Santosh Hegde and former CEC J. M. Lyngdoh to spread this message.[2]

The Delhi High Court passed a judgment in this case (*Association of Democratic Reforms v. Union of India*), on 2 November 2000, that emphasised voters' right to know about a candidate's past. The High Court directed the EC to seek information on whether the candidate was guilty of any offence punishable with imprisonment; the value of assets owned by the candidate; the candidate's spouse and dependents; the candidate's competence, capacity and suitability for law-making; educational qualifications and the ability to judge the capacity and capability of the political party for fielding the candidate (V. Venkatesan, 2002a).

The central government (NDA-I, under prime minister Atal Bihari Vajpayee) challenged this order in the Supreme Court, saying that it is for political parties to bring amendments to the RPA, 1951 (EC, n.d.6: 9–10). It also argued in the court that as the rules do not disqualify a candidate for non-disclosure of the assets or pending charge in a criminal case, the High Court's judgment does not hold weight and should not have been issued. The central government, however, failed to convince the Supreme Court, which upheld the High Court's order on the matter with a few modifications. The apex court gave its judgment on the case on 2 May 2002, where it reiterated that voters had a right to know more about the contestants. The judiciary through this case expanded the scope of Article 19(1)(a) of the Constitution of India, saying that a citizen's right to freedom of speech and expression also includes the right to know about matters that are of public concern.

The Supreme Court emphasised that during elections a voter expresses his or her opinion through casting a vote, and for this purpose he or she ought to have information about the candidates. Discussing previous court judgments, the Supreme Court took the view 'that the members of a democratic society should be sufficiently informed so that they may influence

---

[2] Trilochan Sastry, ADR, personal interview with the author, Bengaluru, 14 November 2016.

intelligently the decisions which may affect themselves and this would include their decision of casting votes in favour of a particular candidate' (ADR, 2002) It further said, 'If there is a disclosure by a candidate as sought for then it would strengthen the voters in taking appropriate decision of casting their votes' (ADR, 2002). It gave the EC the green signal to solicit such information from candidates contesting elections. Giving direction to the EC, it said:

> The Election Commission is directed to call for information on affidavit by issuing necessary order in exercise of its power under Article 324 of the Constitution of India from each candidate seeking election to Parliament or State Legislature as a necessary part of his nomination paper, furnishing therein, information on the following aspects in relation to his/her candidature:
>
> 1. Whether the candidate is convicted/acquitted/discharged of any criminal offence in the past - if any, whether he is punished with imprisonment or fine?
>
> 2. Prior to six months of filing of nomination, whether the candidate is accused in any pending case, of any offence punishable with imprisonment for two years or more, and in which charge is framed or cognizance is taken by the Court of law. If so, the details thereof.
>
> 3. The assets (immovable, movable, bank balances etc.) of a candidate and of his/her spouse and that of dependants.
>
> 4. Liabilities, if any, particularly whether there are any over dues of any public financial institution or Government dues.
>
> 5. The educational qualifications of the candidate. (ADR, 2002: 23)

The EC issued an order on 28 June 2002 that said that candidates contesting any parliamentary or state legislature seat should file an affidavit during their nomination, giving information about their educational qualifications, wealth and criminal antecedents (EC, 2002). As Ronojoy Sen points out, this information on candidates especially about their finances 'is in keeping with the practices of other mature democracies' (R. Sen, 2012: 222).

Political parties did not quite see the same way as civil society and the Supreme Court did. They felt that information on wealth of the candidate and his or her family should be sought after he or she has won the election rather than while filing nominations for contesting as directed by the court (V. Venkatesan, 2003). On details of educational qualification, parties felt that seeking this information was unnecessary and also against the spirit of the debates in the CA, which had rejected a proposal to prescribe minimum educational qualifications for candidates (V. Venkatesan, 2003). There was also an apprehension that insisting on disclosure of educational qualifications might create 'some kind of a negative bias in the minds of the voters against those who are less educated or are illiterate' (S. Kumar, 2002: 3491).

Concerns were raised by the CPI(M) that the judgment and the subsequent EC order did not take into consideration the difference between political offences and criminal offences, where the former are activities like organising rallies, picketing and demonstrations, and these did not make a ground for disqualification (Pillai, 2002). Political leaders routinely took up activities like agitations, *gherao*s (a form of protest in which the protestors block the exit of employers, leaders, managers or officials so that they agree to the protestors' demands) and demonstrations for people's issues that might be 'considered unlawful in the eyes of the law' (S. Kumar, 2002: 3490). According to Sanjay Kumar, at times demonstrations might turn violent, leading to arrests and police cases and, 'If the law is implemented to the letter, even such people will be debarred from contesting election. Are we aiming to ban politicians from participating in demonstrations, *dharna*s (sit-in, peaceful protests) and *gherao*s, which are basic political activities?' (S. Kumar, 2002: 3490). It was also felt that due consideration has not been given to 'false cases' that can be filed against rival candidates (Pillai, 2002). Concerns were also raised that such judgments meant judicial encroachment upon powers that belonged to the legislature (Pillai, 2002). It was felt that only the parliament can legislate on such issues in a democratic system (Pillai, 2002).

Political parties tried to undo the directive of the Supreme Court and the subsequent EC order. The government called an all-party meeting on 8 July on the issue. The then Union Ministry of Law and Justice asked the EC to postpone the implementation of the order by asking the court for more time (V. Venkatesan, 2002b). The EC, however, felt that it was the government which should seek more time from the court rather than the EC (V. Venkatesan, 2002b). The matter came before the Supreme Court, but it did not extend the deadline for issuing the order. As a result, the EC went ahead and issued the order on 28 June 2002 regarding the disclosure of information (V. Venkatesan, 2002b). Leaders of 21 political parties in a 'rare unanimity' (Joshua, 2002) rejected the EC's order at the all-party meeting. Thereafter, the NDA government promulgated an ordinance that negated the judgment and the order of the EC. Section 33B of the ordinance reads as follows:

> Notwithstanding anything contained in any judgement, decree or order of any court or any direction, order or any other instruction issued by the Election Commission, no candidate shall be liable to disclose or furnish any such information, in respect of his election, which is not required to be disclosed or furnished under this Act (Representation of the People Act, 1951) or the rules made thereunder. (Quoted in EC, 2003: 6).

This was subsequently passed as law, and the RPA, 1951, was amended. The Supreme Court and the EC were seen by some as 'encroaching' on the powers of the parliament, and their actions were interpreted as 'judicial legislation' (*Times of India*, 2002). The rejection of the EC's order by the all-party meet was met with some criticism in the media and civil society. *The Tribune* (2002), for instance, saw it as 'most unfortunate'. Its editorial further noted, 'It is the failure of the political parties to appropriately tackle the problem that has led to the entry of criminals into our representative institutions, forcing the Supreme Court to step in and ask the Election Commission to issue the directive in this regard.'

On a petition by the National Campaign for Electoral Reforms (a civil society initiative), the matter again came before the Supreme Court. In its judgment of 13 March 2003, the Supreme Court struck down the law and declared Section 33B of the amended RPA as illegal, null and void. The Supreme Court emphasised that the citizens have a constitutional right to know more about the candidates, and the latter should furnish details of their educational qualification, assets owned by them and their family members, including spouse, and criminal antecedents at the time of their nomination as contesting candidates. Regarding the latter, the court directed that candidates need to furnish information on any pending case for any offence that carried a prison term of two years or more, along with the charges that have been taken cognisance of by a court of law and acquittals or discharges in any criminal case (V. Venkatesan, 2003).

The judgment was 'widely welcomed across the country' (Paul, 2003: 1447). *The Tribune* in its editorial said:

> The Supreme Court has rendered a great service to the country by declaring the new legislation as null and void as it curtails the voters' freedom to vote even though it is equal to the fundamental right to expression as guaranteed under Article 19 of the Constitution. (*The Tribune*, 2003)

Reetika Khera, while discussing the work of the group Rajasthan Election Watch, remarked that the Supreme Court judgment was also seen as possessing 'the potential to change the character/nature of elections and democracy in India' (Khera, 2004). Information about candidates was considered vital because 'as citizens it is important for us to know about the people we elect to make policy' and whether these people are 'honest and capable of making the right decisions for us' (Khera, 2004). The affidavits by candidates are seen as 'another tool (apart from voting them out) to keep a tab on our representatives' and bring about 'some accountability especially vis-à-vis their sources of income' (Khera, 2004). The efforts of civil society groups paved the way for the passing of the judgment which was seen as a 'poor reflection on the quality and vision of our political leadership' (Paul, 2003: 1447). The political leaders 'instead of being leaders in deepening the democratic process ... are being forced to follow the thinking of the civil society and an independent judiciary ... – a "role reversal"' (Paul, 2003: 1447). Jayaprakash Narayan, the founder-leader of the Lok Satta party and a former MLA of Andhra Pradesh, who has advocated for electoral reforms, wrote, '[T]his verdict and people's right to know must be the starting point of democratic reform' (Narayan, 2003). He noted that millions of Indians along with several media and other organisations came together in this 'battle for democracy and liberty' (Narayan, 2003).

The EC in its order dated 27 March 2003, following the directions of the Supreme Court, revised its earlier order and specified:

> Every candidate at the time of filing his nomination paper for any election to the Council of States, House of the People, Legislative Assembly of a State or the Legislative Council of a State having such a council, shall furnish full and complete information in regard to the matters specified by the Hon'ble Supreme Court. (EC, 2003: 8).

The EC's order also made the following clear:

> Non-furnishing of the affidavit by any candidate shall be considered to be violation of the order of the Hon'ble Supreme Court and the nomination of the candidate concerned shall be liable to rejection by the returning officer at the time of scrutiny of nominations for such non-furnishing of the affidavit. (EC, 2003: 8).

However, there was an unease among the political leadership whether the 'judiciary has overstepped its limits and upset the doctrine of separation of powers between the judiciary and the legislature' (V. Venkatesan, 2003). Some contestants found a way to sidestep this requirement. Many of them began leaving the columns where this information had to be furnished blank. The Justice Verma Committee, constituted to look into the Delhi gang-rape of December 2012, raised a concern in its report given in January 2013 that a convicted person might deliberately refrain from disclosing this information in his affidavit or might make the 'false disclosure that he has no charges pending' (J. S. Verma Committee, 2013: 349). The committee called upon the EC to prepare an 'accurate database which is publicly available' on the candidates whose offences have been taken into cognizance by the court (J. S. Verma Committee, 2013: 350).

An NGO called Resurgence India brought this issue to the notice of the Supreme Court. The latter in its judgment of 13 September 2013 made it clear that candidates need to disclose all information in the columns (where this information was sought) and that they cannot leave the columns blank if they want to contest elections. The Supreme Court ordered the returning officers to insist on relevant details from the candidates and reject their candidature if they failed to furnish details despite reminders (see Mahapatra, 2013; J. Venkatesan, 2013). Justices P. Sathasivam, Ranjana Prakash Desai and Ranjan Gogoi in their judgment said:

> [I]t is the duty of the Returning Officer to check whatever the information required is fully furnished at the time of filing of affidavit with the nomination paper since such information is very vital for giving effect to the 'right to know' of the citizens. If a candidate fails to fill the blanks even after the reminder by the Returning Officer, the nomination paper is fit to be rejected. (Supreme Court, 2013b).

The court gave the candidates the option of writing 'NIL', 'not applicable' or 'not known' in the columns. But in case these responses were found to be incorrect, the candidates could be tried for perjury for giving false information to the returning officers (see Mahapatra, 2013; J. Venkatesan, 2013).

Conviction and Disqualification

Just a few months earlier, on 10 July 2013, in another landmark judgment, the Supreme Court had ruled that sitting MPs and MLAs who were convicted (not just charged) would be disqualified with immediate effect, and their seats would thereby be declared vacant. This verdict came on petitions filed in 2005 by advocate Lily Thomas and NGO Lok Prahari on convicted candidates. The Court struck down Sub-Section 4 of Section 8 of the RPA, 1951, which allowed convicted members of the parliament and legislative assemblies to continue in office if they had filed appeals in a higher court within a span of three months from the date of conviction (see ADR, 2014a). This meant that convicted candidates continued in legislatures while their appeals journeyed through courts, often for indefinite periods. The overloaded judicial system as well as the power of politicians meant that the cases against political leaders who were charged with crimes could drag on for years. According to ADR member Anil Bairwal, politicians can use their position to delay their cases 'not just for years, but decades' (quoted in A. North, 2013). The Supreme Court in its judgment said:

> We also hold that the provisions of Article 101(3)(a)[3] and 190(3)(a)[4] of the Constitution expressly prohibit Parliament to defer the date from which the disqualification will come into effect in case of a sitting member of Parliament or a State Legislature. Parliament, therefore, has exceeded its powers conferred by the Constitution in enacting sub-section (4) of Section 8 of the Act and accordingly sub-section (4) of Section 8 of the Act is ultra vires the Constitution. (Supreme Court judgment quoted in A. North, 2013: 34–35)

---

[3] Article 101(3)(a) is about disqualification of MPs.
[4] Article 190(3)(a) talks about disqualification of MLAs.

The court thus made it clear that MPs and MLAs so convicted would stand disqualified with immediate effect, and their seat would fall vacant.

Concerns were raised by the then UPA-II government that the disqualification of even one member of the government might have a 'deleterious' effect on it, destabilising it, especially if it was surviving on a 'razor-edge thin majority where each member counts significantly' (Supreme Court judgment quoted in A. North, 2013: 19). This would have grave consequences for the democratic process. The government argued that there was sufficient possibility of filing of false cases against legislators, which would not bode well for democracy. This meant that time and opportunity of appeal had to be given to them rather than calling for their immediate exit and preventing them from contesting before their appeals were heard.

The UPA-II government, ostensibly backed by support from almost all political parties, introduced a Bill in parliament to override this Supreme Court judgment. It was, however, unable to get the Bill passed. The BJP allegedly changed its opinion on the matter (*Hindu Business Line*, 2013). The government then took recourse to its ordinance-making powers and passed one overriding the judgment in September 2013. This ordinance protected the convicted legislators from disqualification, provided that they appealed to a higher court within 90 days of conviction and that their conviction and sentence were stayed. The ordinance further said that the MPs and the MLAs would neither be able to vote in the proceedings of the House nor be able to draw their salaries and allowances, but they would be able to sit through and participate in the proceedings of the House. The BJP went ahead and sought the intervention of the president to challenge the government's decision to bring an ordinance to overturn the court ruling (*Hindu Business Line*, 2013). The BJP's senior leader Sushma Swaraj termed the ordinance 'illegal, immoral and unconstitutional', and former deputy prime minister and senior leader of the BJP, L. K. Advani, said that the move would harm the dignity of the parliament (ADR, 2013b).

The UPA government withdrew the ordinance following a public uproar on it. According to a former CEC, the ordinance 'would arguably have been a very regressive step in the development of our democratic institutions' (Chawla, 2013). There were differences within the party itself over the ordinance. For example, the then INC vice-president, Rahul Gandhi, and the then minister belonging to the INC, Milind Deora, voiced their unhappiness with the ordinance. There were concerns raised that 'there were problems with the Supreme Court judgment', but the government 'showed disgraceful haste in rushing an ordinance through, rather than going through a proper parliamentary debate' (P. B. Mehta, 2013).[5]

Rashid Masood of the INC, a sitting Rajya Sabha member, was convicted on corruption charges and was the first to be disqualified and formally lose his seat. He got a four-year jail term. The next to lose their seats in the parliament were Laloo Prasad Yadav, the chief of the Rashtriya Janata Dal (RJD) and the former chief minister of Bihar, and Jagdish Sharma of the Janata Dal (United) (JD[U]), who were members of the Lok Sabha and were similarly convicted on corruption charges. They were given five- and four-year jail terms, respectively. The ADR observed:

> This is a very significant judgment, as it would act as a deterrent to political parties from giving tickets to tainted candidates. (ADR, 2013a)

Subhash Kashyap, an analyst of the Constitution, speaking on the judgment, was of the following view:

> This ruling has given clarity for an incongruous position that a person cannot contest election if he is convicted but can continue as a lawmaker if the conviction takes place after he or she becomes a lawmaker. This is a first step. The next step should be to disallow all those charged with criminal cases from contesting elections. (Quoted in Mathew and Anuja, 2013)

Barring convicted leaders from continuing in office is not unusual. The Representation of the People Act, 1981, of the UK has a similar provision regarding disqualification of sitting MPs. It disqualifies a sitting MP if he or she is detained for more than a year or indefinitely for any offence in the UK or the Republic of Ireland – the seat then stands vacant (see Castle, 2009; website of the Electoral Commission of the UK). Similarly, the Constitution of South Africa disqualifies a legislator from membership if such a member is convicted of an offence carrying a sentence of more than 12 months without

---

[5] Pratap Bhanu Mehta draws attention to the ramifications for a democratic verdict if the government has a real thin majority of one or two in the legislature (P. B. Mehta, 2013). In such a case, Mehta points out, an erroneous judgment can cause a major disruption in the government. As a safeguard against this disruptive factor, it might not be unreasonable to have another judge (of a higher court) look at the matter by way of appeals filed before the higher court.

the option of a fine, unless he or she has received pardon (Constitution of the Republic of South Africa, n.d.: ch. 4). In Canada, parliamentarians automatically lose their seat if they are convicted for an indictable offence and are sentenced to imprisonment for two years or more. In such a case, a new election is ordered (M. Roy, 2017).

'NOTA'

On 27 September 2013, close on the heels of the contentious ordinance, came another judgment from the Supreme Court. On a PIL filed by the PUCL in 2004, it ruled that voters, if they so choose, should have the option of rejecting all candidates contesting elections. The EC on the directions of the court added a button for 'NOTA', meaning 'none of the above', to the EVMs. Voters were thus given an option of refusing to vote for any candidate by pressing the 'NOTA' button. This was another move in the direction of furthering the rights of voters, especially in a context of the candidature of those with criminal charges against them.

Data gathered by two NGOs, the NEW and the ADR, in 2013, revealed that 1,460 (30 per cent) out of 4,807 sitting MPs and MLAs had criminal cases pending against them – of these 14 per cent of the MPs and MLAs, numbering 688, had serious criminal charges against them (ADR, 2013c). The report of the two NGOs noted that there was a low rate of conviction, which might be because of the 'excruciatingly slow pace at which hearings of cases proceed in our courts' (ADR, 2013c). The report also stated:

> It is possible that a candidate contesting an election may be refraining from declaring conviction in his/her affidavit once an appeal in a higher court is admitted challenging the conviction. In such a case this candidate may merely mention that an appeal is pending in a court and may not declare the conviction in the appropriate section of the affidavit. (ADR, 2013c)

The report further pointed out the possibility that candidates may not be revealing the conviction at all, taking advantage of an absence of a reliable mechanism in place to scrutinise these affidavits (ADR, 2013c).

In this context, the NOTA judgment came as a significant development, especially when seen together with the judgments in the past about rights of voters to know about the economic, educational and criminal background of their representatives and the judgment disqualifying the representatives who had been convicted. According to former CEC N. Gopalaswami, 'In the face of the government's reluctance to move ahead in bringing meaningful electoral reforms, the courts have had to intervene wherever they could to give some push to the reforms and to restore the public's faith in the system' (Gopalaswami, 2013). The EC had moved the law ministry as early as 2001, proposing a 'button in electronic voting machines in order to protect the identity and secrecy of a voter who does not want to vote for any candidate', but the EC received no response on the proposal (Gopalaswami, 2013). In 2004, the then CEC, T. S. Krishnamurthy, reiterated the proposal after calling the button 'none of the above' but, for the first time, clearly articulating that it was to 'to enable a voter to reject all the candidates, if he chooses so' (Gopalaswami, 2013). By this time, the PUCL had already moved the Supreme Court in the matter (Gopalaswami, 2013).

The NOTA option meant that if a voter did not want to vote for any candidate, he or she had the option of exercising this choice in secrecy – not that the option of not voting did not exist. The Conduct of Election Rules, 1961, provided that one could choose not to vote after identifying oneself to the returning officer, and thereafter appropriate entries would be made in the electoral register, and so on. This procedure, however, did not maintain the secrecy of the negative ballot. As former CEC S. Y. Quraishi pointed out, the EC had been asking for the NOTA option to ensure secrecy and bring down bogus voting and not actually for any other reason (Quraishi, 2013). The PUCL petition on which the Supreme Court based its ruling was on the same issue – maintaining the secrecy of the voting decision. The Supreme Court in its judgment said that in all direct elections, 'secrecy is a must and is insisted upon all over the world' so that 'a voter casts his vote without any fear of being victimized if his vote is disclosed' (Supreme Court, 2013a: 26). The court further said that a voter may refrain from voting because of a variety of reasons, including the one where none of the candidates is considered worthy by a voter, but abstaining from voting is 'not an ideal option for a conscientious and responsible citizen', and the only way this can be handled is 'by providing a button in the EVMs to express that right [to not vote]' (Supreme Court, 2013a: 33). The court felt that the secrecy of a voter who decides not to cast a vote has to be protected in the same manner as the secrecy of one who casts a vote (Supreme Court, 2013a: 39–40). The court also noted, 'Not allowing a person to cast vote negatively defeats the very freedom of expression and the right ensured in Article 21 i.e., the right to liberty' (Supreme Court, 2013a: 42).

The Supreme Court went a little further in its judgment and highlighted the cleansing and participatory dimensions of the negative vote. The court felt, 'By providing NOTA button in the EVMs, it will accelerate the effective political participation in the present state of democratic system and the voters in fact will be empowered' (Supreme Court, 2013a: 44). It felt that negative voting would make political parties introspect about their choice of candidates. The court further said:

> When the political parties will realize that a large number of people are expressing their disapproval with the candidates being put up by them, gradually there will be a systemic change and the political parties will be forced to accept the will of the people and field candidates who are known for their integrity. (Supreme Court, 2013a: 45)

It felt that 'a provision of negative voting would be in the interest of promoting democracy as it would send clear signals to political parties and their candidates as to what the electorate think about them' (Supreme Court, 2013a: 46). It was largely believed that the judgment, though about the secrecy of the act of not voting for any candidate, would bring about some soul-searching among political parties regarding the choice of candidates (the 'tainted' ones) they were putting up for election.

The Supreme Court thereby directed the EC to include the option 'none of the above' in the EVMs. Some confusion arose about this option, which were cleared by the EC. It said that even if the number of NOTA votes were more than those of the winning candidate, they will not invalidate the verdict, and the candidate with the maximum number of votes would be declared elected (EC, 2013a). This meant that more NOTA votes would not nullify an election. The EC also made it clear that if there is only one candidate in the fray for a Lok Sabha or a state legislative assembly seat, he or she would be declared elected, and NOTA would then not be relevant in such cases (EC, 2013a). The NOTA option was thus meant to convey the diminished confidence of the voter in the candidates vying to become people's representatives in a constituency.

Such institutional efforts to enthuse ethical norms in electoral politics were considered important and welcomed, but it was also pointed out that criminalisation of politics, as of other institutions of state and society, is to a large extent a function of the existing socio-economic inequalities and uneven power relations (Katju, 2013: 12). The Supreme Court felt that the NOTA option would contribute to cleansing politics – that the political leadership would formally know that there are people unhappy with the parties' choice of candidates. The logic of this judgment was that it would build moral pressure on political parties and possibly make them rethink their choice of candidates and hold them back from putting up candidates with criminal records.

The NOTA judgment was put into effect from the then upcoming assembly elections in Delhi, Rajasthan, Chhattisgarh, Madhya Pradesh and Mizoram in 2013. In that year, in Madhya Pradesh 1.9 per cent voters used the NOTA option; in Chhattisgarh this number was 3.06 per cent; in Delhi it was 0.63 per cent; in Rajasthan it was 1.92 per cent (Thakkar, 2013); and in Mizoram it was 0.66 per cent (EC, 2013b). In these elections, an interesting trend came to light – the more the number of candidates in a constituency, the less the number of NOTA votes (Shashidhar, 2013), which meant that being given more options at elections, the voters felt a lesser need to opt for NOTA and hence avoided it. Conversely, when choices were reduced, the options were fewer, and a higher percentage of voters went for the NOTA option. Tables 6.1 and 6.2 indicate the range of the percentage of NOTA votes in different legislative assembly elections between 2013 and 2018.

The NOTA count in the Lok Sabha elections of 2014 was 1.08 per cent, and it fell only slightly in 2019 to be at 1.06 per cent. Analysis revealed that in 2019 NOTA votes were relatively high in Scheduled Caste and Scheduled Tribe constituencies, as also in constituencies with a presence of left-wing insurgency (Bansal and Marathe, 2019). In areas of a multi-party contest, the percentage of these votes were relatively low (Bansal and Marathe, 2019). David Damore, Mallory Waters and Shaun Bowler, in their study of the entire history of NOTA voting in the US state of Nevada (the only state in the US that has given the NOTA option to its voters from 1976 onwards), found some support for the position that NOTA voting represents 'a form of purposeful protest as it increases when fewer options are put before voters' (Damore, Waters and Bowler, 2012: 896). They also found no positive relationship between NOTA voting and voter turnout – implying that the provision of NOTA did not mean that more people were turning out to vote (Damore, Waters and Bowler, 2012: 904). Their study further revealed that the NOTA option 'has not fallen out of favour with Nevada voters but instead has increased slightly in use since its implementation' (Damore, Waters and Bowler, 2012: 904).

Table 6.1 'None of the Above' (NOTA) votes (per cent) out of the total votes polled in the legislative assemblies of states and union territories (UTs), 2013–16

State and year	NOTA votes (per cent)	State and year	NOTA votes (per cent)
Chattisgarh, 2013	3.06	Maharashtra, 2014	0.92
Madhya Pradesh, 2013	1.90	Jharkhand, 2014	1.69
Mizoram, 2013	0.66	Jammu and Kashmir, 2014	1.02
National capital territory (NCT) of Delhi, 2013	0.63	NCT of Delhi, 2015	0.40
Rajasthan, 2013	1.91	Bihar, 2015	2.50
Telangana and Andhra Pradesh, 2014	0.64	Assam, 2016	1.12
Odisha, 2014	1.26	Tamil Nadu, 2016	1.30
Arunachal Pradesh, 2014	1.05	Kerala, 2016	0.53
Sikkim, 2014	1.44	Puducherry, 2016	1.62
Haryana, 2014	0.43	West Bengal, 2016	1.52

Source: *Electoral Statistics Pocket Book 2017* (New Delhi: Election Commission of India), 122.

Table 6.2 'None of the Above' (NOTA) votes (per cent) out of the total votes polled in the legislative assemblies of states and union territories (UTs), 2017–18

State and year	NOTA votes (per cent)	State and year	NOTA votes (per cent)
Goa, 2017	1.19	Himachal Pradesh, 2017	0.9
Gujarat, 2017	1.8	Chhattisgarh, 2018	2.1
Uttarakhand, 2017	1.01	Mizoram, 2018	0.5
Manipur, 2017	0.55	Madhya Pradesh, 2018	1.5
Uttar Pradesh, 2017	0.87	Rajasthan, 2018	1.3
Punjab, 2017	0.70	Telangana, 2018	1.1

Source: Pandey (2017); *India Today* (2017); PTI (2018).

The NOTA option raises a few issues about voters' rights and democracy in India. First, NOTA expands the choice of those voters who want to refrain from casting a vote. These voters, because of NOTA, have the choice of coming to the polling booth to cast the NOTA vote instead of completely absenting themselves. Both NOTA and not voting are ways of conveying displeasure (if such a displeasure exists) towards the candidates contesting elections. Coming to the polling booth, however, involves costs compared to not turning up at all, conveying the intensity of discontent or displeasure in a voter that becomes a compelling factor in bringing him or her to the polling booth. However, the extent of displeasure cannot be fully known as many refrain from voting. The NOTA votes, in the current situation, cannot overturn an election. This leads one to the second point that NOTA votes have a status of invalid votes because even if their number is more than that of the votes received by the winning candidate, they do not have the legal status of nullifying an election. Third, when it is a tightly contested election, NOTA votes actually strengthen the position of the more entrenched and powerful candidate in a constituency. He or she might be low on the scale of popular support in an upcoming election but might get elected because the NOTA vote might pull votes away from the rival candidate. If in an election the margin of votes between the winner and the loser is lower than the NOTA votes, this is precisely what happens. This occurred in quite a few seats in the 2013 assembly elections in Chhattisgarh. Though negative voting like NOTA highlights the issue of accountability of the political leadership more sharply, it might lead to endorsing that very political leadership.

Fourth, does the NOTA option have the capacity to raise voter turnout? Evidence is scarce, but from Damore, Waters and Bowler's study (2012) it appears that it does not. A point has also been made that negative voting holds more weight when combined with a system of compulsory voting. Since in this system one has to vote mandatorily, one can give a 'no vote' or 'blank vote' if one does not prefer any candidate. In countries without compulsory voting, the voters who disapprove of all the contesting candidates can sit back and need not come out at all.

Fifth, will electoral participation increase if NOTA votes can nullify an election? In other words, if displeasure of voters with candidates has the power to nullify an election and order re-election, will electoral participation rise? One does not know the answer to this question, but one has to keep in mind that the NOTA vote is mediated by the number of candidates in fray – meaning, the choices available to the voters. As mentioned earlier, evidence suggests that the greater the number of candidates, the fewer the NOTA votes. Also, greater participation in elections is more a factor of engagement with the politics of the day and a feeling of involvement in it. The absence of this involvement is a bigger factor in subduing electoral participation than the dissatisfaction with the contestants. This involvement differs across elections and regions – the parliamentary elections might see a greater or lesser turnout than the state or municipal elections, and elections in certain years (which have seen, say, price rise or 'corruption') might draw out more voters than others. Similarly, certain regions see greater voter involvement in politics than others.

Sixth, does the NOTA vote take away support from smaller parties who might be 'protest' parties but, because they are lesser known or 'weak' parties vis-à-vis entrenched ones, they lose their votes to NOTA? This is a distinct possibility. NOTA can pull away votes from parties that are small and less known. They face resource crunch and limited canvassers to campaign effectively and extensively, rendering them invisible and incapable of taking on entrenched parties. But it has also been seen that the higher the number of candidates contesting an election, the lower are the NOTA votes, implying that the availability of alternatives shrinks the NOTA vote.

Whatever the reasons for or against NOTA, it came as an institutional response to the demand for an expansion of voters' choices. It added the option of 'negative' choice to the 'positive' choice and gave people a chance to say they are not 'happy' with the existing list of contestants. Its incorporation on EVMs reflected an institutional proactiveness in furthering citizen involvement in electoral politics by bringing the individual 'protest' voice in. Organisations like the ADR went a step ahead to suggest that if the NOTA votes are higher than those of all the contesting candidates, there should be a re-election from which the earlier candidates should be barred (*Economic Times*, 2022).

Public Scrutiny and the Right to Information (RTI)

A debate took place some years ago as to whether political parties should be subject to public scrutiny and accountability. Political parties reacted furiously to the EC's directives in this regard in 2013. The Central Information Commission (CIC) had ruled that political parties were 'public authorities' who need to respond to Right to Information (RTI) queries within six weeks (see *Frontline*, 2013; *Indian Express*, 2013; *The Hindu*, 2013b). In June 2013, it directed the six national parties – the INC, the BJP, the NCP, the CPI, the CPI(M) and the BSP – to have mechanisms and personnel in place to give information sought of them by the public under the RTI Act, 2005.

The CIC declared the parties as public authorities and thus covered under the RTI Act, as according to it they had received 'substantial financing' from the government by way of land in prime areas of Delhi, government accommodation at very low rates, unconditional income tax exemptions and free campaign time on All India Radio (AIR) (state-run audio media) and Doordarshan (state-managed television channel) during elections. The CIC ruled that all this amounted to substantial financing by the government, which makes political parties public authorities. It also said that political parties ought to be considered so because they affect lives of citizens in every conceivable way and are engaged in public duties at all times.

The UPA-II government (2009–14), with considerable support from political parties affected by this order of the CIC, went into action and decided to amend the RTI laws to exclude political parties from the definition of 'public authority' and thus make them immune to the requirements of the RTI. This was strongly opposed by RTI activists who warned that this move of the government would 'lead to corruption'. Discussion on the Bill was deferred following criticism, and political parties continued their non-compliance with the RTI Act. With the change in governments after the 2014 general elections, the Bill lapsed.

In 2015, the ADR moved a PIL in the Supreme Court seeking a directive on this matter. The petitioners argued that political parties should be more transparent in their working, be accountable to the public and disclose details of income and expenditure for public scrutiny. According to the petitioners, this was necessitated due to the role of political parties in the formation of government, formulation of policy and enactment of laws. The SC issued notices to the national parties, the EC and the central government seeking their response. The NDA government under prime minister Narendra Modi, like its predecessor, opposed the plea. The DoPT in an affidavit said:

> If political parties are held to be public authorities under RTI Act, it would hamper their smooth internal working, which is not the objective of the RTI Act and was not envisaged by Parliament. Further, it is apprehended that political rivals might file RTI applications with malicious intentions, adversely affecting their political functioning. (Anand, 2015)

The DoPT also said that in 2013 the CIC had a made a 'very liberal' interpretation of the RTI Act, 'leading to an erroneous conclusion' that political parties are public authorities and thus open to RTI queries (Anand, 2015). Regarding financial matters, the DoPT stated in its affidavit that the

RPA, 1951, and the Income Tax Act, 1961, contained provisions that imposed restrictions on political parties and made their financial matters transparent (Anand, 2015). D. Raja, a former Rajya Sabha MP and the general secretary of the CPI, echoed the views of political parties when he said that while they were in favour of transparency, they cannot be considered public authorities under the RTI as they did not get any government funding (see Jebaraj, 2019). Thus, despite the CIC's directives, political parties continued to bypass the law.

Right to Recall

A prominent issue which comes up in democracies is about the voters' right to recall. Recall means calling back. The right to recall implies that citizens should have the right to call back their representatives if they fail to fulfil the responsibilities bestowed upon them as people's representatives. These are elected leaders who fall short of fulfilling their roles as people's representatives or indulge in empty rhetoric or somehow fall out with their constituencies. Such representatives can also be those who do not fulfil promises made in their party manifestos and thus lose the confidence of the people. As legislators they may indulge in activities seen as corrupt practices. It is argued that people should have a right to call back these leaders; they should be 'recalled' before their legislative term expires. In India this debate has come up recently in the context of corrupt practices involving elected leadership. Those who advocate the right to recall as a voters' right argue that such a law should be put in place as it will deter political parties from putting up candidates who have 'tainted' records or indulge in corrupt practices. This right, it is argued, would involve voters more closely with politics and make democracy more participatory. People would also have a closer sense of belonging as they would have more say in how their representatives conduct themselves.

According to BJP MP Varun Gandhi, who is an ardent advocate of the right to recall, 'Logic and justice necessitate that if the people have the power to elect their representatives, they should also have the power to remove these representatives when they engage in misdeeds or fail to fulfil their duties' (Gandhi, 2017). According to him, this right would mean a check on corruption and criminalisation of politics (Gandhi, 2017). The reasoning here is that the fear of removal from office would make representatives do their work responsibly and honestly. Also, as mentioned earlier, political parties would refrain from putting up candidates with 'tainted' records for elections. However, many questions remain about putting such a right into practice. How much time should be given to a legislator before putting him or her to a test of performance? Implementing an election promise might take time; in the meantime, voters might get restless and ask for a recall. A representative might face politically motivated false cases – in this situation, is asking for a recall the correct step? Accusation and conviction of a corrupt practice or a crime usually have a considerable time interval – when should a recall happen? These are some questions that come up while debating the right to recall. However, it remains a peripheral issue in India and has not received much attention.

Apart from civil society organisations, formal institutions like the Supreme Court and the EC have attempted to reform the electoral system by bringing in various provisions in laws to strengthen voters' rights. Through reform measures like candidate disclosures and NOTA, they have tried to infuse more meaning into the idea of democratic citizenship. Though this saw some disagreements between the political representatives and the EC, it did lead to the extension of transparency and accountability norms in the decades of the 2000s and the 2010s.

7

Election Violence

Instances of transgressions of law, especially by political leaders and their supporters, have been a visible part of elections in India. Election-related violence of varied kind, though considerably reduced over the years, still occurs. Blatant violence has become rare. A look at the evolution of electoral violence in India helps in understanding why and in what form election violence occurs and how the EC deals with it. Evidence suggests that this particular violence, while endemic in transitional states or nascent democracies, is not absent in long-standing democracies. However, as democracies get increasingly stable, violence declines or becomes sporadic – indicating institutional strengthening and a greater capability of polities to solve differences through institutional mechanisms non-violently. Violence then becomes confined to specific areas within democratic states where greater economic inequality and acrimonious social relations persist. In contexts of deep division, control over political power becomes a do-or-die situation, and here political incumbents and rivals (and, of course, their supporters) take recourse to violence during elections to change electoral outcomes. Elections are held and accepted because of their legitimate value among the larger public and international community, but violence is perpetrated to deal with insecurities of electoral outcome.

Election violence, as stated, is not unique to India but occurs in other democracies too. Institutional efforts, judicial overreach, initiatives by civil society, media coverage and international attention have done much to help reduce electoral violence and its intensity everywhere. However, in societies facing serious divisions, violence and intimidation related to elections are intense. In India the threat of violence is still considerably high in certain pockets such as J&K, parts of the north-eastern states and those with Maoist presence, making the organising of elections and electoral activity a big challenge here – the logistics of elections takes considerable energy and resources. Interestingly, in states like Bihar that were known for blatant election violence, it has considerably reduced.

Violence and Its Utility

Electoral violence is violence that is carried out to influence elections or electoral outcomes (Rapoport and Weinberg, 2000: 33; Hoglund, 2009: 415). This violence manifests itself both as physical attacks and intimidation of voters (Rapoport and Weinberg, 2000: 33; Hoglund, 2009: 417). What sets election violence apart from other kinds of political violence is its timing and motive (Hoglund, 2009: 415). The motive of this violence is to influence elections, and, as research points out, it can happen in all the three phases of an election process – namely in the pre-election phase, during the voting day(s) and in the post-election phase (Rapoport and Weinberg, 2000: 18–20, 33; Hoglund, 2009: 416). Violence related to electoral outcomes can also take place 'sometimes considerably later' (Rapoport and Weinberg, 2000: 33). Extreme cases of violence 'can prevent an election from taking place or a victor from taking charge of the government' (Rapoport and Weinberg, 2000: 33). Those involved in this violence can be state actors (like the military and the police) or political parties, guerrilla or rebel groups and militia and paramilitary groups (Hoglund, 2009: 416). The military and the police act on behalf of the groups or parties in power.

Research indicates a strong link between the process of democratisation and violence (Pastor, 1999; Rapoport and Weinberg, 2000; Klopp and Zuern, 2007; Hoglund, 2009). These studies indicate a low level of violence in both authoritarian and democratic states as compared to those that are going through a transition – that is, moving towards democracy or trying to build democratic institutional structures. Authoritarian states are more given to repressing violence, whereas democratic states have means and institutions to channelise discontent and anger onto peaceful paths of resolving disputes (Klopp and Zuern, 2007: 128). Therefore, violence in the aforementioned two is low as compared to that in states in transition. States moving towards a democratic form of government are prone to high levels of electoral violence also because they experience 'more political violence of all sorts' (Rapoport and Weinberg, 2000: 21). Research shows that violence has the effect of decreasing voter turnout due to safety reasons; voters prefer to stay back rather than take risks by coming out in public spaces (Bratton, 2008; Trelles and Carreras, 2012).

In transitional states not only is state control shaky, but the institutional set-up is also feeble, and there is much political distrust, prompting the opposition to arm itself. As Robert Pastor puts it, 'If the government refuses to respond to legitimate concerns and continues to manipulate the electoral process, opposition leaders may conclude that the only path to change is violent' – something that happened in Nicaragua in the 1960s (Pastor, 1999: 2). However, not all violence is perpetrated by opposition forces. Incumbents might also take recourse to violence in order to influence elections and hold onto power. Their control of state institutions gives them 'significant advantage in both the production and policing of violence' (Klopp and Zuern, 2007: 131–32). Jacqueline Klopp and Elke Zuern, through their study of South Africa and Kenya in transition, highlight another dimension of violence. They point out, 'Disputes over resources and authority occur in local communities without external prompting and at times grow violent' (Klopp and Zuern, 2007: 138). The uncertain political atmosphere and the 'fears and rumor it breeds provide fertile ground for violent resolution of ongoing disputes'. Also, policing issues – inadequate presence of the police, deliberate withdrawal of the police and improper policing – create conditions for adding to the possibility of violence (Klopp and Zuern, 2007: 138).

Violence in democratising states takes different forms, including ethnic clashes, party clashes, militia activity, repression by incumbents, and so on. Violence in these states, for instance, has had the effect of displacing and disenfranchising voters, such as before the first multi-party elections in 1992 in South Africa, or derailing the constitutional reform process (which included elections), such as in Kenya in 1997 (Klopp and Zuern, 2007: 137). Kenya in 1992 and 1999 saw violent clashes during the run-up to elections indirectly instigated by the ruling Kenya African National Union by organising youth militias (Hoglund, 2009: 417). As stated earlier, violence also takes place in the post-election phase. Steele (2011) shows how elections can become the basis of 'strategic displacement' of sections of population from a given territory. For instance, in north-west Columbia, elections exposed the local cleavages (so far hidden), making it easier for counterinsurgency groups to identify segments of civilian population supporting rival parties and displacing them through use of violence (Steele, 2011: 426–28).

This displacement, according to Steele, is strategic in nature because it is indulged in by armed groups, including state armed forces, to change the politics of an area (Steele, 2011: 426). Once the supporters of rival parties are identified and displaced, the territory can be controlled more easily and with lesser strain on resources (Steele, 2011: 427–8). This affects future electoral outcomes, reflecting a totally different political picture from what it was before the occurrence of strategic displacement.

Electoral violence and malpractices are largely a feature of democratising or institutionally weak states and have occurred in the states of Africa, Asia, Latin America and Eastern Europe. Closer home, such problems have been seen most commonly in South Asia, including the elections held over the years in India, Pakistan and Bangladesh. Violence and malpractices are low in post-industrial democratic states but not absent. Research points to the pervasiveness of malpractices and violence in established democratic states, too, though such activities have declined over the years (Rapoport and Weinberg, 2000; Lehoucq, 2003). According to Fabrice Lehoucq, 'Indeed, it is hard to study any democratic or quasidemocratic system of the past 200 years without acknowledging that governments or their rivals resorted to less than transparent methods to alter the results of the ballot box' (Lehoucq, 2003: 234). There was use of intimidation and violence against undecided or opposition voters in the US between 1850 and 1900 (Rapoport and Weinberg, 2000: 28–9; Lehoucq, 2003: 237) and vote buying in 19th-century England and Ireland (Rapoport and Weinberg, 2000: 29; Lehoucq, 2003: 239). These were familiar scenes in almost all countries where elections were held (Rapoport and Weinberg, 2000: 30).

Violence and riots have been orchestrated to prevent people from coming out to vote and wealth distributed in exchange for votes. The time period of 2000 to 2011 has witnessed electoral violence in places like Northern Ireland and Spain, a fallout of a past of internal strife (Norris, 2014: 159). But the fact remains that in established democracies, also called post-industrial democracies, the instances of electoral violence are far fewer now. According to Pippa Norris, '[I]n general countries are most likely to demonstrate electoral integrity if they combine state capacity (allowing electoral officials to deliver effective public services) with the broader institutional checks on the process derived from power-sharing arrangements' (Norris, 2015: 170). To these she adds freedom of the press that ensures transparency and exposes instances of electoral malfeasance (Norris, 2015: 170). According to Norris, the notion of *electoral integrity* refers to the 'agreed upon international conventions and universal standards about elections reflecting global norms applying to all countries worldwide throughout the electoral cycle' (Norris, 2014: 21). Conversely, the notion of *electoral malpractice* means the violations of these principles (Norris, 2014: 21). She says, '[I]t is no accident that the states observed to rank highest in electoral integrity include long-standing democracies and affluent societies with this mix of characteristics' (Norris, 2015: 170).

How influential is ballot rigging? Does it affect electoral results? Lehoucq's research shows that 'ballot rigging does not appear to be decisive most of the time' (Lehoucq, 2003: 251). In India the presence of the EC, the media and largely the processes of democratisation (for instance, the system of open and public elections) have ensured the neutralisation of rigging through ballot-box capture. Wherever there are instances of rigging, the elections are countermanded by the EC, and repolls are conducted. However, as Lehoucq points out, fraud still undermines political stability and 'robs elections of credibility' (Lehoucq, 2003: 252). For reasons of credibility and voters' faith, electoral institutions should work towards minimising the cases of fraud. Norris on somewhat similar lines argues that electoral integrity has an effect on 'democratic legitimacy, civic activism, political representation, security and the processes of democratization' (Norris, 2014: 10).

Kristine Hoglund lists out four targets of electoral violence. These are *electoral stakeholders* (voters, candidates, and so on), *electoral information* (registration data, vote results, and so on), *electoral facilities* (polling and counting areas) and *electoral events* (campaign rallies, visits to polling booths, and so on) (Hoglund, 2009: 417). These are targeted with the intention of altering the electoral outcome, especially when rivals are seen to be ahead in the race. Electoral violence and fraud bring the issue of 'fairness' to the forefront. Elections no longer remain fair if results are influenced by violence and fraudulent activities on a large scale. David Rapoport and Leonard Weinberg point out that the fairness issue developed with the emergence of modern elections in England (Rapoport and Weinberg, 2000: 28). They also highlight two institutional factors that shape the fairness question: first, the existence of permanent political parties and, second, the 'notoriously complex character of the electoral process' (Rapoport and Weinberg, 2000: 28). Political parties are agents of the first resort that bring about or contain violence, and the electoral process is administered by many at several levels which create ample opportunities for mistakes, frauds and complaints (Rapoport and Weinberg, 2000: 28–29).

Through cross-national data on elections and state-sponsored election violence, Emilie Hafner-Burton, Susan Hyde and Ryan Jablonski show that incumbent leaders are more likely to resort to violence against political opponents, voters or citizens when 'they fear losing power but have few institutionalized constraints on their decision-making powers' (Hafner-Burton, Hyde and Jablonski, 2013: 174). They show that in the pre-election period, the incumbent government or leaders may use violence to prevent an unfavourable verdict, and the chances of this violence are more when there are no or fewer institutionalised constraints on them like the legislature, ruling party, military or court (Hafner-Burton, Hyde and Jablonski, 2013: 150). In the post-election period, the incumbent who has survived an election might face protests that have the potential to dislodge him – here again the leader without strong institutional constraints might use violence (to suppress the protests) to stay in power (Hafner-Burton, Hyde and Jablonski, 2013: 151).

Electoral Violence in India

The history of elections in India, though overall smooth, has had instances of blatant violence. Some areas have been more prone to violence than others. Over the years electoral violence has both declined and become more localised. The nature of violence has varied in the sense that there are different kinds of violence that have occurred. This includes collisions between rival groups, family skirmishes, party clashes, intimidation of voters, kidnapping, insurgent-led violence and booth capturing. Stone-pelting, brickbatting and gunfire have been used by perpetrators of violence, leading to grievous injuries and even death. Brute muscle power to subvert the democratic process is witnessed during these incidents. Secessionist sentiments and deep divisions in local areas based on caste, ethnicity or religion have led to violence in the past. Rising political participation among the previously marginal social groups has brought forth retaliatory anger from entrenched interests who perpetuate violence and intimidation to maintain their social and political dominance. Violence here becomes a means to maintain the social status quo. While areas like Jammu and Kashmir, Nagaland, Assam and Mizoram, among others, have seen militancy and insurgency-related violence, states like Uttar Pradesh and Bihar have witnessed religious and caste violence. Religious riots might also be instigated to alter electoral outcomes. Seen thus, poll violence has incentives attached to it – it is seen as giving accessibility to state office or power.

Electoral violence in India can be classified in different ways, which helps in clarifying the nature of violence. Violence can be classified according to its timing – whether it occurs specifically during election time (that is, around the election date) or occurs anytime (that is, not necessarily during elections but is intended to influence the poll verdict). Violence can also be classified according to its 'target' (Hoglund, 2009) – whether it is directed towards polling facilities, polling personnel, electoral candidates or voters. Vandalising of polling facilities and equipment is aimed at nullifying institutional opportunity – it reflects a discomfort with institutionally generated equality of opportunity. The perpetrators are clearly uncomfortable with everyone participating – supporters of the opposition, social rivals and socially oppressed, among others. Intimidation of or violence against polling personnel shows the same discomfort. The entrenched interests see them as a challenge to their power in the local area, and intimidating them is seen as demonstration of their power to the voters. Violence against rival candidates and parties is to discourage them from contesting, and intimidation of voters is to instil fear in them so that they either refrain from coming to the polling stations or vote for the incumbent or entrenched groups.

Election-related violence is contingent upon enabling conditions – a supportive ground – to break out and escalate. Certain sociological, political and economic factors create such an environment. Bitter rivalries – ethnic or political – provide a fertile ground for violence to occur. Situations of strong patron–client relationships, where supporters of a party or a strongman can be mobilised to take up arms against rivals, also enable electoral violence (Hoglund, 2009: 420). Violence also breaks out in contexts of weak formal institutions that deal with disputes – the culture of impunity that is pervasive in such contexts fosters violence (Hoglund, 2009: 420–21). These, together with an atmosphere of fear and insecurity in economic contexts of deprivation and inequalities, nurture violence. Some or all of these conditions persist in certain pockets of India where such violence has occurred or continues to occur.

The violence mentioned in the first column in Table 7.1 is usually collective in nature – political parties and their supporters are involved. On the other hand, the violence in the second column is both individual-centric and party-centric; it involves individual political leaders as well as supporters of political

Table 7.1 Types of election-related violence in India

Violence on polling day(s)	Violence before, during and after elections
Clashes between rival political parties, contestants and their supporters	Murder
Attacks on poll officers or police personnel	Kidnapping
Attacks on activists of opposition parties	Amassing of illegal arms and explosive material
Booth capturing or attempts to do so	Hate speeches
Destruction of polling booth or equipment	Intimidation through threats of violence
Stone-pelting near polling booths by groups	Stone-pelting on campaign rallies
Intimidation through threat of violence	Communal riots

parties as perpetrators. These two columns list out instances of both physical and verbal violence. Firearms are known to be used in both. Instances of verbal aggression during campaigning have seen a rise over the last few elections. There are increasing numbers of hate, communal and inflammatory speeches by political leaders in India. Such speeches intend to raise communal or ethnic passions and sway voters. In a social environment of deep religiosity and caste inequalities, these may not lead to immediate violence but often have the intended consequence of polarising voters on religious or caste lines. Communal riots also polarise voters. Steven Wilkinson's research shows riots breaking out at the behest of political forces to bring about a desired electoral outcome (Wilkinson, 2005 [2004]).

The police forces in India face a considerable task during elections in these conditions. Due to their competitive nature, difficult terrain, poor infrastructure, limited resources and organisational limitations, elections pose a challenge to the police (Verma, 2005: 354). The sheer magnitude of Indian elections is a challenge in itself. They pose a challenge to not only the police but also the entire electoral personnel. The police have to restrain the illegal ways of influencing elections, which need 'the complete impartiality of police personnel' (Verma, 2005: 355). The issue of impartiality of police personnel during elections has often run into controversy in India. The executive's overbearance on the police makes the EC step in to ensure an unbiased police performance during elections.

States like Bihar, Uttar Pradesh, Assam, West Bengal and Jammu and Kashmir have been particularly vulnerable to instances of coercion and intimidation at work and, consequently, electoral violence. The north-eastern states have also seen blatant instances of violence. Violence in elections was primarily seen as 'the north Indian practice of winning election by *bandookbaji*' (through the gun) (*Economic and Political Weekly*, 1991: 1248). Some states of the north were more prone to violence. 'Booth capturing' that began with the 1957 Lok Sabha elections in Bihar (Chaudhary, 2005) was a feature of poll violence during the ballot-paper era. Booth capturing had been a common occurrence during national and state elections in states like Uttar Pradesh and Bihar. These two states have been seen as 'notorious' and 'problematic' in electoral management (Kaushik, 1982: 162; Murthy, 2008: 142). The report of the fifth Lok Sabha elections (1971) on booth capturing in Bihar says:

> Politicians and their workers and supporters belonging mainly to three dominant castes, to whatever party or parties they may belong, take a leading part in arranging or instigating booth-capturing by organised goondas and hoodlums in large numbers, with the result that in a good number of cases reports are received from the presiding officers and returning officers necessitating repoll or fresh poll in the polling stations concerned. (EC, 1973: 192)

During the 1991 Lok Sabha election campaigning, it was commented, 'News reports are replete these days with reports about the flourishing arms bazar in Bihar' (*Economic and Political Weekly*, 1991: 1249).

Fielding of 'hardened criminals' by all major political parties and 'caste rivalries' was seen as leading to poll violence in Bihar (Bharti, 1990: 429). The state also saw 'competitive booth looting' with every party engaging in it – to demonstrate territorial dominance and political clout through control over polling booths (Witsoe, 2013: 138–39). Polling booths used to be stormed by armed men, ballot papers stamped by them, ballot boxes seized and stuffed with these fake votes. S.Y. Quraishi recalls that during 1995–96, when he was an election observer in Bihar, he was threatened, and there were bomb explosions.[1] The state has seen booth capturing 'of various shades' (Murthy, 2008: 143). This was done by local strongmen and their militias (called *sena*s)

---

[1] S. Y. Quraishi, personal interview with the author, Gurugram (Gurgaon), 23 January 2017.

usually hired by political parties or candidates during polling time.[2] Bihar is especially well known for the activities of local militia, particularly the Ranvir Sena which acted during elections often with impunity (Narula, 1999: 56; Kumar, 2008: 148). Ranvir Sena activists emerged as 'violent political entrepreneurs impacting the electoral outcomes in many places in Bihar' (A. Kumar, 2008: 150). There were other private *sena*s too – namely the Bhoomi Sena and the Lorik Sena, belonging to the Kurmi and the Yadav groups, respectively (Bharti, 1990: 429). Political and caste considerations steered their actions.

The 1980 elections saw a surge in election violence (Kaushik, 1982: 162). On similar lines, S. S. Agarwalla informs that booth capturing reached alarming proportions during the 1989 elections in 12 states but primarily in Andhra Pradesh (united) with 593 cases, Uttar Pradesh with 592 and Bihar with 272 (Agarwalla, 1994: 31). Votes of the economically vulnerable and Dalit communities in many instances would be rigged by the dominant castes who used armed groups to unleash spates of violence, including killings, to prevent the lower castes from reaching the polling booths (Kaushik, 1982: 146–47; S. K. Ghosh, 1997: 129–31). In Tripura during the 1989 elections, where the rival parties were the INC and the CPI(M), it has been noted that there was 'large-scale rigging, booth capturing and false voting' at the hands of the former and its alliance partner (*Economic and Political Weekly*, 1989: 2757). Also, 'Voters were driven away from the queues or were prevented from coming to the polling booths' (*Economic and Political Weekly*, 1989: 2757).

Rigging and booth capturing were attributed to a lack of confidence among the ruling class who felt insecure of the growing political awareness in the economically and socially vulnerable sections (Kaushik, 1982: 147). It was also said that free and fair elections do not happen because the politicians and political parties themselves do not want them (S. K. Ghosh, 1997: 129).

---

[2] S. S. Agarwalla gives a glimpse into the methods of booth capturing, looking at instances of this violence in Bihar. There are several instances of police and other officials stamping ballot papers; often the weaker sections or castes are threatened by higher castes to discourage them to vote; sometimes the miscreants use bombs to scare people away from polling booths; ballot papers are snatched and officials forced to initial them after which they are stamped and stuffed in ballot boxes; ministers of state governments have also been involved in this activity (Agarwalla, 1994: 30–31). The process of rigging starts well before the announcement of names of candidates, and caste and muscle power is deployed for the purpose (Agarwalla, 1994: 31).

The 'feudal' and 'caste and religious' nature of political parties and the state administration were also cited as reasons for violence among political parties (Murthy, 2008: 142–43, 153).

Booth capturing and poll violence was, and in some areas still is, a sign of the social transformation of the Indian electorate. Growing political consciousness and an eagerness to move out of the control of dominant social groups are one of the major reasons of violence perpetrated by the latter. The dominant caste and rich peasantry often resorted to violence when they felt that elections were neutralising their power by making the middle peasantry and agrarian workers potent rivals in the competition for state power. It was felt that violence will instil fear that would keep the aspiring castes and classes as well as their supporters silent and submissive. The local militias like the Ranvir Sena, which protected landed interests like the Bhumihars in Bihar by unleashing ruthless violence on political competitors and landless Dalits, reflected this phenomenon. Insurgent movements in states like J&K and Nagaland also resorted to violence during elections. Reasons of autonomy and secessionism from the Indian state explain the anger and aggression during elections. Stone-pelting and bomb explosions were often witnessed during elections in the strife-torn Kashmir Valley. Inter-party clashes broke out in the past during elections in Nagaland, leading to grievous injuries and even death with arms and locally made grenades (Karmakar, 2018). Regional turmoil, social inequalities and sub-nationalist stances were some of the factors that have led to electoral violence in India.

Hate Speeches

As discussed briefly in Chapter 5, hate or inflammatory speeches have seen a rise on the eve of elections. These speeches represent verbal violence directed against the 'other' – the other religious communities and political rivals. In India such hate speeches use stereotypes about the 'other' and are positioned on the 'us and them' axis which they simultaneously construct. These stereotypes are exaggerated to vilify rivals who are then portrayed as loathsome and not belonging to the nation. The speeches target communities, their beliefs and practices or stereotypes that are built around them and intensify the constructed non-belongingness. They also target prominent individuals who are born into these communities. The objective of this vilification is to polarise voters and morally constrain them from voting for rival political parties. The reach of physical violence is limited – at the most it covers a few polling booths or a locality or a group. Speeches, on the other hand, have a mass reach. Made in rallies that are attended by big numbers, speeches have the potential of vast outreach that far surpasses the spread of physical violence. New media technologies, mainly the chatting apps on smartphones, come in handy to spread this verbal violence over time and space. They fill the speech makers with a feeling of false machismo and their targets with fear and insecurity. They breed distrust and hatred and divide votes on religious and community lines in India, with the benefits usually being directly proportional to the intensity of the hate speech.

Made during election campaigns, these speeches have the potential to sway verdicts towards the maker of the speech – in fact, that is the reason for their creation. They are usually made in constituencies which have a mixed religious population – more precisely, where the population is Hindu and Muslim. Through the speech, the aim of the leadership is to polarise communities so that electoral benefits can be reaped. They are believed to generate more votes for the makers of the speech and their parties. The speeches generate a mass frenzy and incite mob violence as also fear in the community that is targeted through such verbal assaults. Those who make hate speeches display a confidence that suggests they are immune from punitive action and will not be penalised. The EC takes cognisance when such speeches are made and brought to its notice as they breed hatred and aggravate differences between communities and thus divide them. Once these differences are hardened, they have the potential to lead to a riotous situation. Such speeches and statements are barred under the RPA, 1951, and the MCC for elections in India. The EC has also termed them as corrupt practices. In the past the EC has issued show-cause notices to leaders who have made inflammatory speeches. Some prominent political leaders who have come under the EC's radar for making inflammatory speeches in the recent past are Raj Thackeray (Maharashtra Navnirman Sena) in 2008, Varun Gandhi (BJP) in 2009, Akbaruddin Owaisi (All India Majlis-e-Ittehadul Muslimeen) in 2012, Pravin Togadia (Vishva Hindu Parishad) in 2014 and Amit Shah (BJP) in 2014.

The Supreme Court in a verdict in March 2014 said that the existing laws were sufficient to curb hate speech. It said that the 'lack of prosecution for hate speeches was not because the existing laws did not possess sufficient provisions' but that there was a 'lack of enforcement' of the existing laws and procedures (Verma and Roche, 2014). The apex court in its order also said that the law-enforcing agencies 'must ensure that the existing law is not rendered a dead letter' (Verma and Roche, 2014). Hate speeches are made as they are seen to place the political leader at an electoral advantage. One can say that such speeches have a 'winnability' factor attached to them. While direct violence by candidates and their supporters has reduced, verbal violence has grown, leading to embittered social relations and political divisions.

Mechanisation and Use of Technology

The spread of media technologies made it easier for the EC to detect and act against hate speeches. Recordings of speeches and other malpractices through videography and mobile technology enabled the EC to dig deeper and build a case against political leaders in case such speeches were made. Video surveillance teams of the EC from around 2014 recorded all major rallies and public meetings. The EC also released a software whereby the authenticity of videos of malpractices, such as hate speeches and distribution of money or liquor, could be established, reducing the possibility of fake videos being uploaded (PTI, 2014d). The software could detect the area, time and place of the video clip uploaded.

At the polling stations, the EVMs were seen as an effective way of countering instances of booth capturing.[3] They were introduced to eliminate the illegal mass-stamping of ballot papers. During the 1980s and the early 1990s, as discussed earlier, one witnessed several cases of fraudulent voting: according to former CEC V. S. Sampath, 'Those were the days of intimidation of voters and booth capturing.'[4] With the introduction of EVMs, ballot paper voting was discontinued. EVMs were developed by Electronics Corporation of India Limited, Hyderabad, and Bharat Electronics Limited, Bangalore, in 1981. The initial order was for 350 machines that were supplied by April 1982 (Lyngdoh, 2004: 61). Though the order was done, the government dithered in sanctioning their use (Lyngdoh, 2004: 62). This was probably because of a fear of losing out on votes. The EC using its constitutional powers went ahead with them in 50 polling stations in the Paravur by-election in 1982

---

[3] The NCRWC (2002a: para. 4.9, Electronic Voting Machines), among others, strongly recommended the use of EVMs in place of ballot papers in all constituencies as soon as possible to counter large-scale rigging in elections.

[4] V. S. Sampath, email interview with the author, 1 August 2020.

(Gopakumar, 2021). The main contest was between the late INC leader A. C. Jose and the late CPI leader N. Sivan Pillai. Jose lost by a mere 123 votes (Gopakumar, 2021). Though the use of the machines was hailed widely, Jose challenged the result in the Kerala High Court (Lyngdoh, 2004: 62–63). The High Court upheld the use of the machines. The appeal went to the Supreme Court, which ordered a repoll in the 50 stations where the EVMs were used. The Supreme Court was of the view that without legal sanctions the EVMs cannot be used, and the EC could not 'innovate a new method' (Gopakumar, 2021). The repoll took place with ballot papers and ballot boxes and Jose won the election. In December 1988, during Rajiv Gandhi's prime-ministership, the Representation of the People Act was amended and a new section, 61 A, which gave legal sanctity to EVMs, was added to it (*The Hindu*, 2019).

Status Paper on Electronic Voting Machine by the EC informs, 'In 1998, EVMs were used in 16 Legislative ACs across three states of Madhya Pradesh, Rajasthan, and Delhi. The use of EVMs further expanded in 1999 to 46 Parliamentary Constituencies (PC), and later, in February 2000, EVMs were used in 45 ACs in Haryana state assembly polls' (EC, n.d.9: 5–6). It further states:

> In 2001, the state assembly elections in Tamil Nadu, Kerala, Puducherry, and West Bengal were completely conducted using EVMs. All state assembly elections thereafter witnessed the use of this machine. In 2004, the EVMs were used in all 543 PCs for the elections to the Lok Sabha. A new technologically advanced voting system completely replaced the erstwhile voting method of using ballot papers. (EC, n.d.9: 5–6)

Thus, the 2004 election became the first Lok Sabha election where EVMs were used in all constituencies. Voting through EVMs, done through the press of a button, expunged the need for ballot papers and stamps. Names of candidates and their symbols were listed on the machine for the voter to choose from, and the vote was electronically registered. What was also drawn up was a strict security protocol for storing and safeguarding the EVMs. The machines were prepared for elections phase-wise after the list of candidates had been finalised. The prepared machines were kept in storage centres or dispersal centres. Detailed plans were prepared for their distribution, and observers closely monitored this process. The EVMs that were used for training were not used for elections – such machines were separate and stored in separate rooms. After the completion of polling, the

EVMs were kept in strongrooms at the counting centres. State armed police and other security forces guarded these strongrooms (these measures are still in use). This considerably reduced booth capturing and fake voting. The use of EVMs also meant saving huge volumes of paper stationery and their transportation costs, easy storage and maintenance, no invalid votes, fewer hassles in electoral preparation and easy and accurate counting (Sezhiyan, 2006). Staggering the poll to two or more phases also eased the problem. It is true that booth capturing and other fraudulent practices reduced over the years due to political reasons,[5] but institutional measures were no less important in bringing a more orderly electoral system (mechanisation by the EC helped in this regard).

Though it was alleged by some political critics during the 2014 and 2019 elections that the EVMs were mass-hacked (through tampering of software, hardware, and so on), no conclusive proof was given to back these allegations (see *Business Standard*, 2019; Pallavi, 2019). According to leading psephologists Prannoy Roy and Dorab Sopariwala, 'India's electronic voting machines are unique – and ideal for Indian voting conditions' (Roy and Sopariwala, 2019: 65). They highlight that Indian EVMs are neither connected to the internet or any wider cloud network nor do they have Wi-Fi or Bluetooth capabilities – they are stand-alone machines that cannot be 'hacked' (Roy and Sopariwala, 2019: 65–66). According to them, the criticism of EVMs stems from a 'knee-jerk mistrust of technology' (Roy and Sopariwala, 2019: 65–66).

The allegations of tampering or hacking of EVMs came mainly from parties who lost elections. In 2009, L. K. Advani (BJP), the then leader of the opposition in the Lok Sabha, had questioned the integrity of the EVMs during assembly elections and argued for a return to ballot papers (Pallavi, 2019). There were allegations of rigging of EVMs after the NDA victory in the 2014 parliamentary elections (*Indian Express*, 2017). Again, during the BJP's massive victory in the Uttar Pradesh assembly elections in 2017, the opposition parties, including the BSP, the SP, the INC, the left parties and the AAP questioned the functioning of the machines (*Indian Express*, 2017). However, concrete proof of tampering was lacking.

The former CECs interviewed for this research expressed their complete faith in the sanctity of the EVMs. A few of them narrated the criticism

---

[5] The entry of 'strongmen' into the electoral process as candidates and eventually people's representatives changed the nature of electoral malpractice. The presence of these strongmen as political leaders made booth capturing and fake voting redundant.

they had faced regarding EVMs during elections and how they had tried to convince the critics on the foolproofness of the machines. Former CEC Nasim Zaidi emphasised the non-tamperability of EVMs used by the EC. He further mentioned that the EC during his tenure had to bear the maximum brunt of complaints regarding alleged tampering of EVMs during the elections to state assemblies of Uttar Pradesh, Punjab and others in 2017.[6] According to him, an intensive awareness campaign explaining the non-tamperable nature of EVMs to electors, civil societies, media and political parties was launched soon after complaints surfaced in March 2017.[7] Leading technical advisors to the EC were deployed to remove doubts from the minds of people.[8] In June 2017, Zaidi invited all political parties and their technical persons to demonstrate the tamperability of EVMs from polling booths of their choice from states that went in for polls in 2017. The challenge demonstration was conducted at the headquarters of the EC in a transparent manner. Zaidi narrated:

> To our satisfaction, none of the political parties could support their complaints by tampering the EVM under challenge. One or two parties insisted on handing over EVMs to them to take back home, but this was declined by the technical team. It was argued by the technical team that the EC cannot be responsible for EVMs away from their administrative custody and security.[9]

There have been instances of malfunctioning of individual EVM units during each election, but no instance of tampering or usage of tampered machines have been found. 'Malfunctioning' implies some electronic fault and is not the same as 'tampering'. The malfunctioning machines are replaced by EC personnel whenever they find such a case. In 2013, the EC introduced the VVPAT (Voter Verifiable Paper Audit Trail) system in a phased manner to assure the voters that their vote was being registered correctly. The VVPAT machine (connected to the EVMs), by generating a printed slip mentioning the name, serial number and symbol of the candidate voted for as soon as the voter cast his or her vote, was meant to assure the voter

---

[6] Nasim Zaidi, telephonic interview with the author, 4 August 2020.
[7] Nasim Zaidi, telephonic interview with the author, 4 August 2020.
[8] Nasim Zaidi, telephonic interview with the author, 4 August 2020.
[9] Nasim Zaidi, telephonic interview with the author, 4 August 2020.

that his or her vote had gone to the candidate he or she voted for. It was introduced to strengthen the faith of voters in the electronic voting system. An impression was gaining ground that the EVMs were registering votes for a candidate or party for whom the voter had not voted – that when the voter pressed the voting button for a particular candidate, the vote actually went in favour of another candidate. The VVPAT system was another effort of the EC to not only make the perception of the election process error-free but also eliminate malpractice if it existed (though no evidence of tampering of EVMs was found). However, facing trenchant criticism on the functioning of the EVMs, the EC took the step of directing the CEOs of all states and UTs to conduct awareness programmes on the working of the EVMs and the VVPATs before the 2019 parliamentary elections (EC, 2018a). Such awareness campaigns were conducted in various constituencies to assuage fears of tampering of EVMs. Voters were shown how to use the EVMs and were given an opportunity to settle their doubts on the integrity of the same.

The credit for reduction of election-related violence in India goes to a large extent to the EC's efforts. Its attempts at modernisation and mechanisation of the material and tools of an election went a long way in making polling more secure. The use of technology, despite the fears and misgivings expressed by members of civil society and some political groups, helped. Going ahead with the changing times and technological development enhanced the efficacy of the electoral process (as discussed in Chapter 4). Photo identity cards, or election cards, were introduced by the EC in 1993 during the tenure of CEC T. N. Seshan to bring down impersonation.[10] Electoral rolls were computerised to organise the enormous voter data and to make it accurate and error-free (see Chapter 9). The central security forces were made part of the election security to supplement the local police because efforts of the latter were not enough. These institutional efforts systematised the voting process

---

[10] In 1993 the EC issued a notification saying that no election would be held after 1 January 1995 unless all electors had an electoral photo identity card. This order was contested by some state governments in the courts. The matter went to the Supreme Court, which held that elections could not be stopped because the state governments were unable to issue the photo identity cards to all voters within the deadline scheduled by the EC. Elections took place, but slowly photo cards were issued to all voters and became universal across the country. A voter is not permitted to vote unless he or she is carrying his or her elector's photo identity card (EPIC).

and checked duplicity and impersonation. They made the voting behaviour less insecure.

The EC and Electoral Security

Sampath, interviewed for this research, said that the security of the polling stations earlier was organised mostly with the help of local police and other outfits like forest guards and home guards. As a matter of policy, the EC had not been bringing in the army for security during elections. However, during the 1990s it was considered that the EC use the central police forces.[11] This was done not only to supplement the efforts of the local police but also to neutralise any partisan behaviour on its part. It was through the efforts of late CEC Seshan that the Central Armed Police Force (CAPF) was sanctioned by a reluctant central government to assist in the conduct of elections.[12] Seshan not only took the central police force issue to the Supreme Court but also refused to hold elections and by-elections until his demand for central forces was met.[13] According to Sampath:

> One of the pre-election exercises by way of holding discussions with various stakeholders and organisations by the EC includes discussions with the Home Ministry, which is almost the last part of the exercise before the announcement of the schedule for the elections. It is the timing of availability and the quantum of central police force which determines the scheduling and phasing of elections.[14]

The EC's efforts to streamline the electoral process and keeping firmer vigil in real time has helped bring down political violence in India. Concerted thinking, better coordination with the local administration and effective implementation of measures have helped. The EC has resorted to planning, coordinating and strategising of election booth management. It has received much help from civil society organisations and the media. Electoral studies

---

[11] V. S. Sampath, email interview with the author, 1 August 2020.

[12] V. S. Sampath, email interview with the author, 1 August 2020.

[13] V. S. Sampath, email interview with the author, 1 August 2020.

[14] V. S. Sampath, email interview with the author, 1 August 2020. Over 2000 companies of the central police force were used during the parliamentary elections in 2014.

by civil society groups over the long term and reporting by the media at an immediate level have done much to control violence during elections. In any case, the EC stops polling wherever violence takes place and orders a repoll in that polling station. This places an extra layer on making the elections fair.

The practice of holding elections in phases – staggering the poll as discussed earlier – rather than on a single day was started with the view to minimising violence and managing it better.[15] This way the CAPF could be spread out and cover all areas.[16] Table 7.2 shows that it is from the 1991 parliamentary elections that spreading out the election schedule over a few weeks was a regular feature.

The phase-wise elections were seen as a 'turning point' in terms of 'strict enforcement and better management' (Murthy, 2008: 125). The EC and its personnel were able to spread out their onerous tasks over time and thus manage them better. More significantly, the central paramilitary forces could be deployed everywhere in phases and provide more security. This was not only to check violence against the polling staff and facilities but also to provide security to voters (Murthy, 2008: 127). The opposition parties also preferred their presence as they lacked faith in the state police (Murthy, 2008: 127). The phases helped in better administration of elections (though they faced criticism from some quarters that one phase had the potential of influencing voting in the next and making the whole process 'unfair').

Polling booths are classified according to past violence in them. Categorised such, a booth is 'hypersensitive', 'sensitive' or 'normal'. A booth is categorised by the EC as hypersensitive if a life has been lost in poll-related violence in the past, sensitive if there is a history of violence and normal if there is no record of electoral violence. 'Vulnerability mapping' was a practice started by the EC eight or nine years ago – it began in Uttar Pradesh.[17] The EC gets records of all *goonda*s (criminal elements) from the police before elections and keeps a check on them.[18] The EC also does what is called 'poll

---

[15] S.Y. Quraishi, personal interview with the author, Gurugram (Gurgaon), 23 January 2017.

[16] S.Y. Quraishi, personal interview with the author, Gurugram (Gurgaon), 23 January 2017.

[17] S.Y. Quraishi, personal interview with the author, Gurugram (Gurgaon), 23 January 2017.

[18] S.Y. Quraishi, personal interview with the author, Gurugram (Gurgaon), 23 January 2017.

Table 7.2 Election schedule, 1951–2019

Election	Schedule
1951–52	October 1951, December 1951, February 1952
1957	24 February–14 March
1962	19–25 February
1967	17–21 February
1971	1–10 March
1977	16–20 March
1980	3–6 January
1984	24–28 December
1989	22–26 November
1991	20 May–15 June
1996	27 April, 2–30 May
1998	16–23 February
1999	5, 11, 18, 25 September, 3–6 October
2004	20 April–10 May
2009	16 April–13 May
2014	7 April–12 May
2019	11 April–19 May

Source: Murthy (2008: 125) for elections till 2004; open web sources for 2009 elections onwards.

tracking' – it keeps a track of booths where participation is low, where votes largely go to one particular candidate and where there is a history of law-and-order problems. Such booths are a 'red flag' for the EC, and it probes further into why this is so. The EC starts its work a year before the elections without publicity. It has to work 'in real time' to prevent violence and malpractices during election time.[19]

The EC, for instance, issued directives to personnel and police forces to ensure a violence-free assembly election in West Bengal in 2016, failing which they were to be held accountable. The EC made arrangements here to minimise violence by taking 'confidence-building measures' such as 'visits (by police forces) to the identified vulnerable habitations, contacting

---

[19] All information is from S. Y. Quraishi, personal interview with the author, Gurugram (Gurgaon), 23 January 2017.

vulnerable people and also taking preventive measures like seizure of arms and weapons, execution of non-bailable warrants, binding down of history sheeters, anti-social elements by applying relevant legal provisions to ensure fear-free environment' (EC, 2016c). It also said that each and every case of violence 'is being closely monitored and strict action would be taken against such perpetrators irrespective of their political affiliation' (EC, 2016c). The EC plans deployment of security forces meticulously. This is an act that indicates taut centralised planning. The security personnel need to be trained to 'handle tasks of ballot preparation, voter registration and identification. They have to be educated about election laws and rules for counting of votes' (Verma, 2005: 356).

A letter by the EC to the central and state governments and the CEOs of various states and UTs is instructive on this matter. Sent on 7 April 2014 – just before the 16th Lok Sabha elections – the letter directs that the guidelines laid down by it 'will be followed strictly in the matter of deployment of security forces for conduct of elections' (EC, 2014b). The EC in this letter strongly discourages the keeping of the CAPF in reserve or on stand-by by the states and wants them deployed to prevent any untoward incidents. The letter talks about a 'State Deployment Plan', which it says 'will be prepared in consultation with the Chief Electoral Officer of the State', and his recommendations on 'the quantum of forces to be deployed' in various constituencies 'shall merit serious consideration in the drawing of the plan'. In this task, according to the EC, the CEO would be assisted by a state-level force coordinator appointed by the Ministry of Home Affairs (EC, 2014b). This 'State Deployment Plan' would be based on the requirements of the different districts as projected in the District Deployment Plans. The EC puts the responsibility of certifying whether 'the area is insurgency/militancy/naxalite affected or otherwise' on the superintendent of the police of the concerned district. The state and district plans have to be 'finalized at least one week before the day of the poll' (EC, 2014b).

The EC urges states to pay particular attention to polling stations identified as sensitive or hypersensitive and deploy CAPF there. It lays down certain guidelines for identifying sensitive or trouble-prone polling booths, which are 'past history of the constituency or the polling area', incidents of booth capturing, violence and big-time impersonation, 'specific complaints made by political parties and candidates', 'political rivalries', 'number of history sheeters and absconders', 'number of SC/ST [Scheduled Tribe/Scheduled

Caste] electors', and so on (EC, 2014b). For Naxalite and insurgency-affected areas, the EC emphasises the deployment of the CAPF 'for active election related duty other than static duty at polling booths such as mobile patrols with magistrates, area pickets, check gates and quick reaction teams located in specific areas etc'. In normal constituencies, the EC wants the deployment of the CAPF on static duty on the voting day in polling stations as a matter of policy (EC, 2014b).

The EC directs that 'for guarding strongrooms after the completion of poll CAPFs/SAPs [State Armed Police] from other states will be deployed'. It also makes clear in its letter that the state governments would look after the transport and accommodation of the CAPF deployed in their states (EC, 2014b). The EC also states that the Ministry of Home Affairs shall seal international borders 'at least one week in advance to prevent any movement of anti-social elements crossing the borders to disrupt electioneering process'. In the same way, all state governments will 'seal inter-state borders/inter-district borders well in advance to prevent infiltration of antisocial and disruptive elements' during elections (EC, 2014b). All these measures have reduced violence considerably at the booth level. According to former CEC S. Y. Quraishi, 'We have come a long way from the era of violence and booth capturing to an era of peaceful, free and fair elections' (Quraishi, 2014: 208). He says, 'Booth capturing is history. *Goondagardi* [lumpen acts of petty criminals] is history.'[20] But, he continues, 'we still keep our fingers crossed and we take care of everything especially in areas which have seen violence in the past'.[21]

There is also something called vulnerability mapping done by the EC. According to Rajarshi Bhattacharya, 'This starts at the hamlet level. The EC collects information about any problem at the village level whether natural calamity or *goondagardi* [hooliganism]. Feedback is important for vulnerability mapping. Contingency planning is needed too – what the EC's response would be if there is any problem before or during an election.'[22]

---

[20] S. Y. Quraishi, personal interview with the author, Gurugram (Gurgaon), 23 January 2017.

[21] S. Y. Quraishi, personal interview with the author, Gurugram (Gurgaon), 23 January 2017.

[22] Rajarshi Bhattacharya, former DEC, personal interview with the author, New Delhi, 5 August 2017.

Lawmakers and Lawbreakers

What has replaced open electoral violence is a phenomenon referred to as the 'criminalisation' of politics, where political leaders seek help from 'criminals' to win elections, individuals with a criminal record contest elections, crimes are committed by political leaders to win further elections or crimes are committed with impunity. Jagdeep S. Chhokar calls this phenomenon 'the case of riding a tiger' – once you are on it, you cannot get off (Chhokar, 2020: 324). Once ground was ceded to criminals, it was exceedingly difficult to regain it and the political class decided to 'follow the dictum "If you can't beat them, join them"' (Chhokar, 2020: 324).

The decade of the 2000s was a time when civil society worked on collating data on politicians linked to crimes. Civil society also took legal recourse to 'cleanse' politics. The opinion that lawmakers should not be 'lawbreakers' gained substantial ground among rights' activists and media. Concerns were expressed about how laws would be effectively implemented if lawmakers brazenly break laws. Elected representatives' casual attitude towards law would make them ineffective and weak. Laws in such a case would be selectively implemented and political influence would neutralise them, laying the ground for lawlessness and injustices weighing against the weak.

One instance of the anger against the political class was expressed thus:

> A rape or a murder becomes more heinous when the aggressor is the person meant to be the guardian or protector and courts take a harsher view of such cases. Similarly with legislators, who enjoy more privileges than the citizenry they are expected to represent, any transgression should attract a disproportionately higher punishment. (R. Roy, 2007)

There was a rise in 'criminality' with the number of MPs facing serious criminal charges like murder, kidnapping and extortion seeing an increase from 12 per cent in 2004 to 14 per cent in 2009 (Nagarathinam, 2014). There were 125 MPs in the 2004 Lok Sabha against whom criminal cases were pending. This number went up to 162 in the 2009 Lok Sabha and to 186 in the 2014 Lok Sabha (Chhokar, 2017: 95). The ADR wrote to all major parties, listing names of sitting MPs and MLAs from their parties who had criminal cases pending against them, and requested them not to give tickets to these individuals (Chhokar, 2017: 95). The Justice Verma Committee, set up to look into the Delhi gang-rape (Nirbhaya) case of December 2012, was of the opinion that electoral reforms are integral to the Indian political process to bring about gender justice and prevent sexual offences against women (J. S. Verma Committee, 2013: 340). The committee in its report underlined its concern about the political process in the following words:

> This Committee is concerned about the integrity of the legislative process, in particular with regard to the reform of the criminal justice system, if lawmakers themselves have serious charges – of which cognizance has been taken by a court of competent jurisdiction – pending against them. (J. S. Verma Committee, 2013: 340)

It asked the EC about the efforts being made to deal with electoral candidates accused of, charged with and convicted for sexual offences (J. S. Verma Committee, 2013: 340–41).

Contrary to popular perception and given the uproar among the middle class against 'growing criminalisation' of politics, scholars have hinted that criminality and winnability are not adversely related: 'criminals' have popular support and thus a good chance of emerging victorious in an election. It was noted that a candidate facing criminal charges has higher chances of winning an election than a 'clean' candidate (Sastry, 2014: 36; Nagarathinam, 2014; Vaishnav, 2017: 119). A candidate's ability to accomplish tasks and approachability are factors that made people vote for candidates with criminal charges (Nagarathinam, 2014). This means that voters might not be unaware of the 'predilections of the political class: many voters vote for politicians *because*, rather than *in spite*, of their criminal reputations' (Vaishnav, 2017: xi, emphasis original). In situations of 'deep social cleavages and weak rule of law', coupled with the state's inability or unwillingness to 'fulfil its core obligations vis-à-vis its citizenry', people would look for 'alternatives' and go for political strongmen as their representatives (Vaishnav, 2017: 21).

Money and muscle power are also close cousins. It is said that 'there are more candidates as well as MPs with criminal backgrounds in the top 25 per cent of declared asset value than in the bottom 25 per cent' (Nagarathinam, 2014). According to Trilochan Sastry, who looked at the records of candidates of Lok Sabha and state assembly elections between 2004 and 2013, 'Wealth increases the chances of winning, and a combination of wealth and criminal record increases it even further as 23% of tainted candidates win compared to only 12% of clean candidates' (Sastry, 2014: 37). According to him, unless the flow of black money in elections is 'minimised, we cannot get good governance' (Sastry, 2014: 37).

Former union minister for external affairs and the 12th prime minister of India, Inder Kumar Gujral, writing in 1997, noted that muscle power is 'on ascendance', and the 'anti-social elements who till yester years were playing a supportive role have now come to the fore.... Quite a few of them have been elected to the legislatures and local bodies' (Gujral, 1997: 2). Arvind Verma makes a similar point and says that political leaders take the help of offenders to win elections, and political parties often put them up as their candidates seeing their winning potential (Verma, 2005: 360). Echoing this, Milan Vaishnav highlights that political parties put these strongmen up as their electoral candidates, and people vote for them despite knowledge of their criminal profile. Factors such as elections becoming expensive affairs, parties becoming organisationally and ideologically weak and electoral finance laws being ineffectual make parties pick individuals with criminal records as they have the money as well as an interest in investing in politics (Vaishnav, 2017: 121–22).

To prevent criminals from gaining entry into the legislatures, U. C. Agarwal suggests some measures that can be taken up by recognised political parties. They can publish the list of their potential candidates in the press three months in advance of any election (Agarwal, 2002: 85). This way 'at least the hardcore criminal elements could be thus found out and exposed' (Agarwal, 2002: 85). It would enable political parties to avoid 'formally nominating the candidates with doubtful records' (Agarwal, 2002: 86). 'Requirements of such advance information about potential candidates may be made legally compulsory' (Agarwal, 2002: 86). Some see civil society (or NGO) activism as important in containing the effects of black money and criminality in politics and upholding democratic safeguards (Godbole, 1998: 950; U. K. Singh, 2004; Chhokar, 2017: 98; Sastry, 2014: 41). It is felt that civil society activism in tandem with the media, the judiciary and the voter would help in cleansing the system (Sastry, 2014: 41; Chhokar, 2017: 98). 'Voter education' (Agarwal, 2002: 85; Godbole, 1998: 949; Sastry, 2014: 41) and efforts of 'all stakeholders' are further seen as bulwarks to ensure a healthy democracy.

Institutional effort and coordinated action of the EC, the Supreme Court, civil society and the media have reduced open violence during elections. The modernisation of procedures and equipment under the guidance of the EC has gone a long way in helping with a peaceful election. The EC's efforts, helped by the use of technology, have created enabling conditions to draw out more people to the polling booths. The decline of violence at polling sites has meant that the potential victims of violence can exercise their voting rights with a sense of security. However, the fact that lawbreakers can become lawmakers has become a cause for concern for many – in the long run this has the potential to make elections trail away from the fair path.

8

Campaign Funding and Spending

Funding of political parties and financing of their election campaigns are important issues seen as influencing politics in democratic countries. Scholars have highlighted the issue of campaign finance reform as well as the relation between campaign spending and electoral outcomes (Nice, 1987; Cox and Thies, 2000; Stratmann, 2006; Rekkas, 2007; Milligan and Rekkas, 2008; Gowda and Sridharan, 2012; Magee, 2012; Weintraub and Brown, 2012; Kapur and Vaishnav, 2018). Electoral contests are occasions when colossal amounts of money are splurged by candidates and political parties to raise their winning chances. Both the incumbents and challengers spend money to win elections. It is generally believed that there is a complementary relation between high campaign spending and high vote share, leading to favourable electoral outcomes, but research studies point out that this is not as linear as it appears to be.

In India it is the EC that regulates campaign finance and spending. Political parties are known to spend money often in excess to the legally permissible limits on campaigning, including distribution of cash, liquor and 'gifts' in the constituencies, to strengthen their electoral chances. The use of 'black', 'dark' or unaccounted money has often been reported in Indian elections. Elections are an expensive affair in India. A considerable amount of money is needed to compete in an election. How do political parties finance their campaigns? How is this money raised by them? Where do they get the money from? What do they spend the money on apart from campaign material and rallies? Financial contribution to and campaign expenditure by political parties in India have come under much focus in contemporary times.

What Is the Money Spent On?

Election campaigns are expensive affairs. The spatial spread of campaign territory necessitates substantial expenditure for mobilising support. The larger the territory, the bigger are the resources needed for an effective campaign in contemporary democracies. Each party needs to take its ideas and programmes to the citizens to keep itself alive in the public mind. Maintaining a constant presence in the public space needs resources. A constant supply of propaganda paraphernalia requires considerable spending capacities. Funds have to be raised and allocated to all campaign modes, such as rallies, roadshows, advertisements, signages, broadcasts, and so on. Raising funds itself is contingent upon an initial capital, organisational capacity and infrastructure. Established systemic parties liaison with business and industries to finance their campaigns besides raising small funds from individual supporters. Big parties with big money and organised capacity to raise funds have an advantage over smaller parties with smaller resources. The latter, because of fewer resources, weaker organisations and thinner on-ground presence, do not have enough capability to cast their nets wide. Bigger parties have an all-encompassing advantage, implying that the level playing field needed for fair elections is not actually levelled. Many a time the very survival of small parties becomes difficult.

There are specific activities on which money is spent by contesting candidates and political parties during elections. These activities range from travel campaigns and rallies to virtual and audio-visual canvassing. Advertisements and messages in print and television media, radio broadcasts and online and postal campaigns are some ways of political campaigning across the world. Social media is another channel tapped by political parties for political campaigning. In India, wall writing, wall posters and use of cut-outs are popular forms of campaigning, though restrictions have been placed on defacement of public property by writing or pasting posters. Roadshows, rallies, public meetings and bus tours are conducted in different regions to canvass. Door-to-door campaigns are also a popular form of campaigning to reach voters. Market research by political parties and their support groups has caught on in recent times to gauge the extent of support in different constituencies. Campaign material like posters, banners, flags, banners, pamphlets, caps, t-shirts, and so on, are prepared and distributed. Party manifestos are printed and distributed, too, to reach electors.

The expenditure which is permitted under law (within limits) is for canvassing door-to-door, holding public meetings, printing leaflets, posters and banners for rallies, hiring vehicles for campaigning and placing advertisements in print and electronic media. The EC revises spending limits from time to time. Spending which is illegal and comes within the definition of 'bribery' includes distribution of money, liquor, food items, or any other thing which is seen as being done with the intent of influencing the voters – these are corrupt practices under the RPA, 1951. They are also 'offences' under the Indian Penal Code. The phenomenon of 'paid news', which was discussed in Chapter 5, is another malpractice that has grown in the recent past.

Saye Sekhar, writing in *The Hindu*, lists out the main areas of spending by a candidate during an election:

> The major heads of poll spending are: engaging at least 2,000 active men for campaigning, poll management and counting; hiring or purchasing, and maintaining, vehicles; organising publicity material; opening village-level offices; preparing and distributing voter slips; fetching electors to polling stations; getting star speakers and picking up the tab for their travel, lodging and boarding; and other miscellaneous expenditure. (Sekhar, 2009)

Campaign material, transport, labour and personnel costs make up a substantial amount of the canvassing bill. In India money is spent on 'purchase of votes', too, though it remains outside account books or formal computation. Money is also spent on 'selling' candidature. It is an open secret that political parties sell tickets to aspiring individuals to contest elections as their nominees. This is again expenditure that is unaccounted for and remains outside the conventional purview of campaigning, which is about party programmes and issues and is seen as buttressing the former. In the experience of many political leaders (in erstwhile united Andhra Pradesh), purchase of votes forms 'the major chunk of election expenditure' (Sekhar, 2009). For the 2009 general elections, the cost of each vote was between INR 200 and INR 500 (Sekhar, 2009). Including liquor, this had come to about 65–70 per cent of the costs incurred (Sekhar, 2009). Rama Lakshmi informs that Tamil Nadu voters were handed INR 1,000 notes rolled up in pens before elections in 2014. They were also given train tickets to be later exchanged for refunds (Lakshmi, 2014). In Uttar Pradesh, INR 1,000 crore (10 billion) were distributed among voters during the 2017 assembly elections (PTI, 2017), and in Nagaland voters were offered INR 1,000 for a vote during the assembly elections in 2018 (H. K. Singh, 2018).

Distribution of liquor, goods and cash is a common practice. It is indulged in to ensure votes. According to former MP P. J. Kurien, 'The most outrageous thing about these practices is that there is an underlying presumption in it, namely that the ordinary illiterate voters can be easily corrupted with liquor, a little money or a pair of sarees' (Kurien, 1997: 19). *Laddu*s (a kind of Indian sweets that are round in shape and made from a mixture of flour and sugar) are distributed, too. Parliamentary or state assembly elections are not the only occasions when money is spent. Big expenditures have been seen even at the level of local government elections. Village-level *gram panchayat* elections see a big splurge of money as well – no wonder elections in India are termed as 'festivals of unaccounted cash' (Deka, 2018). It has been reported that a candidate spent INR 25 lakh (2.5 million) in *gram panchayat* elections in Bundelkhand (Uttar Pradesh) in 2015 (Anuja, 2016). The main expenses included distribution of liquor, holding feasts and distribution of cash. Here expenditure on alcohol topped the list followed by cost of meat that had to be cooked in feasts (Anuja, 2016). Personal and household goods like shawls, sarees, blankets, shoes, watches, and so on, are also distributed. At times the candidates also provide for hospital treatment or wedding gifts (Anuja, 2016). Cash distribution was another way of catching votes. According to Anuja's findings, the cost of a single vote was between INR 1,000 and INR 1,500 (Anuja, 2016) in the 2015 *gram panchayat* elections in Uttar Pradesh.

In Punjab, banned substances or drugs in record measures have also been caught during elections, making the purpose of their circulation obvious (Miglani, 2014). Interestingly, trenchant criticism of these forms of 'bribery' – cash, goods, alcohol, and so on – come from the city-based civil society, the middle class and the media. The former sees it as political corruption that needs to be curbed by state authorities, particularly the EC. For the mass of the electorate, however, these 'events' or 'gifts' become occasions of feasts and small monetary gains in the larger setting of economic hardship and insecure employment.

The EC and Expenditure Limits

In India the EC has the responsibility to see that the legal limits of expenditure are not crossed. It prescribes spending limits for candidates during campaigns, which have been revised at regular intervals. However, it has not been able to strictly enforce these limits. Candidates breach these prescribed limits and spend money in excess during campaigns. Political parties can spend any amount of money because they are not bound by limits. The end result is that Indian elections see expenditure that is far above the permissible limits.

The 2014 elections saw 'a disconcerting growth in gross electoral spending' (Collins, 2014), where the spending was about USD 5 billion, which includes a cost of USD 600 million to the government exchequer and is among the costliest in the democratic world (Collins, 2014). Elections in the US are usually the most expensive. However, the Indian elections of 2014 far surpassed US elections. The total cost of the presidential election in 2012 in the US was about USD 2 billion (*The Economist*, 2014). This went up to USD 2.4 billion in 2016 (Ingraham, 2017). In the Canadian national elections of 2015, the candidates of Liberal Party, the Conservative Party, the New Democratic Party and the Green Party, which ran full or nearly full campaigns in all the 338 federal electoral districts across the country, were entitled to spend CAD 296 million, but their actual spending fell far short – it was just under CAD 63.1 million in total (Press and Bryden, 2016). It was reported that third-party interest groups had spent five times more on the 2015 federal elections compared to the previous ones – they put in more than CAD 6 million on ad space and airtime in the 78-day campaign (Duggan, 2016). In 2015, 115 third parties registered with Elections Canada (the poll management institution of Canada) – this was up by more than half from 2011, when 55 registered with Elections Canada (Duggan, 2016). The top spenders in 2015 were largely unions. Many of those groups had either not spent anything in 2011 or not nearly as much (Duggan, 2016).

Coming back to India, 'bribing' of electors by distribution of goods and cash in India is, in the words of former CEC V. S. Sampath, a 'major challenge during elections' (Sengupta, 2013). According to former CEC T. S. Krishnamurthy, 'Money has been allowed to play a dangerously negative role.'[1] Conversations with young researchers and voters have highlighted that in India the relation between campaign spending (distribution of cash and goods) and electoral victory is not straightforward. Voters are not necessarily inclined towards the party or the candidate from whom they receive the

---

[1] T. S. Krishnamurthy, email conversation with the author, 7 October 2020.

largest bounty – they might not even vote for that party. On the other hand, voters are not averse to receiving 'gifts' from political parties during elections. In fact, as one report from Tamil Nadu points out, opposing such distribution has become quite unpopular, and political rivals refrain from doing so (Kannaiah, 2019). Voters have, in some instances, paid off their debts with the cash they received or made small financial gains, and thus the indications are that they are not against such distribution.

During the 2013 assembly elections (in a few states), the EC asked the candidates to 'open a separate bank account and incur all expenditure through cheques from the said bank account' (Kannaiah, 2019). It also asked political parties to advise its workers not to carry more than INR 50,000 cash to the constituencies during election. It kept a close vigil on the production, distribution and storage of liquor through the Excise Department in the poll-going states (Kannaiah, 2019). Along with these measures, the EC took steps to campaign for 'ethical voting through print and electronic media' and also by involving students, resident forums and citizen organisations (Kannaiah, 2019).

In the 2014 Lok Sabha elections, the EC roped in security and financial intelligence agencies like income tax intelligence and the financial intelligence units to help it track the movement of illegal money (PTI, 2014b). Flying squads (FS) and video monitoring teams were also put into service.[2] In the 2016 Tamil Nadu assembly elections, 702 FS were deployed (EC, 2016d). Their task was to intercept illegal money and distribution of goods to voters and monitor lavish spending on party functions. In Punjab, the EC teams even took a count of *laddu*s distributed by political parties to voters (after the parties had weighed candidates against them) and took their cost as elections expense (Lakshmi, 2014). While the regional party that had been in power

---

[2] The EC passed revised orders (EC, 2015) for three or more FS in each assembly constituency. The number had to be more in what EC terms as 'expenditure sensitive constituencies'. The FS function from the date of announcement of elections till their completion. Their work includes attending to complaints regarding violations of the MCC and other complaints of threat, intimidation, movement of criminal elements, liquor, arms and ammunition, as well as cash. They also have to attend to complaints regarding spending on elections after elections have been announced. They are also given the work of videographing, along with the Video Surveillance Team, all major rallies and public meetings. The FS include members of the police and the Income Tax Department and are led by a magistrate.

claimed that the same bunch of *laddu*s was carried from one village to the next, the EC teams found video evidence to the contrary as the *laddu*s were eaten right there after the weighing was done (Lakshmi, 2014)!

While monitoring and tracking by the EC has become more stringent now as compared to the previous elections, parties are always in search of 'innovative' means to attract voters. Rajendra Kondepati writes that the EC once raided a marriage reception where there was no bride or groom but an assembly of voters brought together 'for distribution of goodies' (Kondepati, 2011: 71). Economist Arun Kumar points out that what could have been legally spent in the parliamentary elections of 2019 would be an aggregate INR 3,700 crore (37 billion), but, as per his calculations, in 2019 parties spent at least an aggregate of INR 16,000 crore (160 billion) (the figure could be higher), making the gap between what was permissible and what was actually INR 12,300 crore (123 billion) (A. Kumar, 2019).

Unaccounted-for cash is also caught before and during elections. According to Sampath, cash worth INR 53.09 crore (0.5309 billion) was seized from five states of Madhya Pradesh, Chhattisgarh, Rajasthan, Mizoram and Delhi. The amount of cash seized during elections in Assam, West Bengal, Kerala, Tamil Nadu, Puducherry, Punjab, Uttar Pradesh, Goa, Manipur, Uttarakhand, Himachal Pradesh and Gujarat was INR 101.16 crore (1.0116 billion) (Sengupta, 2013). According to Sampath, the role and influence of money power on elections is not uniform over the entire country – it is largely felt in the southern and western parts of the country where the wealth created by the information technology (IT) industry and of contracts is felt significantly.[3]

Just after the first day of polling on 7 April 2014, the EC seized INR 195 crore (1.95 billion) throughout the country, of which INR 118 crore (1.18 billion) was seized from the state of Andhra Pradesh (before the bifurcation of the state) itself (PTI, 2014c). Overall, INR 300 crore (3 billion) was caught in the 2014 election (Collins, 2014). During the Tamil Nadu assembly elections in 2016, cash amounting to about INR 5.2 crore (0.052 billion) was seized in and around the capital city of Chennai on 22 April (EC, 2016d). In the words of the EC, 'The money seized was not related to normal business activity of the group and major part of it is suspected to be linked with hawala operations and was likely to be used in the upcoming election of Tamil Nadu'

---

[3] V. S. Sampath, email conversation with the author, 1 August 2020.

(EC, 2016d). On the same day, INR 4.77 crore (0.047 billion) was seized in Karur district. Also, '[g]oods worth over 1 crore [0.01 billion] rupees in the form of dhotis and sarees etc, suspected to be used for inducement of voters, were found in the premise and the same has been placed under restraint' (EC, 2016d).

Parties find novel ways of transporting prohibited items. Expenditure-monitoring officials have found money in dashboards of cars, alcohol in milk vans and narcotics in trucks carrying vegetables (Miglani, 2014). Unaccounted-for money stashed in sacks has been found in vans carrying ATM (automated teller machine) money (Miglani, 2014). Cash has also been found in an ambulance in Odisha (Miglani, 2014). Sampath does feel that the EC's efforts to clamp down on use of money power have seen some success, evident from the cash that has been seized from time to time (Sengupta, 2013). He says, 'The seized amount has certainly created deterrence for huge amounts from being distributed among the electors' (Sengupta, 2013).

Those asking for more accountability on the part of contestants note that once an election is won, political parties and victorious candidates focus on recovering the money they spent on winning an election. Their attention is often on accumulating wealth to recover the amount spent and to gather more resources to be used for the next round of elections. Incumbency gives them an advantage over rivals. This leads to apathetic governance and neglect of public issues. Dependence on big corporations and businesses leads to interest re-prioritisation that places corporate interests above public ones. According to H. R. Khanna, a former judge of the Supreme Court, 'It would also be unrealistic to expect hard-headed industrialists and businessmen to pay huge amounts out of altruistic considerations.' They are 'bound to seek, due and very often undue, concessions and favours as quid pro quo for money paid by them' (H. R. Khanna, 1997: 43). This tilts the focus of the government from public issues onto corporate interests. S. N. Sangita lists out some implications of huge election expenses on the quality of governance. According to him, elections being costly affairs discourages good candidates with limited means from contesting; it makes parties and candidates dependent on big businesses and wealthy individuals, which in turn gives excessive power to the latter two; it promotes corruption and resultant poor performance – big businesses expect high returns on their investments; and it makes political parties dependent on black money (Sangita, 2013: 73–74). The EC, in its 'Background Paper on Political Finance and Law Commission Recommendations', says, 'If wealthy individuals and corporates pay to the political party or the candidate in order to make them listen to them, this undermines the core principles of democracy and transfers the economic inequality to political inequality' (EC, 2014c).

Civil society groups and smaller political parties have sought reform of campaign finance and more openness about election funding. The efforts of these groups have brought about some stringency in laws on campaign financing over the years. But as discussed earlier, the amount of money that gets spent on elections is far higher than what is legally allowed. The EC has made efforts to curb this but has not been able to strictly enforce limits because of the 'absence of express legal provisions' (EC, 2014c).

Expenditure limits have been revised periodically to tackle this unaccounted-for money (see Table 8.1). These limits vary between big, small and very small states. In October 2003, the ceiling for a Lok Sabha candidate was raised to INR 25 lakh (2.5 million) and for an assembly candidate to INR 10 lakh (1 million) in big states like Maharashtra, Madhya Pradesh, Uttar Pradesh, West Bengal, Karnataka, and so on. This limit was raised in 2011 to INR 40 lakh (4 million) for Lok Sabha and INR 16 lakh (1.6 million) for assembly candidates in big states. In small states like Himachal Pradesh and Uttarakhand, the expenditure limit was placed at INR 11 lakh (1.1 million), while in very small states like Nagaland and Tripura it was INR 8 lakh (0.8 million).

The limit was raised further to INR 70 lakh (7 million) for Lok Sabha candidates in big states, INR 54 lakh (5.4 million) in smaller states (the

Table 8.1 Spending limits put in place by the Election Commission of India, 2003–20

Year	Election	Big states (in INR lakh [million])	Small states (in INR lakh [million])
2003	Lok Sabha	25 (2.5)	–
	State assembly	10 (1)	–
2011	Lok Sabha	40 (4)	40 (4)
	State assembly	16 (1.6)	11 (1.1)
2014	Lok Sabha	70 (7)	54 (5.4)
	State assembly	28 (2.8)	20–28 (2–2.8)
2020	Lok Sabha	77 (7.7)	59.4 (5.94)
	State assembly	30.8 (3.08)	22 (2.2)

Source: Information in the public domain.

north-eastern states, Himachal Pradesh, Goa, and so on) and INR 28 lakh (2.8 million) for assembly candidates in March 2014. The Conduct of Election Rules, 1961, were amended accordingly. Often these limits are discussed lightly, highlighting the hiatus between official view and real spending. According to a party worker, 'We spend Rs. 70 lakh [7 million] just on cups of tea in election days' (Malhotra, 2014). While these curbs continue to focus on candidates, the parties carry on spending on their nominees, leaving excessive spending intact. This neutralises the effects of spending curbs.

There has been some back-and-forth on this issue between the Supreme Court and the parliament (Ranjan, 2012). Section 77(3) of the RPA, 1951, keeps out the spending by political parties on an election campaign. This means that expenditure of any amount by a political party is not calculated as expenditure on an election; it is only expenditure done by a candidate that becomes 'electoral spending'. There is an interesting history to this, and concerns have been expressed on this matter by no less an authority than the apex court of India, which gave its specific direction to law. In 1975, the Supreme Court set aside the election of Amarnath Chawla on the grounds that his electoral expenditure crossed the ceiling limit and was therefore 'corrupt practice' (*Kanwar Lal Gupta v. Amar Nath Chawla and Others*, 3 October 1974). The Supreme Court had included as expenditure the spending done by the party on this candidate – it had ruled that the two should be clubbed, and this amount should be within the prescribed limit.

In this judgment, the Supreme Court emphasised that the objective of enacting ceilings on spending was that everyone should be able to contest elections on a 'footing of equality'; no individual or political party should be able to have an advantage over others for reason of greater financial strength. It observed that the democratic process can function efficiently and effectively only when all participate in the democracy, howsoever lowly or humble. The other objective to limiting spending, according to the court, was to prevent political parties that were supported by the wealthy and big money from becoming the representatives of this economic class. The court was of the view, 'The small man's chance is the essence of Indian democracy and that would be stultified if large contributions from rich and affluent individuals or groups are not divorced from the electoral process' (see *Kanwar Lal Gupta v. Amar Nath Chawla and Others*, 3 October 1974).

The government of the day, led by prime minister Indira Gandhi, in response added an explanation to Section 77, exempting the expenditure by political parties and individuals from the candidate's expenses (see Ranjan, 2012). This exchange, however, did not end here. The Supreme Court again stressed the need to bring the spending by political parties within the ceiling limits. In 1994, in its ruling in the *Gadakh Yashwantrao Kankarrao v. E. V. Alias Balasaheb Vikhe Patil and Others* case, the Supreme Court noted that the 'existing law does not measure upto [*sic*] the existing realities' (EC, n.d.4). It said that the money spent on a candidate's election by the party or anyone else is 'safely outside the net of legal function', that the ceiling on spending by candidate is a 'mere eye-wash and no practical check on election expenses' (EC, n.d.4). It went on to note that this lacuna in law is for the parliament to fill 'lest the impression is reinforced that its retention is deliberate for the convenience of everyone' (EC, n.d.4). Again, in 1995, in the *Gajanan Krishnaji Bapat v. Dattaji Raghobji Meghe* case, the apex court took note of the excessive spending during elections by political parties and felt that the 'naked display of black money, by violating the mandatory provisions of law, cannot be permitted' (see ADR, 2014b: 32).

In April 1996, the Supreme Court gave a judgment in the *Common Cause v. Union of India and Others* case where it made clear that expenditure incurred by a political party or anybody (other than the candidate and his or her election agent) to advance the election chances of a candidate will be excluded from the expenditure incurred by the candidate if, and only if, that expenditure has been shown in the account of the party, body, association or individual concerned and that account has been duly audited and submitted to the income tax authorities; otherwise such expenditure shall be presumed to be that of the candidate (EC, n.d.4).

The EC, following the *Kanwar Lal Gupta v. Amar Nath Chawla and Others* case (1974), reiterated that expenditure incurred by political parties in general and not for any particular candidate or candidates will be treated as expenditure of the political party on general party propaganda. However, if the party through an advertisement seeks support for a particular candidate or group of candidates or promotes their prospects, it would be treated as expenditure of the candidate or the group of candidates (in case of a group the expenditure would be equally divided between the individual candidates) (see EC, 2014d: 154–55, 192–93). According to Sampath, it is 'unrealistic' that spending limits exist for candidates but not for political parties (R. Chopra, 2015). The party can spend 'three to four times the money spent by a candidate' in the name of general party propaganda and campaigning (R. Chopra, 2015).

According to the RPA, 1951, all candidates must keep separate and correct accounts of the expenditure incurred by them on elections between the date of the election notification and the date of the declaration of election results, both days inclusive. In 1998, the EC directed that the candidates had to maintain daily accounts of electioneering expenditure. It designed a register with proper formats where all the details of the money spent by candidates had to be noted. It also said that these accounts had to be submitted to the electoral officer for scrutiny once in three days. Some political parties asked for a review of this decision 'as visiting the office of the Returning Officer on every third day was inconvenient to the candidate in many cases' (EC, 2009a: 119). The EC thereafter reviewed and revised this decision in 2004 and said that the scrutiny of accounts was to be done only on three occasions during the entire election period, but there had to be a gap of four days between each inspection. In 2014 the EC instructed that the accounts register (with supporting documents) had to be made available for inspection by the candidates any time during the process of election. It said that failure to produce this register on demand would be considered a 'major default' (EC, 2014d: 185).

In a letter in 2010, the EC instructed that for the conduct of free and fair elections, political parties should avoid transactions in cash and carrying large amounts during campaigns (EC, 2014d: 61). CEOs were given the charge of identifying constituencies that were prone to 'high expenditure and corrupt practices' (EC, 2014d: 7). Termed as 'expenditure sensitive constituencies', these had to be observed by 'expenditure observers', 'flying squads', 'static surveillance teams' and 'video surveillance teams' (EC, 2014d: 7) to track over-the-limit spending.

According to Trilochan Sastry of the ADR, the raising of spending limit does 'not address the real issues' (*Business Standard*, 2014). He stresses the need for a 'level playing ground so that any public minded citizen with a desire for public service should be able to contest elections and not be at a disadvantage. Raising the ceiling has no impact on that' (*Business Standard*, 2014). Spending on elections by established political parties is so heavy that it is difficult for a small party or an individual to compete with them. Sastry also emphasises the need for more transparency in funding, sources of funding, along with penalties for not being transparent, which are not addressed by the increase in the ceiling limit. He also says that one needs penalties for crossing the new limit of INR 70 lakh (7 million). This again is not taken care of (*Business Standard*, 2014). Also, the huge amount of black money spent in elections is not curbed. In other words, according to him, none of the major concerns of unaccounted spending are addressed by the cabinet decision to raise the ceiling (*Business Standard*, 2014). According to Jayaprakash Narayan of the Lok Satta party, the EC knows fully well that in most parts of India the money spent for parliamentary elections is an average of INR 20–30 crore (0.2–0.3 billion), and for assembly elections it is INR 5–10 crore (0.05–0.1 billion), but it can do nothing (Narayan, 2013: 316). According to him, 'If the giver and the taker, both are content, the Commission can do precious little' (Narayan, 2013: 316). Much does depend on the social acceptability of a political practice – the absence of large-scale disapproval of campaign spending, where the money is used to mobilise underprivileged voters, means that the EC's directives can do little.

Election Finance and Legal Obligations

Campaign finance laws in India are more comprehensive at least in theory but have had less success in implementing expenditure disclosure requirements (Weintraub and Brown, 2012: 241). The laws place limits on expenditure by candidates as mentioned earlier and are thus stringent about how much they spend on campaigning (it is another matter that the money spent is far higher than what law permits as there is little scrutiny of the amount spent by political parties on candidates). However, the candidates can raise funds from any source – there are no restrictions on fundraising. The candidates do not have to maintain or reveal the names and addresses of the donors. Though spending limits are placed on candidates in India, there is no ceiling imposed on pre-nomination spending, and the candidate need not disclose the same. In contrast, laws in the US are strict about disclosure of contributions to parties and impose contribution limits, but there are no expenditure limits (Weintraub and Brown, 2012: 244). The Federal Election Commission of the US does not manage elections but regulates the role of money in the elections, which includes imposing limits on contributions and seeing that parties adhere to the existing disclosure norms (Weintraub and Brown, 2012: 249). Spending in US elections is a concern, but some argue that more should be spent to motivate apathetic voters to come out to counter historically low turnouts (Grant, 2005: 73). In the UK there are legal limits on the amount that can be spent by a candidate on elections. Also, there are curbs placed on the sources of funding. The candidates also have to file spending returns with the returning officer.

Australia has a 'minimalist approach' to regulating campaign expenditure. The parliament of Australia (Odgers, 2016 [1953]: ch. 12) lists the following provisions:

1. the provision of public funding
2. candidate campaign expenditure disclosure requirements
3. donation disclosure requirements
4. broadcasting and publisher disclosure statements
5. three-day electronic advertising ban to 6 p.m. on polling day – broadcasters have to provide opportunity for advertising prior to this period, and
6. the 'caretaker convention' which limits all government advertising once an election is called

The parliament of Australia also notes that in Australian elections, because of deficiency of funds, parties and candidates rely on 'financial support garnered from fundraising events and from donations by organisations and private individuals' (Odgers, 2016 [1953]: ch. 12). It is estimated that 'more than 80 per cent of funding gained by political parties comes from private sources' and that this amount has been growing.

Advocacy groups in South Africa have demanded more transparency in election finance. The African National Congress, which has been a ruling party for long, and the major opposition parties have often faced criticism that they have opposed campaign finance reform to keep the names of their donors a secret (Onishi, 2019). It has been noted that there is little information on private donations to party campaigns – this means that there have been 'only hints about how much parties have spent on previous campaigns' in South Africa (Onishi, 2019). In the UK and the US, similar concerns have come up on electoral reform regarding transparency in donations to parties and candidates, spending in campaigns, rising campaign costs, unequal access to funding and influence of large donations, among others (Grant, 2005: 71). Also, questions have been raised as to what extent the taxpayer should subsidise campaigns by parties and candidates (Grant, 2005: 71). Canada follows limits on both campaign expenditure by candidates and donations. Interestingly, as discussed earlier, money spent on campaigns and winnability are not always positively correlated. Spending huge resources did not guarantee victory in the 2015 national elections as was revealed by a study (Press and Bryden, 2016). However, 'not spending enough to at least stay competitive with rival candidates was an almost certain path to defeat' (Press and Bryden, 2016). In close races, the amount of money spent mattered for a victory (Press and Bryden, 2016).

In Japan electoral finance rules prohibit donations by individuals directly to candidates (Yuda, 2017). Each candidate is permitted to set up one support organisation which people can donate to. Corporations, industry organizations and unions can only donate to political parties and their fund-managing organisations, 'which is one reason why it helps to run on a party ticket rather than as an independent' (Yuda, 2017). Money is spent by candidates to print posters and leaflets, give ads in newspapers and television, rent campaign offices and hire staff (Yuda, 2017).

Democratic countries have tried to level the electoral field by formulating and imposing capping laws on donations and spending (see Table 8.2). Where caps are absent, disclosure norms try to bring about an environment of self-restraint. Elections have become an expensive affair everywhere. Parties that can spend more tend to disrupt the equilibrium or the level playing field and tilt the balance in their favour. Caps and disclosure regimes encourage small players, and this works in favour of equalising democratic functioning. Evidence indicates that increasing pressure is being brought upon incumbent governments to bring about more transparency in election finance – both in incoming and outgoing resources.

As Eswaran Sridharan points out, regulation on election funding usually takes four forms: (*a*) limits on expenditure on an election, (*b*) limits on contributions that are made to a candidate or party, (*c*) state funding of elections (which can be full or partial or in the form of subsidies or reimbursements after an election) and (*d*) the reporting and disclosures of contribution and expenditures incurred on an election (quoted in Chatterjee and Sahoo, 2012: 6). In India this regulation is weak. And since there is no cap on spending by political parties, and they do not have to disclose how much they are spending on a candidate's election, the ceiling imposed on the candidate becomes farcical. A party can spend a huge amount of money, way beyond the legal limit, in the name of general propaganda in constituencies going to polls. This, according to former CEC Sampath, 'poses a major hurdle in controlling money power' (Sengupta, 2013).

Table 8.2 Campaign finance limits (federal or parliamentary elections)

Country	Donation or contribution limits	Limits on campaign spending	Remarks
United Kingdom	No (Political parties must report information on donations to the Electoral Commission every quarter.)	Yes (Before the 2001 general elections, there were no limits on political party spending.)	Parties and candidates must report their spending to the Electoral Commission.
United States	Yes (Regular disclosures by candidates are required in the form of a report.)	No (Super political action committees [PACs] must file regular reports of expenditure with the Federal Election Commission.)	One of the conditions for receiving public funding is that presidential candidates must agree to abide by spending limits.
Japan	Yes (Corporations and other organisations can donate only to political parties.)	Yes (on candidates contesting elections and not their respective parties)	
Canada	Yes (Limits apply to both political parties and candidates.)	Yes (on candidates contesting elections and not their respective parties)	
Australia	No (Disclosures must be made.)	No (Political parties and candidates have reporting and disclosure obligations.)	Political parties and candidates must file financial disclosure returns with the Australian Electoral Commission. Foreign donations have been banned.

(Contd)

Table 8.2 *(Contd)*

Country	Donation or contribution limits	Limits on campaign spending	Remarks
South Africa	No (Disclosures to be made by political parties if donations are above ZAR 100,000.)	No (Reporting and disclosure requirements to the Electoral Commission of South Africa exist.)	Donations by government departments, state-owned entities and foreign governments and agencies are not permissible under the new 2021 laws. Anonymous donations are permissible.
India	No (Only anonymous cash donations are limited to INR 2,000, brought down from INR 20,000 in 2017.)	Yes (on candidates contesting elections and not their respective parties)	Each candidate must keep a separate and correct account of all expenditure incurred by him or her or his or her election agent for the elections contested. New laws of 2017 permit anonymous funding through electoral bonds and also foreign funds to political parties.

Source: Information in the public domain.

Political parties have to submit details of donations and contributions of more than INR 20,000 from individual donors to the EC, but they do not come out openly on these. The details of donations or contributions have to be filed annually – that is, once a year to the EC – as prescribed under Section 29C of the RPA, 1951. These donations can come from individuals, companies, election trusts, and so on. The EC can seek withdrawal of tax exemption benefits on the contributions if political parties fail to file the expenditure contribution reports on time. The party need not maintain details of donations less than INR 20,000 or disclose the same to the EC. Political parties are also not required to disclose the total amount of contributions received by them, which means that anonymous donations are permissible.

An ADR report points out that between 2004–05 and 2014–15, political parties (national and regional) received INR 7,832.98 crore (78.329 billion) from unknown sources, which is 69 per cent of their total income. From known donors they received 16 per cent. Another 15 per cent was generated through other known sources like sale of assets, membership fees, bank interest, sale of publications, party levy, and so on. Their total income was INR 11,367.34 crore (113.673 billion) (ADR, 2017). ADR also brought out that the total declared donations of national parties in 2017–18 came down by INR 119.49 crore (1.194 billion), a 20 per cent decrease from the previous financial year of 2016–17 (ADR, 2019).

The central government also began a scheme of 'electoral bonds', announced in 2017, supposedly to bring about transparency in election finance. The scheme where the donor can buy these bonds from an authorised bank and then deposit these bonds in the designated account of political parties to whom he or she wants to donate was introduced through the budget in February 2017 by the NDA government. A bond has a life of 15 days. The income tax authorities and the EC need not be informed about the donor, amount and beneficiary of such donations – in fact, no one needs to know about these transactions. Though the transaction is done in 'white' money, it need not be disclosed by the donor or the beneficiary – apart from these two nobody else needs to know about these transactions. This government action on funding of political parties removed all caps on corporate donations that existed earlier. Till this scheme came, companies could donate only up to 7.5 per cent of their average net profit in the past three years to political parties. Also, the obligation on companies to disclose to their shareholders the name of parties they were contributing to and the amount was discontinued.

This scheme was seen by the NDA government as a way of bringing about more transparency in electoral funding since the transactions are through banks and not in cash. The then union finance minister, Arun Jaitley, called it a 'substantial improvement' over the existing funding modes (*The Hindu*, 2018). However, critics have referred to it as a 'massive retrograde step' (Sundaresan, 2018) and a 'great leap backwards' (Yadav, 2017) in the history of finance reforms as it has brushed aside the issue of transparency in a single stroke. Critics have also claimed that it 'legalises political corruption' (Anuja and Prasad, 2019). The former chief of the Law Commission of India, A. P. Shah, in a letter to prime minister Narendra Modi, raised a concern that this system 'may lead to increase in black money and corruption' (*Times of India*, 2018). He feared that this would lead to the 'creation of shell companies and rise of benami transactions[4] to channelise the undocumented money into the political and electoral process' (*Times of India*, 2018). Section 13A(b) of the Income Tax Act, 1961, and Section 29C of the RPA, 1951, were amended accordingly by the government to operationalise this law. Doubts about transparency associated with the scheme were also expressed by former CEC Nasim Zaidi, who said that if the EC does not get to know about the donations, even the people would not get to know (B. Jain, 2017). In other words, secrecy cloaks these transactions, which goes against the demand for more transparency in political funding. Also, the government of the day can have access to information on these as such information resides with the public sector banks. The system which was put into operation a few years ago has so far not settled the doubts expressed by critics about its openness.

Suggestions and Proposals on Funding

One suggestion to regulate funding that has come from some political leaders is to separate the executive power from legislative power (Manish Tiwari and Rajiv Pratap Rudy in Chatterjee and Sahoo, 2012: 9, 12–13). The belief that underlies this suggestion is that to get executive power, legislators spend huge amounts to win elections. The expenditure knows no bounds and goes beyond spending limits. It is believed that the delinking of the executive from the legislature would act as a disincentive, and candidates would refrain from spending huge amounts to ensure a victory (Manish Tiwari and Rajiv Pratap Rudy in Chatterjee and Sahoo, 2012: 9, 12–13). But as it has been pointed out, this delinking is not possible in a parliamentary system. Even in systems where the two are separate – that is, in a presidential system (like the US) – there are instances of overspending and illegal money being used by senators (Eswaran Sridharan in Chatterjee and Sahoo, 2012: 14).

Suggestions on state contributions to funding of elections have been discussed by various official committees and commissions positively. The Dinesh Goswami Committee (1990) recommended state assistance but

---

[4] *Benami* transactions are related to property and assets where the person in whose name the property is registered is not the real owner – such transactions are done to bypass legal obligations like disclosures and tax rules.

only in kind and not in cash (GoI, 1990). This help, for instance, could be extended for fuel spent, additional copies of electoral rolls, hiring a certain number of microphones for campaigning, and so on. This assistance could be given to candidates of recognised political parties and not others. The committee recommended a ban on company donations. Some of these suggestions of in-kind support have been incorporated by subsequent governments. For instance, free airtime to political parties to campaign on state-run media – Doordarshan and AIR – is provided. Also, one copy of the electoral roll of a constituency is given free of cost to the candidates of recognised parties contesting from that constituency. Free space is given for offices of recognised political parties in state capitals. The income of political parties is tax-exempt. Tax exemptions are also given to those who donate to political parties. Till 2018, such donations could not come from foreign sources, government companies and other companies as per Section 293A of the Companies Act, 1956. However, the government through the Finance Bill, 2018, amended the Foreign Contribution (Regulation) Act (FCRA), 2010, to exempt political parties from scrutiny of funds received from abroad since 1976.[5]

The proposal for state funding also came from former prime minister Inder Kumar Gujral when he was the union minister for external affairs, from former MP and Lok Sabha speaker Somnath Chatterjee and former MPs P. J. Kurien, Vasant Sathe, and so on (Gujral, 1997: 2; S. Chatterjee, 1997: 32; Kurien, 1997: 19; Sathe, 1997: 9). Gujral was of the view that 'the only visible way out' for unhealthy party funding was through state funding of parties – both for elections and day-to-day functioning (Gujral, 1997: 2). The Indrajit Gupta Committee (1998) also recommended state funding of elections but only to recognised national and state parties. It felt that such a move would lead to a level playing field and help cash-strapped parties. Political parties, according to it, played an important role in sustaining representative democracy. It suggested that if the state is not able to fund elections entirely, it should do so partially. It also recommended a separate election fund made up of contributions from both the central and state governments to the tune of INR 600 crore (6 billion) annually. However, most state governments

---

[5] The FCRA dates back to 1976. It was replaced by the FCRA, 2010, which banned foreign funding to political parties. The NDA government in 2016 made it easier for political parties to get donations from foreign companies by amending the Act, and in 2018 it completely lifted the ban on foreign funding.

expressed their inability to do so and wanted the centre to finance such a scheme (S. Jain, 2001: 502). The committee recommended that the state should provide help, to start with, only in kind and not in cash. It suggested that parties should maintain and submit their annual returns of receipts and expenditure to income tax authorities, failing which they would not receive any state funding. It felt that corporate contributions should be fully regulated and made transparent. State funding, at least partially, is seen not only as a way of reducing the costs of elections but also as a way of controlling the use of illegal wealth to finance elections (B. Kumar, 1999: 1888).

The Law Commission, in its 170th report (1999), also recommended partial state funding and saw it as a 'first step towards total state funding', but it felt that such provisions could be put in place only if political parties fulfilled the conditions of internal democracy and maintenance and auditing of accounts and their submission to the EC (Law Commission of India, 1999: ch. 3). The commission felt that without these preconditions, state funding would become another source of funds for political parties and candidates at the cost of the public exchequer (Law Commission of India, 1999: ch. 3). It stood for total state funding eventually, but with the condition that the other sources of funding to political parties should stop (Law Commission of India, 1999: ch. 3).

The NCRWC, in its report (2002), felt that the proposals for reform of political funding should keep the following objectives in view: (*a*) diminishing the very impact of money (by shortening campaigns, establishing expenditure limits and putting curbs on individual contributions), (*b*) improving the use of money by spending on productive activities for the sake of democracy and not squandering it on propaganda and negative campaigns, (*c*) stopping, or at least limiting, the current levels of influence peddling and political corruption, (*d*) strengthening public disclosure and transparency mechanisms, including the source and the use of funds and (*e*) promoting fairer requirements for elections, particularly concerning access to the media (NCRWC, 2002b: book 1, consultation paper vi). It was of the view that state funding should not go ahead until regulatory mechanisms are firmly in place regarding the working of political parties and strict implementation of financial limits (NCRWC, 2002a: para. 4.14.5).

The Second Administrative Reforms Commission (2007) recommended partial state funding in line with the Indrajit Gupta Committee, mainly in-kind support for certain essential items (Second Administrative Reforms Commission, 2007: 12–13). A proposal of partial state funding by way of 'matching grants' has also been put forward (Kondepati, 2011: 73). Anyone contesting elections can provide 'receipts for a minimum sum of contributions from a certain number of donors [who] will be given a matching grant from the state, subject to verification of the genuineness of contributions' (Kondepati, 2011: 73). This grant would be treated as a loan 'until the expenditure receipts for the sum of contributions and grant are provided' (Kondepati, 2011: 73). However, the Law Commission, in its 255th report (2015), felt that complete state funding of elections or providing matching grants to political parties was not feasible given the economic conditions of the country.

It is felt by some that India's campaign finance laws seem to have created more problems than sorted them out. The then prime minister, Indira Gandhi, put a complete ban on corporate donations to political parties in 1969 (the ban was lifted in 1985) without introducing any other source of legitimate funding. While the government stopped corporate funding, it did not put in place state funding of elections or financial help to political parties to contest elections. This is seen as an elimination of 'the most important legal source of funds for elections', which 'effectively pushed campaign finance underground' and led to 'tapping black money' (Vaishnav, 2017: 96; Sridharan and Vaishnav, 2016; 70). Kickback practices grew by leaps and bounds often to finance elections (for the undulating history of campaign finance in India, see Sridharan and Vaishnav, 2016).

Party funding and election spending laws are seen by some as 'flawed' in the sense that they have led parties and political leaders 'to misuse the government's discretionary powers over resource allocation to raise funds for election campaigns and political parties' (Gowda and Sridharan, 2012: 226). M. V. Gowda and Sridharan argue that campaign finance laws in India have 'tended to have unintended, counterproductive, and perverse effects on the electoral system' (Gowda and Sridharan, 2012: 231). Costly elections and not enough legal sources of money to contest these elections have led parties to go for 'illicit sources of funds in the form of black money' (Gowda and Sridharan, 2012: 232) and 'self-financing candidates' (Vaishnav, 2017: 142). The re-legalisation of corporate donations to poltical parties in 1985 did not help much – the dependence on black money did not reduce (Gowda and Sridharan, 2012: 232).

Gowda and Sridharan suggest a look at successful initiatives in other countries to change corrupt fundraising and the lack of financial accountability (Gowda and Sridharan, 2012: 236–37). They favour 'public funding of parties in proportion to the amounts they raise openly from identified small-sum private donors' (Gowda and Sridharan, 2012: 239). This resembles the matching grant proposal mentioned earlier. They also suggest that 'public funding be conditional on parties' adherence to internal democracy, transparency and accountability; otherwise, the existing party leadership can be expected to deploy public funds for their discretionary use' (Gowda and Sridharan, 2012: 239) – suggestions which have come from former committees. Partly, as it is said, 'the solution lies with the political parties themselves to evolve the necessary mechanism to collect funds in a more transparent manner' (S. Jain, 2001: 510-11).

To put matters in perspective, the US presidential campaigns are partly public-funded. The eligible presidential candidates are supported by federal government funds to finance their campaigns. The presidential public-funding programme helps these candidates to meet the expenses of primaries and general elections (Federal Election Commission, n.d.) by giving them matching funds. The presidential candidate must establish that he or she is eligible to receive this fund by showing that he or she has broad-based support among the public. He or she has to show that he or she has received financial support from the public in at least 20 states. The Federal Election Commission lays down the detailed criteria for receiving government funds. Between 1976 and 2012, the programme also funded the presidential nominating conventions of major parties. In 2014 this financial support to conventions was revoked (Federal Election Commission, n.d.).

Canada follows a system of partial state funding for federal elections by way of reimbursement of costs to political parties. Parties that get 2 per cent of the national vote or, alternatively, 5 per cent of the vote in the districts in which they contested get back 50 per cent of the money they spent (Jansen, 2020 [2006]). Candidates who get at least 10 per cent of the vote receive 15 per cent of the election-expenses limit in their district. If the candidate has spent at least 30 per cent of the limit during the elections, he or she receives 60 per cent of the candidate's expenditure (Jansen, 2020 [2006]). Canada also has a system of tax credits for donations to political parties and candidates:

> The first $400 of donations receives a 75 per cent tax credit. An amount between $400 and $750 receives a 50 per cent credit. Amounts over $750 receive a 33 per cent credit. An individual's total tax credit in one year cannot exceed $650. (Jansen, 2020 [2006])

Countries like Australia, Germany, the UK and New Zealand, among others, follow partial state funding for elections through help lent to political parties in their administrative costs and/or campaigning. This specially helps towards levelling the electoral terrain and benefitting those parties that are not well-to-do.

This discussion showcases that institutional regulations and caps, though violated often by the political leadership, have induced a sense of restraint in financial conduct, which has drawn boundaries on the transactional dimension of elections. The election administration under the EC has put limits on spending and donations to bring about a more levelled competition floor. This has enhanced the sense of what ethical spending is and what is not among the electoral stakeholders even if expenditure limits are regularly transgressed.

9

Initiatives to Raise Voter Participation*

Amidst the talk of electoral reform, there were appeals made by civil society that the EC should make efforts to educate voters (Proceedings of the Seminar on Electoral Reforms, 1985: 28). It was suggested that this could be done in different ways like broadcasting educative programmes and advertisements, publishing pamphlets, and so on, so that people can vote without fear or favour (Proceedings of the Seminar on Electoral Reforms, 1985: 28). As mentioned in the previous chapters, the EC made efforts to both encourage voters to exercise their ballot and modernise election machinery by introducing provisions like EVMs, photo identity cards for voters, computerised electoral rolls, and so on, for the convenience of voters and prevention of malpractices.

The EC put in a lot of effort to increase voter turnout from the decade of the 2000s. Its promptness in implementing rules and regulations brought forth the accusation that it has killed the festival of democracy. About this accusation, former CEC S. Y. Quraishi feels that it is only now that the festival of democracy has ushered in because voter participation has gone up, violence during elections has considerably reduced, the EC has ensured peace, and voters, especially women, are coming out in larger numbers to vote.[1] It is said that elections in India are 'carnivalesque' and that this 'carnival' happens

* This chapter is derived in part from an article published in *Contemporary South Asia* on 7 June 2020, available online at https://doi.org/10.1080/09584935.2020.1775179. I am grateful to the journal and its editor for publishing the article and for granting permission to use parts of the article in this book.

[1] S. Y. Quraishi, personal interview with the author, Gurugram (Gurgaon), 23 January 2017.

in more or less an orderly manner under the supervision of the EC (Banerjee, 2014: 10). The EC over the last few elections has made huge efforts to make the electoral process more participatory. A couple of years before the general elections in 2014, it went into an overdrive to register new voters and persuade existing voters to renew their names on the electoral rolls. More than 800 million people were eligible to vote in the 2014 elections. In addition to the conventional ways of spreading voter awareness, the EC used the upcoming media technologies to reach out to voters. It used messaging apps and social media platforms to persuade them to register themselves with it.

Efforts to Raise Voting

Institutional efforts were made to extend the system of universal adult suffrage, which was put in place by the Constitution of India through Article 326. The voting age in elections was brought down from 21 years to 18 years[2] through the 61st constitutional amendment (1988), during the tenure of the then prime minister, Rajiv Gandhi. This came into effect from the 1989 elections onwards, when voting rights became a possibility for 50 million more people (Hazarika, 1988). Rajiv Gandhi, in his announcement of the reduction in voting age, called it a 'major step' (Gandhi's speech [1988] reproduced in Mukherjee, 2011: 349). He said:

> We have full faith in the youth of India. The youth of India have demonstrated their wisdom, their maturity in panchayat elections, local body elections, and we feel that they are now ready to participate fully in the democratic process. This amendment will bring in almost fifty million people into the electoral system. (Quoted in Mukherjee, 2011: 349–50)

It was felt by the parliament that the present-day youth were 'enlightened' and 'politically conscious', and bringing down the voting age would bring

---

[2] Proposals have been made to further reduce the voting age to 16 years. The debate in India resembles the one in a few other democracies that showcases the point that voting age should be lowered to reduce voter apathy, encourage the youth to engage with politics and bring electoral practices in tune with the shifting definitions of adulthood (see Mccue, 2018).

a large number of them into the political process. It was also believed that this measure would generate among the youth 'a sense of participation in the democratic process' (Bhandari, 1988: 115). The Parliamentary Joint Committee on amendments, appointed on 25 June 1971, in its second report, said, '[T]here are no valid reasons for denying the right to vote to persons above the age of 18 years, particularly when for all other purposes of law they are treated as majors and deemed competent to handle their affairs' (quoted in Bhandari, 1988: 122). In the words of former Lok Sabha member Era Sezhiyan of the Dravida Munnetra Kazhagam (DMK), 'As per the law of the land, a citizen becomes an adult at the age of 18 and there is no valid reason why he should wait for three more years to get the benefits of adult franchise' (quoted in Bhandari, 1988: 123). There were also some arguments made against proposals to lower the voting age (Bhandari, 1988: 116). First, it was felt that because of the substantial rise in the number of voters, election expenditure would go up. Second, because of the high rates of illiteracy, the 18-year-olds, it was argued, would not have the maturity to exercise voting rights. And, third, the age group of 18–21 years was deemed incapable of being trusted because of the indiscipline indulged in by the youth (as elaborated in Bhandari, 1988: 116). However, the parliament favoured lowering the voting age and gave its nod to reducing it to 18 years. In order to be eligible to vote, registering oneself with the EC is required; without registration, voting is not possible.

Voter apathy becomes a cause for concern often. Turnout numbers, however, are steadily rising in India as Tables 3.2 and 3.3 show. More rural voters turn up to vote than urban ones. Urban apathy to voting, according to former CEC Krishnamurthy, is due to a variety of reasons like deficiency in voter roll preparation, migration of voters without intimating election authorities, lack of confidence in political parties and leaders, poor civic consciousness, poor governance and violence (Murthy, 2008: 187). One indeed hears urban voters remark that 'politics is a corrupt affair', 'all political parties are corrupt', 'elections do not make a difference to politics which is a dirty terrain' and 'things will never improve in India' – these become pretexts for not voting.

The EC has been making efforts to bring people to the polling booths. In 2008, it wrote to the CEOs, emphasising its efforts to 'rationalise' the polling stations (EC, 2008). The effort was to bring polling stations closer to the people, even in small habitations, for their convenience and also to eliminate the scope of intimidation or force that prevented people from coming out to vote. The EC undertook efforts to provide each village with its own polling station if that village had more than 300 electors and had a suitable building for setting up a polling station. It clarified, however, that villages that have less than 300 electors but already have a functioning polling station would not be deprived of it. It also said that new polling stations might be needed because of the delimitation exercise and should be set up (EC, 2008).

The EC launched a special initiative called Systematic Voter's Education and Electoral Participation (SVEEP) in 2009 to enthuse voters to come out and vote. The SVEEP webpage describes it as 'a programme of multi-interventions through different modes and media designed to educate citizens, electors and voters about the electoral process' (see EC, n.d.10). This initiative aimed at increasing awareness and participation of voters in elections. The webpage also highlights the specific features of SVEEP, saying that it is 'designed according to the socio-economic, cultural and demographic profile of the state as well as history of electoral participation in previous rounds of elections and learning thereof' (EC, n.d.10). The initiative had an underlying concern that low participation in elections would affect the quality of democracy (EC, n.d.10). SVEEP's first election was for the Bihar assembly in 2010. After that it was extended to assembly elections in Tamil Nadu, Kerala, Assam, West Bengal and the UT of Puducherry in 2011.

It was observed by the EC that women and younger voters constituted a major proportion of the non-voting or low-voting sections (Press Information Bureau [PIB], 2014). It therefore took steps to encourage them to vote. For instance, it directed the electoral officials to conduct special programmes as part of SVEEP activities for motivating women to vote in the Madhya Pradesh assembly elections in 2013 (Sirothia, 2013). In some districts in the state, the difference between men and women voters was more than 10 percentage points (Sirothia, 2013). Assistance of *anganwadi* (childcare centres in rural India first set up by the Indian government in 1975 to combat child malnutrition and growth problems) workers and the Department of Women and Child Development was taken to spread messages about the importance of voting. (Sirothia, 2013). The EC also appointed 'campus ambassadors' in 1,300 colleges in Madhya Pradesh to enthuse college-goers to vote in the 2013 assembly elections (Sirothia, 2013). The EC as a part of the SVEEP scheme made efforts to disseminate information, motivate voters and simplify the voter registration process (PIB, 2014). It brought in eminent personalities and celebrities like former president A. P. J. Abdul Kalam, badminton champion Saina Nehwal, cricketer M. S. Dhoni, actor Aamir Khan, boxer Mary Kom, and so on, to spread awareness about elections and motivate people to come to the polling booths (Sirothia, 2013). Money was allocated to carry out SVEEP activities (INR 1 lakh [0.1 million] per district) like hoardings to educate people on voting, mass-media programmes, street plays, and so on (Chinnappa, 2014).

The efforts of the EC to raise voter participation among younger voters, women and areas were because turnouts are low (Nambiar, 2014; PTI, 2014a; *Indian Express*, 2014; *Indian Express*, 2016; Waghmode, 2017) yielded a good response. An EC official in Delhi during the enrolment drive for women said that as many as 6,000 women applied for enrolment as electors of Delhi, and a signature campaign was held at Maitreyi College, University Of Delhi, where girls took a pledge to vote (PTI, 2014a). Such enrolment drives are regularly held in colleges. The EC held a special voter registration camp in Delhi before the 16th general elections for the residents of the city who hail from the north-eastern states. Many turned up during this occasion to enrol themselves as Delhi voters because, as one of them, said, 'When you vote, you matter' (*Indian Express*, 2014).

It was officially acknowledged that a gap exists between what the voters 'should know' and what they 'actually know' on issues of voter registration, EPIC (or identity proofs), the location of polling booths, the use of EVMs, the timings of polls, the provisions of the MCC and the use of money, muscle and liquor power by candidates or their associates to influence vulnerable sections of the electorate (PIB, 2014). It was observed that informed and aware voters did not always cast their vote (PIB, 2014). SVEEP was launched to take care of these issues. In the words of a returning officer in Karnataka, who worked towards motivating younger voters to vote, the SVEEP activities aimed at 'achieving cent per cent polling' (D. K. Ravi quoted in Kundapura, 2014).

A pledge for voters was also formulated by the EC as part of the SVEEP initiative, which read:

> We, the citizens of India, having abiding faith in democracy, hereby pledge to uphold the democratic traditions of our country and the dignity of free, fair and peaceful elections, and to vote in every election fearlessly and without being influenced by considerations of religion, race, caste, community, language or any inducement. (PIB, 2014)

Official sources attributed higher voter turnouts in subsequent elections to SVEEP. It was said, 'Being a landmark initiative by ECI, SVEEP has stimulated every aspect of election processes to ensure enhanced voters' participation in the polling' (PIB, 2014). It was claimed that during 'the last three years [2011–14], voter registration, especially among youth, has gone up from 10–15 percent to 30–35 percent and almost all the state assembly elections held since 2010, recorded high voter turnout with greater participation from youth and women' (PIB, 2014).

The EC continued its drive to raise voter turnouts. In 2019 it proposed to the government to extend postal voting to citizens above 80 years, those engaged in essential services and those with disabilities. The government accepted the recommendation and amended the Conduct of Election Rules, 1961, accordingly. Postal voting till 2019 had existed for members of the armed forces and their spouses, paramilitary forces, government personnel working abroad and those who are in preventive detention. Demand for postal voting for overseas Indians has been growing. The EC in 2021 recommended the facility of postal voting for overseas Indians – a proposal yet to be cleared by the government.

One must note here that there are a few sections in India who are not eligible to vote. For instance, according to Section 62(5) of the RPA, 1951, a person cannot vote while serving a prison sentence and is in the lawful custody of the police. In 2014 the EC made it clear that both convicts and undertrials are not eligible to vote in elections (EC, 2014e: 166). However, persons under preventive detention can vote through postal ballots (EC, 2014e: 166). An opinion exists that prisoners should have voting rights since they are as much citizens of the country as anybody else (R. Chopra, 2016). Human rights activists have also argued that this is a blanket debarment that does not differentiate between the seriousness of the crime or the quantum of punishment awarded (R. Chopra, 2016). For instance, undertrial prisoners are not proven convicts, and it happens that they spend years in jail without their crime being proved. The EC received representations on this count. It decided to look into these and in consideration appointed a panel in April 2016 (EC, 2014e: 166). According to Jagdeep Chhokar of the ADR, '[U]ndertrials should be allowed to vote. This is because there are many people, awaiting trial, who have spent more time in prison than the actual term their alleged crime merits. Their numbers are much bigger than convicts' (EC, 2014e: 166). He adds, 'As for convicts, I am not entirely convinced that each one of them should be disenfranchised' (EC, 2014e: 166). According to him, there are different kinds of punishments – corrective, repudiative, exemplary – and this issue needs to be further debated (EC, 2014e: 166).

Rise in voter participation can be attributed to procedural changes like the simplification of registration procedures, increasing accessibility of the registration centres, lowering of voting age, awareness drives and motivational programmes, among others. Voting percentages are also said to rise because of political factors like anti-incumbency, economic dissatisfaction, social unrest, and so on. However, it was felt by the government as well as the EC that the increase in voting percentages, after SVEEP was introduced in 2009, was because of the SVEEP initiatives (PIB, 2014; the then CEC, Nasim Zaidi, interviewed by R. Rao, 2015). Table 9.1 was projected by the government to indicate this.

Sanjay Kumar of the Centre for the Study of Developing Societies (CSDS), an institution which analyses elections and politics in India, says, 'The Election Commission of India is putting in considerable effort to motivate the youth to vote, and these initiatives have shown a degree of success, especially in the urban centres' (S. Kumar, 2014). According to former CEC Nasim Zaidi, the SVEEP project has over the years given creditable gains in a relatively short period of time (*The Hindu*, 2016). He highlights:

In the areas of enrolment, turnout, women's voting and youth participation, the achievements have been praiseworthy. However, the jewel in the crown was the 66.4 per cent voter turnout in an electorate of 834 million in the national elections held in 2014, which is the highest voter participation in the last six decades. Most significantly, women's participation was at a record high of 65.6 per cent. (*The Hindu*, 2016)

During the tenure of Zaidi, the EC stressed the importance of continuous communication between itself and the voters.[3] Accessibility of election personnel, particularly during the election period, at the grassroots level was a significant element of the communication strategy and redressal of voters' grievances. An online system of registering grievances and their real-time tracking was introduced during his tenure, including other options such as call centres with a universal telephone number, which was 1950.[4]

---

[3] Nasim Zaidi, telephonic interview with the author, 4 August 2020.
[4] Nasim Zaidi, telephonic interview with the author, 4 August 2020.

Table 9.1 Comparison of polling percentages of the state assembly elections held since 2009 with the one before

S. No.	State	Year of election	Polling percentage		
			Male	Female	Total
1	Assam	2006	76.49	74.89	75.77
		2011	76.85	74.94	75.92
2	Bihar	2005	–	–	45.85
		2010	51.12	54.49	52.67
3	Goa	2007	69.70	70.30	70.51
		2012	78.86	84.57	81.73
4	Gujarat	2007	62.31	57.02	59.77
		2012	72.94	69.50	71.30
5	Himachal Pradesh	2007	68.36	74.01	71.61
		2012	69.39	76.20	72.69
6	Jharkhand	2004	–	–	57.03
		2009	59.13	54.53	56.96
7	Karnataka	2008	66.20	63.10	64.68
		2013	71.84	70.1	71.00
8	Kerala	2006	73.17	71.08	72.38
		2011	75.08	74.78	74.92
9	Manipur	2007	85.88	86.82	86.73
		2012	76.94	81.36	79.19
10	Meghalaya	2008	88.62	89.36	88.99
		2013	85.17	88.44	86.82
11	Nagaland	2008	85.99	86.39	86.19
		2013	89.09	91.33	90.19
12	Punjab	2007	75.36	75.47	75.45
		2012	77.58	78.90	78.20
13	Pondicherry	2006	84.48	86.29	86.00
		2011	83.97	86.97	85.52
14	Tamil Nadu	2006	72.41	68.75	70.82
		2011	77.53	78.51	78.01
15	Tripura	2008	90.74	91.72	91.22
		2013	90.73	92.94	91.82

(*Contd*)

Table 9.1   (*Contd*)

S. No.	State	Year of election	Polling percentage Male	Female	Total
16	Uttar Pradesh	2007	49.35	41.92	45.96
		2012	58.68	60.28	59.40
17	Uttarakhand	2007	58.95	59.45	59.45
		2012	64.41	68.12	66.17
18	West Bengal	2006	82.34	80.75	81.97
		2011	84.22	84.45	84.33
19	Rajasthan	2008	67.10	65.31	66.25
		2013	74.92	75.52	75.20
20	Chhattisgarh	2008	71.80	69.20	70.51
		2013	77.37	77.21	77.32
21	Delhi	2008	58.34	56.62	57.58
		2013	65.98	65.13	65.60
22	Madhya Pradesh	2008	72.30	65.91	69.28
		2013	73.95	70.11	72.66
23	Mizoram	2008	78.77	81.24	80.02
		2013	80.3	82.2	81.2

Source: PIB (2014).

A document published by the EC titled 'Experiences and Lessons Learnt from the Poll Gone States 2016' is informative regarding various electoral matters (EC, 2017b). It brings together the experiences of the CEOs of the states and UTs that went to polls in 2016 (Assam, West Bengal, Tamil Nadu, Kerala and Puducherry) and those that were going to polls in 2017 (Goa, Gujarat, Punjab, Uttarakhand, Uttar Pradesh, Manipur and Himachal Pradesh). From the experiences of poll officers in the aforementioned states and UTs, the document lists out the 'learnings' regarding SVEEP. These learnings are that SVEEP should be based on objective base-line surveys (like done in Kerala) which identify 'gaps' in voting in various assembly constituencies, such as problems in registering as voters, gender gaps, lower turnout in some constituencies, apathy among young or urban voters, problems faced by people with disabilities, and so on (EC, 2017b: 13–15). The learnings also emphasised that campaigns should focus on low cost and high visibility; out-of-the-box ideas should be used like printing messages on shopping bags, milk packets, ATM screens and development of SVEEP merchandise like wrist bands, friendship bands, T-shirts, and so on (EC, 2017b: 13–15). It was felt that to implement SVEEP, decentralisation works best – districts should be given scope to choose their icons, strategies, and so on, and citizens should be involved in the election process right from the beginning of the election process (EC, 2017b: 13–15). The learnings also highlighted that there should be an extensive use of social media to cover the SVEEP events (EC, 2017b: 14).

Compulsory Voting?

A discussion about voter turnouts necessitates a mention about compulsory voting. It is one of the ways of raising voting in a legalistic or statist way. The logic of compulsory voting is based upon the understanding that voting is a civic duty rather than an individual right – that as a citizen an individual has a responsibility towards a democratic and participatory government. Upholders of compulsory voting argue that it not only raises voter turnout, which is important in a democracy, but also 'strengthens the public commitment to democratic norms', 'increases at least the descriptive legitimacy of a political system' and is 'associated with a higher reported satisfaction with democracy' (see Chapman, 2019: 105). It also neutralises the 'cycle of disengagement in marginalized communities' (Chapman, 2019: 104); marginalised communities can vote without the threat of violence. Compulsory voting is thus associated with more public involvement, solid majorities, mitigation of intimidation and civic responsibility, as argued by its upholders. If democracy is 'people's rule', then it makes sense that citizens see casting their vote as a duty towards strengthening democracy. A PIL was filed in 2014, seeking compulsory voting in India, where the petitioner argued that different governments in India do not fairly represent the people as only 55–66 per cent of the people exercise their franchise (*The Telegraph*, 2017), and thus the governments are not actually democratic governments. Compulsory voting, as it involves everyone, it is argued, will make democracy a 'true' democracy.

Arguments have also been made against compulsory voting. Those arguing thus claim that compulsory voting is a form of compulsion and places undue constraints on individual rights. Voting should be a right and not a compulsion in a democracy. It is argued that the legal compulsions to vote may lead to 'harassment of the citizens' (Agarwal, 2002: 85). To escape harassment from criminal elements and legal battles, voters 'may be forced to vote for those who threaten to harm them'. Such elected persons 'could hardly qualify to be true representatives of the voters' (Agarwal, 2002: 85). In any case, the act of not voting also implies a political choice. It might be based on a feeling of satisfaction with the incumbent government or a complete disillusionment with the electoral exercise or apathy towards the political process. Compulsion to vote might lead to an increase in invalid votes or meaningless or random votes. Logistical issues also confront the enforcement of compulsory voting, especially those to do with state capacities to monitor and impose penalties. The EC already is overstretched with handling franchise for over a 900-million strong electorate. It will have to expand its capacities enormously to handle compulsory voting. The Law Commission of India, in its report of 2015, found the idea impractical. The International Institute for Democracy and Electoral Assistance (International IDEA), Stockholm, raises some of these issues: How strongly is the compulsory voting law enforced, if enforced at all? What are the penalties for not voting? Can a country be seen as following compulsory voting if there are no penalties for not voting? What if the penalty is negligible or only in name (International IDEA, n.d.)?

The idea of compulsory voting in India has found few takers. It is seen as an idea 'whose time has not come' (Jayaram, 2017), besides being viewed as a task overburdening the EC which already has too much on its plate while it is grappling with criminality and scams (Jayaram, 2017). It is also said that there is 'a real fear that compulsory voting may lead to more vote buying by candidates especially in a country like India, where we have seen instances of – cash-for-vote scams – [sic] where legislators were bought over by money power' (*Hindustan Times*, 2017). It might also lead to 'donkey voting', an Australian experience, where voters, when compelled to vote, voted for the candidate whose name topped the list (*Hindustan Times*, 2017). Another strong plausible reason for not going with this idea is that voter turnouts are rising in India (as compared to industrial democracies where voter turnouts are falling), which makes compulsory voting not very persuasive.

For the first time in India, a step towards compulsory voting was taken by the state of Gujarat in 2015. The Bill to make voting compulsory in local body elections was introduced in 2009 when Narendra Modi was the chief minister of Gujarat. The Bill was earlier passed twice with a majority vote by the Gujarat government, but it faced stiff resistance from former governor Kamla Beniwal in 2010 and 2011 (*Indian Express*, 2015). She stated that forcing people to vote violates Article 21 of the Constitution – it is against the 'principles of individual liberty' (*Indian Express*, 2015). The state decided to make voting compulsory in local body elections in 2014 after the incumbent governor, O. P. Kohli, signed the Bill. Rules were framed for the same by the state government in 2015, and the law empowered the State Election Commission to declare an absentee voter a 'defaulter' except in the case of illness or being out of station (Langa, 2015). An amount of INR 100 was specified in the law as fine to be paid by those who did not vote. However, the law could not be implemented. A PIL was filed against the law in the Gujarat High Court. The petitioner contended, 'The right to vote cannot be termed as the duty by the state and therefore the provision of Compulsory Voting Act is violative of fundamental rights given to any citizen under the Indian Constitution' (quoted in Rajya Sabha TV, 2015). The petitioner also argued that the state legislature is not empowered to enact a law regarding voting as it comes under the purview of the Constitution, and any such law can only be amended or enacted by the parliament (Rajya Sabha TV, 2015). The Gujarat High Court stayed its implementation (Rajya Sabha TV, 2015), saying that the 'right to vote' itself provided the right to refrain from voting. It instructed the state government and the State Election Commission not to implement the law (see Lok Sabha Secretariat, 2015).

Electoral Rolls

The EC has been tasked with the responsibility of preparing electoral rolls for elections to the parliament and state legislatures, through Article 324(1) of the Constitution. The EC's job of registering new voters or revising and updating the electoral rolls is a major responsibility. It is a perpetual task – revisions have to be done continuously to include those who have attained the age of 18 years and also new residents, and to erase the names of those who have died or no longer reside in a constituency. Intensive revisions are done every five years, and summary revisions every year. Summary revisions are considered more important as they update the rolls annually. According to historian Ornit Shani, the preparation of the electoral roll to operationalise universal franchise for the first general elections was a 'bold operation', a 'staggering bureaucratic undertaking' not only because of the number of the people who had to be enrolled but also because this led to an 'institutionalisation of procedural equality' (Shani, 2018: 4–5). The enormity of the task at that time can be gauged from Ramachandra Guha's words, 'Each one [of the 176 million Indians aged 21 or more] had to be identified, named and registered' (Guha, 2008: 133). The vastness, diversity and numbers made it a colossal exercise. Preparation of electoral rolls looks like a smooth and straightforward task, but it is a process which has numerous challenges.

Large-scale anomalies in electoral rolls come to light during almost all elections. While there have been several cases of genuine voters being left out, non-existing names and those that are ineligible find their way into the electoral rolls.[5] Problems like forging of signatures of applicants, filling of false content and non-visits of enumerators in areas from where complaints of non-enrolment or deletions are received also come up (V. Venkatesan, 2002c). The biggest anomaly is missing or deleted names. Objections have arisen from time to time about the authenticity of the electoral rolls. Political parties have often highlighted the irregularities in the rolls. Allegations of names being struck off the electoral rolls were raised during elections in West Bengal in 2006 (CPI[M], 2006: 4). About these deletions, the CPI(M) said, 'Our experience has been that to a large extent such deletions were carried out at the behest of the observers through oral instructions on the unsubstantiated complaints of political rivals' (CPI[M], 2006: 4). Complaints of missing names display the enthusiasm for voting. During election days, disappointment and anger are often seen among voters who find their names missing from the voters' list. The increasing number of complaints received by polling authorities reveal the keenness to participate in the 'carnival' of democracy.

A customary deletion of names from the electoral rolls is part of the process of updating them. Names of voters who have moved out of the constituency precincts or died have to be removed. However, such deletions, as far as possible, should be put up in the public domain. Political parties and civil society groups should be informed of such deletions so that corrections can be carried out within reasonable time – that is, before the electoral roll is published – and eligible voters do not lose the opportunity to vote. Several instances have been reported where eligible voters have found their names missing from the electoral rolls when they visited the polling stations – for instance, in Salem (*The Hindu*, 2008), Patna (Raj, 2010) and Bengaluru (*The Hindu*, 2013a), among others. Unless complaints are filed, corrections

---

[5] A well-known case was that of forest brigand and smuggler Veerappan, whose name found its way in the electoral roll of Tamil Nadu in 1999 (Krishnaswamy, 2001).

are hard to carry out. In Mumbai, in one instance, the number of deleted names was 1,200,000 (the EC could not trace these people), while in the state of Maharashtra the number of deletions crossed 2,900,000 in 2015 (Rahman, 2015).[6] The EC handed the draft list to all corporators, political parties and members present in the Brihanmumbai Municipal Corporation's (BMC) general body meeting (Rahman, 2015) so that they could help in contacting those whose names were missing from the draft list. There were many instances of large-scale deletions or faulty entries due to delimitation. Families in Delhi found their names, gender and photographs jumbled up after delimitation, leading to problems in exercising their franchise (*Times of India*, 2008).

It was also reported that the number of Muslim voters has been declining over the years because they are finding their names missing from the electoral rolls with every passing election. A study found that the exclusion of Muslim voters was disproportionately high and substantially higher than others in Karnataka (Shariff and Saifullah, 2018). According to Abusaleh Shariff, of the US–India Policy Institute, Washington, and the former member secretary (2004–06) of the then prime minister's (Manmohan Singh's) high-level committee for the preparation of a report on the social, economic and educational status of the Muslim community, while members of other communities also find their names missing, the corresponding number for Muslims is higher – 15 per cent for other communities and 25 per cent for Muslims. This 'threatens to make a mockery of our democracy' (Salam, 2019).

Duplication is another common error. Duplication of names, same EPIC numbers for different voters, same house address for different voters and same records for different voters are some common anomalies in the electoral rolls.[7] P. G. Bhat, a resident of Bengaluru, who has closely looked at the problems in electoral rolls, pointed out that there might be different reasons for anomalies in the electoral rolls in different constituencies, which

---

[6] The electoral authorities claimed that booth-level officers were sent to the addresses of the missing voters to trace them and *panchnama*s were pasted on some doors. When no contact was made for over two months, due process was followed to remove these names (Rahman, 2015).

[7] Ordinary citizens like P. G. Bhat (a resident of Bengaluru) have come forward to help reduce the errors through developing software that takes care of the problem (see T. Singh, 2015).

might range from arrogance of the enumeration authorities to act timely on applications and apathy of citizens to get their names included.[8] He also pointed out that more than any other state, in Kerala and West Bengal where the political atmosphere is charged and active, voters enthusiastically come forward to make sure that their names are present in the electoral rolls.[9] He said that the delimitation exercise while leaving out lakhs of names from particular constituencies did not see the transfer of these names to the newly carved ones – names were easily dropped by the enumeration authorities, but efforts were lacking to include these names in the lists where they belong. There were several other errors. This led to large-scale disenfranchisement.[10] According to Bhat, summary revisions are more important than intensive revisions as it is easy to clean up and update rather than start the work of making the rolls all over again.[11] Such discrepancies in the electoral rolls have been highlighted by political parties, media and voters themselves. This has made the electoral authorities take note of the problem and publicly acknowledge the complicated nature of the task and the need for remedies.

In 2015 an election based on an error-free electoral roll was seen as one of the major challenges before the EC, according to the then CEC, Zaidi (R. Rao, 2015). According to Zaidi, 'Even today there are errors, mismatches, multiple entries and other discrepancies in the electoral rolls' (R. Rao, 2015). He continued, 'Also enrolment of all the eligible electors is equally major task' (R. Rao, 2015). Rajarshi Bhattacharya, a former DEC, echoed that updating of electoral rolls is a major area of work.[12] According to him, the inclusion of new names and removal of non-existing ones in the voters' list is a challenging task.[13]

The EC has made efforts to bring about error-free electoral rolls. It launched a scheme called the National Electoral Roll Purification and Authentication Programme (NERPAP) on 3 March 2015, with the purpose of creating an error-free electoral roll. The programme culminated on 15 August 2015. Through this programme the EPIC data of electors were linked

---

[8] P. G. Bhat, telephonic interview with the author, 22 September 2017.

[9] P. G. Bhat, telephonic interview with the author, 22 September 2017.

[10] P. G. Bhat, telephonic interview with the author, 22 September 2017.

[11] P. G. Bhat, telephonic interview with the author, 22 September 2017.

[12] Rajarshi Bhattacharya, personal interview with the author, New Delhi, 5 August 2017.

[13] Rajarshi Bhattacharya, personal interview with the author, New Delhi, 5 August 2017.

to Aadhaar[14] data. This mechanisation drive focused on improving the quality of electors' photos along with sorting issues like incorporating corrections of errors, and so on. Electors were provided the facility to put in their respective Aadhaar numbers through SMS, email, mobile application and the National Voters Service Portal (NVSP) using web services through the EC website (PIB, 2015). However, problems persist.

D. Anandan, the district collector-cum-magistrate (at the time of writing), East Sikkim, Gangtok, listed out the challenges in the management of an electoral roll. The first challenge is the sheer magnitude of the electoral population – maintaining this database is a herculean task. This enumeration has to be done at least once a year, which means a lot of work. In contrast, he points out, the census enumeration is done once every 10 years – indicating the massiveness of the task of election officials. The delimitation exercise (2002) made the task tougher because it meant that the entire electoral roll had to be recalibrated. The second challenge is the remoteness of certain areas, which makes it difficult for enumerators to add, check and verify voters' names living in these hard-to-access areas. The third challenge is a lack of awareness as well as illiteracy among voters about registration procedures, which makes it difficult for them to complete forms, procedures, and so on. Fourth, there is a lack of motivation, enthusiasm and training among field functionaries of the EC. The fifth challenge is the repeated revisions of rolls, which acts as a further dampener for field officials. Sixth, there is an indifference among political parties and voters, with the former become active only during elections and accusing the electoral machinery of bias and partiality, especially when they see that the names of their likely supporters are missing from the rolls during a particular election. The seventh challenge is the lack of technological equipment and know-how, especially in remote areas. Breakdown of computers and other similar problems cause delays and incompleteness of work. Finally, Anandan says, the very dynamic nature of the rolls throws up a challenge. Rolls keep changing every day. The entries which are there today may not be correct tomorrow. Repeated revisions have to be undertaken to keep the roll up to date. Anandan highlights that the inclusion of names in the electoral rolls can be done only through an application by a voter himself or herself and is not a *suo moto* activity taken

---

[14] The Aadhaar system, which was introduced in India in 2009, is a unique identification system, whereby each citizen is given a unique number for identification purposes as well as to avail benefits of official schemes.

up by the registration authorities. This implies that unless the voters take a proactive interest in revising their details, the errors would not be erased. However, in case of voters who have died, it is the responsibility of the authorities to revise the roll themselves.

The document 'Experiences and Lessons Learnt from the Poll Gone States 2016' also discusses how the EC has attempted to improvise its work on the preparation of electoral rolls. From the experiences of poll officers in various states, the document listed out the 'learnings' regarding electoral rolls that can guide subsequent steps on improving them. These learnings include: (*a*) summary revisions should be carried out as per the schedule, and the final roll should be published latest by mid-January of the election year; (*b*) corrections should be carried out during the summary revision period much before the announcement of elections; (*c*) more clarity is needed on the ways in which *suo moto* deletions can be carried out in an election year by the electoral registration officer (ERO), because if the EROs remove names through the *suo moto* route they are accused of bias, and if they do not take any action they are accused of ignoring the problem; (*d*) proper management of work is needed through breaking of the summary revision work into manageable tasks with clear timelines and monitoring of work of block-level officers (BLOs); (*e*) voter awareness camps in corporate houses and companies should be conducted to motivate employees to vote; (*f*) mobile enrolment vans should be used but within fixed areas and with fixed time schedules; and (*g*) facilities should be arranged to send EPICs through Speed Post (EC, 2017b: 1–3).

Updating of Rolls

Updating of rolls continues till the last date of nomination in an election. This task involves a number of government personnel, including schoolteachers, who have to take leave from their regular work and take up the task of updating the rolls.[15] The intensive revision work is strenuous as it involves moving door to door and revising the rolls. Computerisation, however, has brought about some ease to the largely manual efforts of updating the

---

[15] There have been concerns that engaging schoolteachers in enumeration work leads to neglect of their professional responsibilities, such as their teaching responsibilities, which in turn negatively affects their students.

rolls and including all eligible voters. As P. G. Bhat observed, 'The use of technology has certainly helped in improving electoral rolls.'[16] According to him, 'It is a simple system (software) but handled non-professionally. With some attention to quality, the software and process can be improved, and human efforts reduced further.'[17] It is impossible to have an error-free electoral roll. The aim should be to minimise errors. After the roll is updated, it has to be published to be effective in an election. The rolls have to be published by the CEOs of the various states on their websites – a non-published roll cannot be used. Only after it is published can objections in the form of appeals be made to the CEO of the state against inclusion or exclusion of names in the rolls.

In India separate electoral rolls are prepared for Lok Sabha and state assembly elections on the one hand and the municipal and *panchayat* elections on the other. For the former it is the EC which prepares and revises electoral rolls, and for the latter it is the State Election Commissions. The latter's powers are delineated in Articles 243K and 243ZA of the Constitution. The making of two separate rolls has its own complications. These parallel enumeration exercises not only create confusion through duplication of names but also lead to wastage of resources and efforts. Besides, they give rise to electoral malpractices. Various committees and the EC have suggested a common electoral roll to tide over these problems. The NCRWC emphasised that there should be 'no duplication of effort and a single exercise should be enough' to prepare the electoral rolls (NCRWC, 2002a: para. 4.8.3, Electoral Rolls and Voter ID). It said that the 'task could be handled by the EC or by the SECs or by the two in coordination' (NCRWC, 2001: para. 4.7.5, Electoral Rolls and Voter ID). Its report further states:

> [A]t the level of gram panchayat (or the relevant local level), a voter must have his/her name properly placed on the electoral roll. This would automatically identify the voter to be a part of the electoral roll of the assembly constituency, which contains this particular panchayat. Likewise, the voter would be automatically identified on the electoral roll of a particular Lok Sabha constituency, in which both his assembly constituency and panchayat are included. (NCRWC, 2001: para. 4.7.5, Electoral Rolls and Voter ID)

---

[16] P.G. Bhat, email conversation with the author, 29 August 2017.
[17] P.G. Bhat, email conversation with the author, 29 August 2017.

In its reform proposals in 2004 and in its letter to the then prime minister, Atal Bihari, Vajpayee, on 22 November 1999, the EC also suggested a common electoral roll 'on the grounds of national interest in saving time, effort, and expenditure; reducing duplication of work and confusion amongst voters; and the fact that it would not pose any problems to the electoral machinery in the field as it is the same at the ground level' (see Law Commission of India, 2015: 213). The Law Commission, in its report, fully endorsed the suggestions of the EC regarding the introduction of common electoral rolls for parliamentary, assembly and local body elections (Law Commission of India, 2015: 214). It further said that since 'introducing common electoral rolls will require an amendment in the State laws pertaining to the conduct of local body elections, the Central Government should write to the various States in this regard' (Law Commission of India, 2015). According to Inderjit Khanna, '[T]he unanimous view is that there should be a common electoral roll for elections to the Lok Sabha, legislative assemblies and local bodies' (I. Khanna, 2008). Khanna adds, 'Besides being a logical requirement since the voter is the same, the common electoral roll will result in considerable savings and avoid disruption of normal work since government staff has to be withdrawn from their normal duties. A common electoral roll will also curb some of the electoral malpractices' (I. Khanna, 2008).

The ADR and the NEW, in their recommendations on electoral reforms to the Ministry of Law and Justice and the EC, made similar points. They stated that the use of different electoral rolls is 'a totally unacceptable practice' (ADR and NEW, 2011: 25). According to them, 'It results in unnecessary duplication, extra expenditure, and tremendous confusion in the minds of the voters at the time of polling' (ADR and NEW, 2011: 25). They highlighted that the NCRWC had also recommended a common electoral roll in its report (ADR and NEW, 2011: 25). They also felt that in today's times of advanced information technology, the EC can 'make suitable arrangements for every citizen to be able to (a) register her/his vote at any place of his choosing and any time of the year, and (b) be able to cast one's voter wherever one happens to be on the date of polling' (ADR and NEW, 2011: 24). They also suggested that whether this is 'done by using Post Offices as agencies for preparation and maintenance of electoral rolls (as suggested by the Goswami Committee in 1990), or through an automated online database to be created by the Election Commission or through an outside agency under the supervision of the Election Commission (as recommended by the NCRWC in 2001) should be left to the best judgment of the Election Commission' (ADR and NEW,

2011: 24). If accepted, this suggestion can save time and resources that can be used to incentivise voting.

In August 2018, the EC held a meeting with all the recognised national and state parties where they gave suggestions on various aspects of the elections (EC, 2018b). They asked the EC to share with them the copies of the list of deleted names from the electoral rolls. They also suggested that the office of the BLOs should be strengthened for work on the electoral rolls. Some parties came up with the suggestion that festival seasons should be avoided for updating the rolls as people move about during holidays (EC, 2018b). They also asked the EC to link the Aadhaar number of voters with their electoral details for better management of electoral rolls (EC, 2018b). These suggestions from the stakeholders have helped in the task of preparation and updating of electoral rolls.

Education and encouragement by the EC have led voters to see voting as a serious matter. The EC has worked towards extending franchise and raising consciousness about the value of a vote. 'Vote consciousness' in the electorate has grown over the years, especially from the early 2000s. Efforts by the EC to update electoral rolls in an error-free way have also gone on. Considering the enormity of the exercise, errors still creep in. Political parties, civil society organisations and the media have contributed to raising voter consciousness, but the credit for it in a substantial measure goes also to the EC.

10

Conclusion

State institutions are products of history and social contexts and have a layered character that defines their overall nature. Their position within power structures and entrenched hierarchies need to be accounted for in their biographical sketches for a better understanding of their nature and practices. However, as this book argues, the embeddedness of state or formal institutions does not take away from them their agency which influences politics and marks the boundaries of permissible conduct. They are hardly, as is sometimes assumed, mute and passive spectators of political currents and counter-currents. On the contrary, they are agents of changes themselves and embody operative procedures that structure behaviour and stabilise democratic functioning. Through their pursuits and actions, they shape political histories over the long term. Institutionalised pathways are compendium of standardised procedures and coherent rules that sculpt political acts. This operationalisation is repeated from case to case to follow a path-dependent course that is marked by its predictiveness.

Theoretically, the work of institutional structures in any collective endeavour is to make it functional, orderly and goal-oriented. In a democratic system, the multiplicity of demands and interests have the potential of derailing or complicating decision-making. This necessitates a smooth regulatory institutional structure to channel demands into effective and fulfilling outcomes. Institutional structures are expected to work on principles of rationality and be just and equal to all citizens. Modern political systems, where multiple functions need to be fulfilled, possess differentiated structures. Each function of a modern polity, whether of legislation, implementation or adjudication, is performed by a separate institution with its own responsibilities and modes. This is needed to avoid excessive centralisation and to bring in the required expertise and skill for each task at hand. It goes without saying that collective activity often involves tensions, clashes, confusions, disorder and delays. Institutions, signifying procedures and regulations, smoothen out these tensions and remove stumbling blocks to timely and democratic outcomes. These outcomes, whether to do with economic development, affordable healthcare, inexpensive housing, cleaner environment, mainstreaming gender in policy or conducting free and fair elections, provide the mainstay of an effective political order. Powers are divided between institutions that balance each other in performing tasks and taking decisions. Mutual checks and restrictions prevent them from crossing boundaries of permissible behaviour and encroaching on prohibited institutional territory. This differentiated and specialised mode of functioning while leading to a deliberative decision-making also checks authoritarian tendencies in a government.

In the case of India, institutions evolved as an embodiment of the project of post-colonial modernisation. They emerged in a colonial setting and subsequently went through modern rejuvenation and innovations. The Constitution of free India divided responsibilities between different institutions and entrusted the work of multiparty elections to the EC. The EC began its work from the first general elections held in 1951–52 and over the years evolved into a robust regulatory mechanism to carry out the mammoth responsibility of conducting elections in a federated set up. It was structured in a way such that it would function within the purview of the parliament but remain above party politics and social contestations. The parliament shaped the EC's functioning, which both expanded and restricted the scope of its powers. The EC's position was also strengthened by the Supreme Court from time to time. The Supreme Court judgments affirmed the EC's status as the final voice in taking decisions on electoral matters and disputes. The apex court acknowledged the EC's views as carrying substance. This moulded the EC as a regulatory institution, and it worked on its tasks as a distinct entity but integrated with other state institutions. It improved the procedures of holding regular, free and fair elections and sculpted electoral behaviour among contestants and voters. Its regular recommendations to the government, the parliament and the judiciary proved indispensable for keeping elections a regulated and smooth competition within the logic of participatory democracy.

The EC was (and is) also helped in its task of conducting elections smoothly by the administrative institutions. It sought help from income tax agencies and police forces to minimise the use of money and muscle power. They coordinated their work and took recourse to technology to minimise glitches and wrongdoing in elections. The use of EVMs and videography helped in bringing down financial and force-driven malpractices. This help from other state institutions enabled the EC to play its supervisory role with minimal problems.

While the EC's hands were strengthened by regular interactions with the parliament, the judiciary and administrative institutions, its functioning on the ground was made more effective by citizens' initiatives and media inputs. Their help and constant 'vigil' enthused the EC personnel on the field. Citizens' organisations and media raised issues of reform and streamlining the electoral process and highlighted the need for enhancing voters' rights. They also brought issues of electoral malpractice to the forefront and suggested remedial measures to minimise them. For instance, citizens' right to know more about electoral candidates and to make an informed choice while casting their ballot was highlighted with continued momentum by civil society organisations. Thus came the institutional provision of mandatory disclosures – that it was binding on electoral candidates to disclose their educational, economic and criminal background while filing their nominations papers for an election. This information strengthened the right of an elector to cast his or her vote with a more holistic knowledge of the prospective representatives. Citizens became increasingly vocal about the lacunas in efficient electoral management during the actual event of elections that brought problems like anomalies in electoral rolls, faulty functioning of EVMs, inaccessibility of booths for senior citizens and the physically challenged, and so on, to the attention of election managers. This citizen activism helped the EC in continuously working on infusing efficiency into the electoral system.

The media, on its part, also played an invaluable role in improving the electoral terrain and making it fairer. It brought instances of violations of the MCC and the spending limits at the hands of political leaders to the notice of the EC. For example, distribution of freebies and announcement of welfare schemes after the scheduling of election dates were often brought to the EC's attention by the media. Hate speeches were also highlighted. The media also brought incidents of violation of spending limits to the forefront and before the EC's eyes. Excessive spending and inflammatory speeches during election campaigns publicised by the media helped the EC keep a stronger vigil on the election activities of political parties and candidates. The

EC also penalised such violations. The media's role concerning accountability and transparency of the political process and public figures made the EC more attentive to issues of smooth regulation of the electoral process. The EC, the parliament, the Supreme Court, the administration, civil society and the media thus often worked in tandem to 'cleanse' the electoral process and level the playing field.

The EC gained recognition for regulating party competition and political behaviour that helped minimise disruptions during elections. It streamlined electoral rules to make elections more transparent and voter-friendly. In doing so, it not only worked towards institutionalising electoral democracy but also oversaw its own growth as an agent of political change. Though the EC faced enormous challenges of enumeration and mobilisation in the first round of elections itself, several peculiar challenges emerged only in the late 1980s – a time of great churn in Indian politics and society.[1] The diversification of political opinion and the consequent party competitiveness meant an increased intervention in the electoral arena for interpretation and streamlining of rules and making of fresh ones. It also meant standing up for the rights of voters and weaker parties primarily vis- à-vis the state power of ruling parties. The electoral machinery in India faced political pressures, too, and had to take decisions under the strain of executive demands. At times, its actions came under the scanner and criticism for favouring the prevailing regime and not taking action against violations of the MCC at its hands (see Yadav, 2019; Chishti, 2021).[2] Nevertheless, it contributed to moulding a participative political culture and taking it in a particular direction in an environment of intense activity prone to friction. Partisan mobilisations amidst spatial and cultural diversity that had the potential to grow into combative situations were smoothened and regulated to make the political environment conducive to a peaceful exercise of franchise and amicable competition. The EC carried its role forward here as a mediator and constructive steerer of democratic politics.

---

[1] This churn was evident in the weakening of the one-party dominant system, or the 'Congress system', as also in the strengthening of politics of identity and the growing rights' movements, among others. In other words, political fragmentation, growing politicisation and increased contestation for state power were the marked features of the Indian scene at that historical juncture.

[2] Concerns have been expressed lately on the EC's functioning and its reported proximity to the ruling party, the BJP, especially after the 2014 parliamentary elections.

Also, as discussed earlier in the book, conducting elections meant the need for enormous state capacity to handle the costs and logistics of an election, especially for a country of the size and with a population of India. A moral agreement on the regularity of free and fair elections at the level of principles and ideas was a clear requirement. What was also needed was a proper infrastructure, technical know-how, means of communication, smooth transportation, trained personnel and the capability to manage these. This involved considerable resources and expertise. In a large measure, the proactiveness of the EC and its effective management style led to an overall successful handling of elections in India. It was able to work through difficulties and optimise the use of capacity, strengthen procedures and put in place the logistics of an election through its professional staff and planning capabilities.

Important here is to highlight that the EC's main task of refereeing elections brings it in close interaction with political parties and the electorate underlying the importance of mutual trust and confidence. It regulates the electoral exercise by putting to work the rules and regulations of elections. Between 1990 and 2019 (the time span covered in this book), the EC's tasks increased manifold because of the structural transformations in the Indian polity that had begun in the late 1980s, as stated earlier, and furthered themselves more markedly. The outward manifestations of these were the creation of new states, birth of new parties, increased dissatisfaction with the old parties, increased internal migration, growing politicisation of voters and growth in media technologies. The EC found its hands full with the huge quantum of work and varied electoral challenges. Violations of the MCC, rise in election-related corruption and use of dark money made for a frenzied time for the EC. The relation between the EC and political parties, which constitutes a crucial aspect of political functioning, underwent ups and downs. Political parties found electoral orders as unnecessary constraints on them. But what needs to be showcased is that in the given situations the EC was able to lead the electoral administration to conduct elections within the set time schedules and was able to handle problems in a reasonable way within the prescribed procedures. The political parties too, after the EC's censures, modified their conduct, at least ostensibly, to carry out their work within the pathways laid out by the EC.

The EC gradually became an institution which was always 'at work'. The task of registering new voters and conducting elections is an ongoing process. Election work begins with enrolling voters and registering political parties.

The names of voters are listed out in what are called electoral rolls that are updated every year. In case of political parties, their names go through an approval process, and they are granted symbols by the EC before they contest. There are disputes which come up within parties, leading at times to a split. The EC intervenes and decides which faction should retain the name and the symbol of the original party and which has to be allotted a new name and symbol. Apart from this, there are parliamentary and legislative assembly elections that follow different time schedules, and then there are by-polls too. This makes the EC an institution which is forever at work. Its 'always on the move' mode has made for a regular electoral exercise and legitimate processes of party recognition and functioning.

The EC, through its experience, has taken on a reformist role as well. Electoral management under the EC in the 8 parliamentary and about 189 state assembly elections between 1990 and 2019 has shown that a streamlined and equalised process of selection of representatives goes a long way in keeping the political system fair and receptive to popular aspirations. Time and again it has proposed reforms to strengthen voters' rights and to reduce costs, inefficiency and malpractice related to elections. It has taken steps to modernise the electoral apparatus and has come up with proposals and suggestions to strengthen its own independence. Its reformist stance has made it an entity which is viewed as a proactive institution committed to strengthening the participatory processes of Indian democracy. Suggestions from it, such as a common electoral roll for all elections, enhancement of penalties for filing false affidavits, the provision of more than one qualifying-age date for registration of new voters, and so on, show that the EC is involved actively in streamlining and improving the electoral system, besides conducting elections on a regular basis. The experience of its personnel on the field has led to proposals to further upgrade election procedures. It is thus continually involved in defining and reworking the logic of appropriateness.

The EC in the past and contemporary times has had to often safeguard its autonomy against the influences of the incumbent government and maintain the inter-institutional balance that sustains democracy. The perils of becoming a 'committed bureaucracy' or 'government mouthpiece' is ever present to engulf the EC when differences come up between the ruling and other political parties over electoral norms. It has had to preserve its neutral voice and equalise the field of electoral competition so that all political parties, whether big or small, in government or outside, participate in elections within permissible limits and without trampling upon each other.

It needs to be mentioned here that in a democratic context the party in power or the ruling coalition has a decisive influence over state institutions because of the majority principle and popular support. Under this institutional design, the various institutions of state at times tend to move in a direction as visualised by the executive. Occasions might also arise when a regime would like to alter institutional character and design to suit itself. The electoral administration's, and particularly the EC's, functioning in India must be assessed in this larger political ecosystem. The EC has had to work within this institutional arrangement and guard its autonomy within a structural design that prioritises the interest of a parliamentary majority. In this system it is the parliament which holds supremacy and gives direction to policy.

In such a political environment, regulatory institutions like the EC may have their work neatly cut out for them by those at the helm of the parliament, but they also play an important role, as constitutional institutions, in strengthening the democratic work cultures. They restrain those in government and maintain checks and balances. They contribute to moderating the excessive behaviour of entrenched political forces and also become active agents of democratisation by expanding people's choices, building a fairer political domain and drawing the marginalised voices into the public arena. This makes them active agents of setting the logic of appropriateness.

The functioning of the EC shows that it has made sincere efforts to put these practices in place, which have institutionalised collective functioning through adherence to procedures. It has inculcated considerable ease into a mass activity that happens throughout the country at a given time. It has made new rules and brought clarity to the existing ones, making political praxis more methodical, orderly and moderated. It was visualised as an institution that would ensure a fair game to all and restrain the government of the day from misusing its hold over state power to put itself ahead of others and have the upper hand in the electoral race. Within its institutional field, the EC's work went a long way in checking this dominant tendency and maintaining the institutional equilibrium. This helped in easing the entry of the marginal into the competition. Citizens, on their part, reposed a lot of faith in it despite errors, slip-ups and allegations of biases; they also increasingly valued their involvement in the polling process. Thus, its work of procedural fine-tuning added to democratic functioning, accountability and expansion of choices. It tried to direct the system towards more transparency and energised the citizen voter towards an increased political participation.

Thus, as a state institution it paved a distinct path towards the fortifying of electoral democracy in India. Herein also lay the incentives for maintaining its own autonomy.

The EC's efforts in this arena of procedural fairness have made democracy more substantive and meaningful as a form of government to a greater number of citizens. Both at the level of ideas and ground-level work, elections conducted by the EC have had considerable support among the electorate. Aberrations such as election-related violence reduced considerably through the vigilance of the EC so as not to reach levels which disrupted polling on a large scale. This indicates the growing legitimacy of the process of elections across regions and sections. Elections gradually became celebratory occasions and participatory carnivals. Voters enthusiastically came out to get their finger inked and mark their involvement in them. The credit for this in a large measure goes to the EC.

Bibliography

Agarwal, U. C. 2002. Non-titled article. In *National Resurgence through Electoral Reforms*, edited by Subhash C. Kashyap, 81–87. Delhi: Shipra Publications.

Agarwalla, S. S. 1994. *Contemporary India and Its Burning Problems*. New Delhi: Mittal Publications.

Agrawal, Ravi. 2018. *India Connected: How the Smartphone Is Transforming the World's Largest Democracy*. New Delhi: Oxford University Press.

Ahuja, M. L. 2000. *Handbook of General Elections and Electoral Reforms*. New Delhi: Mittal Publications.

Ali, Mohammad. 2013. 'Over 30% of MPs, MLAs Face Criminal Charges'. *The Hindu*, 22 July. https://www.thehindu.com/news/national/over-30-of-mps-mlas-face-criminal-charges/article4938403.ece. Accessed on 11 September 2013.

Anand, Utkarsh. 2015. 'Political Parties Can't Be under RTI Act: Centre Tells SC'. *Indian Express*, 25 August. http://indianexpress.com/article/india/india-others/political-parties-cant-be-under-rti-act-centre-tells-sc/. Accessed on 17 April 2017.

Anandan, D. n. d. *Challenges in the Management of Electoral Rolls*. http://eci.nic.in/eci_main1/sharingportal/D.Anandan.sikkim.doc. Accessed on 19 September 2017.

Andersen, Walter K. 1991. 'India's 1991 Election: The Uncertain Verdict'. *Asian Survey* 31(10): 976–89.

———. 2015. 'The Bharatiya Janata Party: A Victory for Narendra Modi'. In *India's 2014 Elections: A Modi-Led BJP Sweep*, edited by Paul Wallace, 46–63. New Delhi: SAGE Publications.

Ansari, Javed. 1994. 'The Unsparing Rod'. *India Today*, 15 December. http://indiatoday.intoday.in/story/cec-t.n.-seshan-tightens-electoral-reform-screws-to-clean-up-entire-election-process/1/294621.html. Accessed on 6 July 2016.

Anuja. 2016. 'Panchayat Polls: Small Elections, Big Money'. *Mint*, 5 April. https://www.livemint.com/Politics/W2ERq6OrzlAaCSMKc5mALO/Panchayat-polls-Small-elections-big-money.html. Accessed on 15 June 2021.

Anuja, and Gireesh Chandra Prasad. 2019. 'Electoral Bonds Boon or Bane for India's Political Funding System?'. *Mint*, 4 December. https://www.livemint.com/politics/policy/electoral-bonds-boon-or-bane-for-india-s-political-funding-system-11575424422379.html. Accessed on 26 June 2021.

Anuja, and Utpal Bhaskar. 2014. 'EC Now Says It Can't Enforce Its Guidelines on Manifestoes'. *Mint*, 10 April. https://www.livemint.com/Politics/H2EnGkV4cI28oeKxTgcnhN/EC-now-says-it-cant-enforce-its-guidelines-on-manifestos.html. Accessed on 24 August 2022.

Aslany, Maryam. 2019. 'The Indian Middle Class, Its Size, and Urban–Rural Variations'. *Contemporary South Asia* 27(2): 1–18. DOI: 10.1080/09584935.2019.1581727.

Association for Democratic Reforms (ADR). 2002. 'In the Supreme Court of India Civil Appellate/Original Jurisdiction Civil Appeal No. 7178 of 2001'. https://adrindia.org/sites/default/files/Supreme_Court%27s_judgement_2nd_May_2002.pdf. Accessed on 18 June 2017.

———. 2013a. 'FAQ on the Supreme Court Judgement Declaring Immediate Disqualification of Convicted MPs/MLAs'. http://adrindia.org/sites/default/files/FAQ%20-%20Excerpts%20from%20the%20SC%20Judgement%20to%20disqualify%20convicts%20v4.pdf. Accessed on 6 June 2017.

———. 2013b. 'BJP Urges President Not to Sign Ordinance on Convicted Lawmakers'. 27 September. http://adrindia.org/media/adr-in-news/bjp-urges-president-not-sign-ordinance-convicted-lawmakers. Accessed on 8 June 2017.

———. 2013c. '30 Pct of Elected MPs, MLAs Have Declared Criminal Cases: ADRNEW Report'. 27 September. http://www.adrindia.org/media/adr-in-news/30-pct-elected-mps-mlas-have-declared-criminal-cases-adrnew-report. Accessed on 16 June 2017.

———. 2014a. 'Judgements and PILs'. 19 September. http://adrindia.org/legal-advocacy/judgements-and-orders. Accessed 2 June 2017.

———. 2014b. 'Writ Petition on Election Expenditure'. https://adrindia.org/
sites/default/files/ADR_Writ_Election_Expenditure.pdf. Accessed on 21
March 2018.

———. 2017. '69% Funding of Political Parties from Unknown Sources'. 25
January. https://adrindia.org/content/69-funding-political-parties-unknown-
sources-says-report. Accessed on 10 March 2018.

———. 2019. 'Analysis of Donations Received Above Rs. 20,000 by National
Political Parties: FY 2017–18'. 16 January. https://adrindia.org/content/
analysis-donations-received-above-rs-20000-national-political-parties-
%E2%80%93-fy-2017-18. Accessed on 19 September 2022.

———. n.d. 'Mission and Vision'. https://adrindia.org/about-adr/mission-and-
vision. Accessed on 19 September 2022.

Association for Democratic Reforms (ADR) and National Election Watch (NEW).
2011. *ADR/NEW Recommendations for Electoral Reforms*. April. https://
adrindia.org/sites/default/files/ADR_and_NEWs_recommendations_for_
electoral_and_political_reforms_Final_April_20_2011.pdf. Accessed on 5
October 2017.

Attri, Vibha. 2014. 'Awareness on Political Issues'. In *Indian Youth and Electoral
Politics: An Emerging Engagement*, edited by Sanjay Kumar, 1–17. New Delhi:
SAGE Publications.

Australian Communications and Media Authority. n.d. 'Election Blackout
Periods'. https://www.acma.gov.au/election-blackout-periods. Accessed on
8 November 2021.

Australian Electoral Commission. 2022. *Electoral Communication*. https://www.
aec.gov.au/About_AEC/electoral-communication.htm. Accessed on 19
August 2022.

Banerjee, Mukulika. 2014. *Why India Votes?* New Delhi: Routledge. Paperback
edition.

Bansal, Aanchal. 2019. 'Women Turn Out in Greater Numbers than in Previous
Elections'. *Economic Times*, 20 May. https://economictimes.indiatimes.com/
news/elections/lok-sabha/india/women-turn-out-in-greater-numbers-than-
in-previous-elections/articleshow/69405687.cms. Accessed on 6 June 2019.

Bansal, Ishaan, and Mrunal Marathe. 2019. '2019 LS Polls: Most NOTA Votes
in SC & ST Reserved Seats, Naxal-Hit Areas'. *Business Standard*, 25 August,
https://www.business-standard.com/article/elections/2019-ls-polls-most-
nota-votes-in-sc-st-reserved-seats-naxal-hit-areas-119081900121_1.html.
Accessed on 23 February 2023.

Bansal, Shuchi. 2016. 'Indian Media Industry Likely to Touch Rs. 2.26 Trillion by 2020'. *Mint*, 31 March. http://www.livemint.com/Consumer/7cMLq 2Q02wiIBC9T2IEfeO/Indian-media-industry-likely-to-touch-Rs2260-billion-by-202.html. Accessed on 11 September 2016.

Barley, Stephen R., and Pamela S. Tolbert. 1997. 'Institutionalization and Structuration: Studying the Links between Action and Institution'. *Organization Studies* 18(1): 93–117.

Barros, Robert. 2003. 'Dictatorship and the Rule of Law: Rules and Military Power in Pinochet's Chile'. In *Democracy and the Rule of Law*, edited by Jose Maria Maravall and Adam Przeworski, 188–219. Cambridge, UK: Cambridge University Press.

Baweja, Harinder. 1994. 'Assembly Elections: Crisis on the Cards'. *India Today*, 15 October.

Ben-Dor, Gabriel. 1975. 'Institutionalization and Political Development: A Conceptual and Theoretical Analysis'. *Comparative Studies in Society and History* 17(3): 309–25.

Bhandari, Kusumlata. 1988. *India: Electoral Reforms*. New Delhi: Election Archives.

Bhargava, Rajeev (ed.). 2008. *Politics and Ethics of the Indian Constitution*. New Delhi: Oxford University Press.

Bhargava, Yuthika. 2015. 'Use of Social Media Doubles in Rural India'. *The Hindu*, 20 June. http://www.thehindu.com/sci-tech/technology/internet/social-media-use-doubles-in-rural-india/article7334735.ece. Accessed on 11 September 2016.

Bharti, Indu. 1990. 'Bihar Elections Violence Inevitable'. *Economic and Political Weekly* 3(3): 429.

Blumstein, James F. 1981. 'The Resurgence of Institutionalism'. *Journal of Policy Analysis and Management* 1(1): 129–32.

Bratton, Michael. 2008. 'Vote Buying and Violence in Nigerian Election Campaigns'. *Electoral Studies* 27(4): 621–32.

Broom, Leonard, and Philip Selznick. 1955. *Sociology: A Text with Adapted Readings*. New York: Row, Peterson & Co.

Brownlee, Jason. 2007. *Authoritarianism in an Age of Democratization*. Cambridge, UK: Cambridge University Press.

Business Standard. 2014. 'Expenditure Limit for Lok Sabha Elections Raised to Rs 70 Lakh'. 4 March. http://www.business-standard.com/article/politics/expenditure-limit-for-lok-sabha-elections-raised-to-rs-70-lakh-1140304011 42_1.html. Accessed on 8 January 2018.

————. 2019. 'Cyber Expert Says 2014 Poll Rigged, EVMs Hacked; EC Stands by Its Machines'. 21 January. https://www.businessstandard.com/article/elections/cyber-expert-says-2014-polls-rigged-evms-hacked-ec-stands-by-its-machines-119012101234_1.html. Accessed on 7 January 2021.

Castle, Bob. 2009. 'MPs with Criminal Records'. https://www.whatdotheyknow.com/request/mps_with_criminal_records. Accessed on 10 June 2017.

Census of India. 2001. 'Age Structure and Marital Status' (Census Data). New Delhi: Office of the Registrar General and Census Commissioner of India. https://censusindia.gov.in/census_and_you/age_structure_and_marital_status.aspx. Accessed on 30 October 2021.

————. 2011. 'Chapter 2: Population Composition'. In *Sample Registration System Statistical Report 2011*. New Delhi: Office of the Registrar General of India, Ministry of Home Affairs, Government of India. https://www.censusindia.gov.in/vital_statistics/srs_report/9chap%202%20-%202011.pdf. Accessed on 31 October 2021.

Census of India and United Nations Population Fund (UNFPA). 2014. 'A Profile of Adolescents and Youth in India'. New Delhi: Office of the Registrar General and Census Commissioner of India, Ministry of Home Affairs, Government of India. https://india.unfpa.org/sites/default/files/pub-pdf/AProfileofAdolescentsandYouthinIndia_0.pdf. Accessed on 14 February 2023. (Office of the Registrar General and Census Commissioner of India, Ministry of Home Affairs, Government of India) https://india.unfpa.org/sites/default/files/pub-pdf/AProfileofAdolescentsandYouthinIndia_0.pdf

Chapman, Emilee B. 2019. 'The Distinctive Value of Elections and the Case for Compulsory Voting'. *American Journal of Political Science* 63(1): 101–12.

Chatterjee, Partha. 2011. 'The State'. In *The Oxford Companion to Politics in India*, edited by Niraja Gopal Jayal and Pratap Bhanu Mehta, 3–14. New Delhi: Oxford University Press.

Chatterjee, Somnath. 1997. 'Some Aspects of Electoral Reforms'. In *Electoral Reforms*, edited by Sharad Dighe and R. B. Sundriyal (the Institution of Constitutional and Parliamentary Studies), 22–33. New Delhi: Shree Publishing House.

Chatterjee, S., and N. Sahoo. 2012. 'Campaign Finance Reforms in India: Issues and Challenges'. http://www.observerindia.com/cms/sites/orfonline/modules/orfseminarseries/attachments/ss_8_1337325945061.pdf. Accessed on 10 April 2014.

Chaudhary, Pranava K. 2005. 'Where Booth Capturing Was Born'. *Times of India*, 14 February. https://timesofindia.indiatimes.com/city/patna/Where-booth-capturing-was-born/articleshow/1020435.cms. Accessed on 18 December 2017.

Chawla, Navin B. 2013. 'Criminality in the Indian Political System'. *The Hindu*, 21 November. http://www.thehindu.com/opinion/lead/criminality-in-the-indian-political-system/article5372634.ece. Accessed on 12 July 2017.

Chhibber, Pradeep, Francesca Refsum Jensenius and Pavithra Suryanarayan. 2014. 'Party Organization and Party Proliferation in India'. *Party Politics* 20(4): 489–505.

Chhokar, Jagdeep S. 2017. 'Black Money and Politics in India'. *Economic and Political Weekly* 52(7) (18 February): 91–8.

———. 2020. 'Criminalisation of Politics: The Malady and the Remedy'. In *Constitutional and Democratic Institutions in India: A Critical Analysis*, edited by Sudha Pai, 317–342. Hyderabad: Orient BlackSwan.

Chinnappa, Jeevan K. 2014. 'SVEEP to be Intensified to Create Voter Awareness'. *The Hindu*, 15 March. http://www.thehindu.com/news/national/karnataka/sveep-to-be-intensified-to-create-voter-awareness/article5785690.ece. Accessed on 2 October 2017.

Chishti, Seema. 2021. 'The Biased Referee: Why the Election Commission's Neutrality Is in Doubt'. *The Caravan: Indian Journal of Politics and Culture* (April): 22–27.

Chopra, J. K. 1989. *Politics of Election Reforms in India*. Delhi: Mittal Publications.

Chopra, Ritika. 2014. '2014 Worst Poll Campaign in 30 Years: Election Commissioner HS Brahma'. *Economic Times*, 10 April. http://articles.economictimes.indiatimes.com/2014-04-10/news/49031750_1_azam-khan-amit-shah-political-parties. Accessed on 28 July 2014.

———. 2015. 'We Need Reform in Political Parties: Veeravalli Sundaram Sampath, Chief Election Commissioner of India'. *Economic Times*, 15 May. https://m.economictimes.com/opinion/interviews/we-need-reforms-in-political-parties-veeravalli-sundaram-sampath-chief-election-commissioner-of-india/articleshow/45892530.cms. Accessed on 6 June 2021.

———. 2016. 'Should Prisoners Be Allowed to Vote?: Election Commission Panel to Seek Answers'. *Indian Express*, 14 September. http://indianexpress.com/article/india/india-news-india/should-prisoners-be-allowed-to-vote-ec-panel-to-seek-answer-3029960. Accessed on 27 August 2017.

Clark, Alistair. 2019. 'The Cost of Democracy: The Determinants of Spending on the Public Administration of Elections'. *International Political Science Review* 40(3): 354–69. DOI: 10.1177/0192512118824787.

Collins, Michael. 2014. 'Money Power in Indian Elections'. *Business Line*, 29 July. http://www.thehindubusinessline.com/opinion/money-power-in-indian-elections/article6261173.ece. Accessed on 8 January 2018.

Colyvas, Jeannette A., and Stefan Jonsson. 2011. 'Ubiquity and Legitimacy: Disentangling Diffusion and Institutionalization'. *Sociological Theory* 29(1): 27–53.

Communist Party of India (Marxist) (CPI[M]). 2000a. 'Reply to Election Commission's Notice on Derecognition'. 18 August. https://cpim.org/content/reply-election-commissions-notice-derecognition. Accessed on 29 March 2017.

———. 2000b. 'Election Commission's Notice: Deregistration'. 18 July. https://cpim.org/content/election-commissions-notice-deregistration. Accessed on 29 March 2000.

———. 2006. *Election Commission: A Case for Reform*. New Delhi: Hari Singh Kang (A. K. Gopalan Bhavan).

Constitution of the Republic of South Africa. n.d. http://www.africa.upenn.edu/Govern_Political/SouthAf_Const_4.html. Accessed on 5 July 2017.

Cox, Gary W., and Michael F. Thies. 2000. 'How Much Does Money Matter?: "Buying" Votes in Japan, 1967–1990'. *Comparative Political Studies* 33(1): 37–57.

Damore, David F., Mallory M. Waters and Shaun Bowler. 2012. 'Unhappy, Uninformed, or Uninterested? Understanding "None of the Above" Voting'. *Political Research Quarterly* 65(4): 895–907.

Dash, B. C. 2004. 'Civil Society Initiatives and Electoral Reforms'. *Economic and Political Weekly* 39(37): 4136–37.

De, Rohit. 2018. *A People's Constitution: The Everyday Life of Law in the Indian Republic*. Princeton (NJ) and Oxford: Princeton University Press.

Deka, Kaushik. 2018. 'Political Funding: Who Pays for the Party?'. *India Today*, 9 November. https://www.indiatoday.in/magazine/the-big-story/story/20181119-political-funding-who-pays-for-the-party-1384158-2018-11-09. Accessed on 14 June 2021.

deSouza, Peter R. 1998. 'The Election Commission and Electoral Reforms in India'. In *Democracy, Diversity, Stabilitiy: 50 Years of Indian Independence*, edited by D. D. Khanna, Lakhana Maharotra and Gert W. Kueck, 51–70. New Delhi: Macmillan Publishers.

Dimaggio, Paul J., and Walter W. Powell. 1983. 'The Iron Cage Revisited: Institutional Isomorphism and Collective Rationality in Organizational Fields'. *American Sociological Review* 48(2): 147–60.

Dixit, Neha. 2019. 'India's Poll Body Accused of Bias as Election Complaints Pile Up'. Al Jazeera, 15 April. https://www.aljazeera.com/news/2019/4/15/indias-poll-body-accused-of-bias-as-election-complaints-pile-up. Accessed on 20 February 2023.

Dube, M. P. 1992. 'Electoral Reforms in India'. In *Electoral Reform in India*, edited by Agarala Easwara Reddi and D. Sundar Ram, 64–70. New Delhi: Uppal Publishing.

Duggan, Kyle. 2016. 'Election 2015 Saw Large Influx of Third-Party Spending: Elections Canada'. *iPolitics*, 30 March. https://ipolitics.ca/2016/03/30/election-2015-saw-large-influx-of-third-party-spending-elections-canada. Accessed on 7 September 2021.

Economic and Political Weekly. 1989. 'Parliamentary Elections: Tripura Style'. *Economic and Political Weekly* 24(50) (16 December): 2757–58.

———. 1991. 'Poll Violence: High Stakes'. *Economic and Political Weekly* 26(20) (18 May): 1248–49.

Economic Times. 2022. '1.29 Crores Votes Cast for NOTA in Last Five Years: ADR'. 4 August. https://economictimes.indiatimes.com/news/politics-and-nation/1-29-crore-votes-cast-for-nota-in-last-five-years-adr/articleshow/93343612.cms?from=mdr. Accessed on 25 February 2023.

Election Commission of India. 1973. *Report on the Fifth General Elections in India, 1971–72*. http://eci.nic.in/eci_main/eci_publications/books/genr/FifthGen Election-71-72.pdf. Accessed on 29 December 2017.

———. 2002. 'Press Note'. 28 June. http://eci.nic.in/archive/press/current/PN_28062002.htm. Accessed on 23 April 2017.

———. 2003. Order, 27 March, 1–14. https://eci.gov.in/files/file/144-commissions-order-dated-27th-march-2003-regarding-criminal-antecedents-assets-and-liabilities-and-educational-qualifications-of-candidates. Accessed on 23 August 2021.

———. 2004a. *Proposed Electoral Reforms*. New Delhi: Publications Division, Government of India.

———. 2004b. *Political Parties and Election Symbols*. New Delhi: Publications Division, Government of India.

———. 2008. 'Rationalisation of Polling Stations – Regarding'. Letter, 8 May. https://eci.gov.in/files/file/5706-rationalisation-of-polling-stations-regarding. Accessed on 4 June 2021.

———. 2009a. *Compendium of Instructions on Conduct of Elections*, vol. 4. New Delhi: Publications Division, Government of India.

———. 2009b. 'Press Note: Schedule for General Elections, 2009'. 2 March. https://pib.gov.in/newsite/erelcontent.aspx?relid=48192. Accessed on 18 February 2020.

———. 2013a. 'Supreme Court's Judgement for 'None of the Above' Option on EVM – Clarification'. 28 October. http://pib.nic.in/newsite/mbErel. aspx?relid=100291. Accessed on 13 June 2017.

———. 2013b. *Statistical Report on General Election, 2013, to the Legislative Assembly of Mizoram*. http://eci.nic.in/eci_main/StatisticalReports/AE2013/MizoramAE_2013_stat_report.pdf. Accessed on 14 June 2017.

———. 2014a. 'General Elections 2014'. http://eci.nic.in/eci/eci.html. Accessed on 10 July 2015.

———. 2014b. 'Security Plan and Force Deployment to Ensure Free, Fair and Peaceful Conduct of Elections to Lok Sabha and Sate Assemblies'. 7 April. http://eci.nic.in/eci_main1/current/CI_07042014.pdf. Accessed on 10 November 2017.

———. 2014c. 'Background Paper on Political Finance and Law Commission Recommendations'. http://eci.nic.in/eci_main1/Current/BackgroundPaper 23032015.pdf. Accessed on 8 January 2018.

———. 2014d. *Compendium of Instructions on Election Expenditure Monitoring*. New Delhi: Publications Division, Government of India.

———. 2014e. 'Chapter 43: Salient Features of the Representation of the People Act 1951'. *In General Elections 2014: Reference Handbook*, 161–67. http://mea. gov.in/Uploads/PublicationDocs/23192_Election_2014.pdf. Accessed on 27 August 2017.

———. 2015. 'Order: Standard Operating Procedure for Seizure and Release of Cash and Other Items'. 29 May. http://eci.nic.in/eci_main1/current/SOP_ English_01072015.pdf. Accessed on 8 February 2018.

———. 2016a. Notification. http://eci.nic.in/eci_main/ElectoralLaws/Orders Notifications/year2015/Amenment%201968%20English.pdf. Accessed 18 April 2017.

———. 2016b. Notification. http://eci.nic.in/eci_main/ElectoralLaws/Orders Notifications/year2016/letter%20to%20CBDT_21122016.pdf. Accessed 23 April 2017.

———. 2016c. 'Press Note: Steps Taken by Commission to Curb Pre and Post Poll Violence in West Bengal'. 23 April. http://eci.nic.in/eci_main1/current/ pn3423416.pdf. Accessed on 6 January 2018.

———. 2016d. 'Measures Taken by the Commission for Control of Illegal Money during General Elections to the Legislative Assembly of Tamil Nadu, 2016'. 24 April. http://pib.nic.in/newsite/PrintRelease.aspx?relid=141103. Accessed on 9 February 2018.

———. 2016e. Letter. 7 October. https://eci.gov.in/files/file/1206-instruction-wrto-hon%E2%80%99ble-delhi-high-court%E2%80%99s-order-dated-070716-in-wpc-83632010-directing-the-political-parties-not-to-use-public-fundspublic-places-for-propagating-the-election-symbol-of-the-party/?do=download&r=2768&confirm=1&t=1&csrfKey=57c42786935d512699dc1660f418fd55. Accessed on 6 June 2021.

———. 2016f. *Proposed Electoral Reforms*. New Delhi: Nirvachan Sadan.

———. 2017a. 'Notification'. 24 January. http://210.212.18.116/ceobihar_materials/judgement/seeking_votes.pdf. Accessed on 7 July 2017.

———. 2017b. 'Experiences and Lessons Learnt from the Poll Gone States 2016'. http://eci.nic.in/eci_main1/current/Experiences_Lessons_poll_gone_States2016_06102016.pdf. Accessed on 3 October 2017.

———. 2017c. 'The Election Symbols (Reservation and Allotment) Order, 1968 (As Amended up to August, 2016)'. New Delhi: Election Commission of India (Nirvachan Sadan).

———. 2018a. 'Conduct of Awareness Programmes on EVMs and VVPATs'. https://eci.gov.in/files/file/8977-conduct-of-awareness-programmes-on-evms-and-vvpats-%E2%80%93-reg. Accessed on 6 January 2021.

———. 2018b. 'Press Note: Election Commission of India Holds a Meeting with all the Recognised National and State Political Parties at New Delhi on Various Electoral Reforms'. 27 August. https://eci.gov.in/files/file/5022-election-commission-of-india-holds-a-meeting-with-all-the-recognised-national-and-state-political-parties-at-new-delhi-on-various-electoral-reforms. Accessed on 8 June 2021.

———. 2018c. 'The Setup'. 26 October. https://eci.gov.in/about/about-eci/the-setup-r1 Accessed on 6 September 2021.

———. 2019. 'List of Political Parties Participated'. https://eci.gov.in/files/file/10989-3-list-of-political-parties-participated. Accessed on 7 October 2021.

———. n.d.1. *Compendium of Instructions*, vol. 1. New Delhi: Election Commission of India.

———. n.d.2. 'Corrupting Influence of Money Power'. http://eci.nic.in/archive/handbook/CANDIDATES/cch11/cch11_3.htm. Accessed on 20 March 2018.

———. n.d.3. *Handbook for Candidates: Accounts of Election Expenses – Measures to Check*. New Delhi: Election Commission of India.

———. n.d.4. *Handbook for Candidates: Accounts of Election Expenses – Maintenance of Accounts of Election Expenses*. New Delhi: Election Commission of India. http://eci.nic.in/archive/handbook/CANDIDATES/cch11/cch11_1.htm. Accessed on 20 March 2018.

———. n.d.5. *Landmark Judgements on Election Law*, vol. 2. New Delhi: Election Commission of India. http://eci.nic.in/eci_main/ElectoralLaws/Judgements/LandmarkJudgementsVOLII.pdf. Accessed 4 February 2017.

———. n.d.6. *Landmark Judgements on Election Law*, vol. 4. New Delhi: Election Commission of India. http://eci.nic.in/eci_main/ElectoralLaws/judgements/LandmarkJudgementsVolIV.pdf. Accessed on 6 August 2014.

———. n.d.7. 'Model Code of Conduct for the Guidance of Political Parties and Candidates'. https://eci.gov.in/mcc. Accessed on 24 August 2022.

———. n.d.8. 'Provisions of the Section 126 of the Representation of the People Act, 1951'. https://eci.gov.in/files/file/9433-provisions-of-section-126-of-the-representation-of-the-people-act-1951-reg. Accessed on 26 August 2022.

———. n.d.9. *Status Paper on Electronic Voting Machine*. http://eci.nic.in/eci_main1/current/StatusPaperonEVM_09052017.pdf. Accessed on 29 December 2017.

———. n.d.10. 'Systematic Voters' Education and Electoral Participation (SVEEP)'. http://ecisveep.nic.in/about.aspx. Accessed on 8 September 2017.

———. n.d.11. 'FAQ on Paid News'. https://eci.gov.in/files/file/13752-faq-on-paid-news. Accessed on 8 November 2021.

Elections Ontario. n.d. 'Rules for Political Advertising'. https://www.elections.on.ca/en/political-entities-in-ontario/political-advertising.html#accordion32. Accessed on 8 November 2021.

Electoral Commission of South Africa. 2021. 'The Electoral Code of Conduct, South Africa'. https://www.elections.org.za/pw/Parties-And-Candidates/The-Electoral-Code-Of-Conduct. Accessed on 29 June 2021.

Electoral Commission of the United Kingdom (UK). 2017. *Guidance for Candidates and Agents*. April. https://www.electoralcommission.org.uk/media/1214. Accessed on 10 June 2017.

———. 2019. *UK Parliamentary General Elections: Guidance for Candidates and Agents*, part 4: *The Campaign*. https://www.electoralcommission.org.uk/sites/default/files/2019-11/UKPGE-Part%204-The%20campaign_1.pdf. Accessed on 7 July 2021.

————. 2021. *Joint Guidance for Candidates in Elections: When It Goes Too Far.* http://www.electoralcommission.org.uk/sites/default/files/2021-03/ Joint%20Guidance%20for%20Candidates%20in%20Elections%202021_0. pdf. Accessed on 30 June 2021.

Evans, Peter B., Dietrich Rueschemeyer and Theda Skocpol (eds.). 1985. *Bringing the State Back In.* Cambridge, UK: Cambridge University Press.

Ezrow, Natasha M., and Erica Frantz. 2011. 'State Institutions and the Survival of Dictatorships'. *Journal of International Affairs* 65(1): 1–13.

Federal Election Commission (United States of America). n.d. *Public Funding of Presidential Elections.* https://www.fec.gov/introduction-campaign-finance/ understanding-ways-support-federal-candidates/presidential-elections/ public-funding-presidential-elections. Accessed on 28 January 2021.

Ferris, Lindsay. 2014. 'In Japan, "Fair" Elections Breed Apathy and Destroy Competition'. Sunlight Foundation, 19 December. https://sunlightfoundation. com/2014/12/19/in-japan-fair-elections-breed-apathy-and-destroy -competition. Accessed on 26 August 2021.

Financial Express. 2006. 'BJP Supports Collegium for Appointment of EC Members'. 13 May.

Firstpost. 2013. 'Keeping Political Parties Out of RTI Will Lead to Corruption: Aruna Roy'. 5 August. https://www.firstpost.com/politics/keeping-political -parties-out-of-rti-will-lead-to-corruption-aruna-roy-1012111.html. Accessed on 11 November 2013.

————. 2019. 'Silence Period Explained: 48 Hours before Polls, Use of Digital or Television Media Verboten for Political Campaigning'. 17 April. https://www.firstpost.com/india/silence-period-explained-48-hours- before-polls-use-of-digital-or-television-media-verboten-for-political- campaigning-6462181.html. Accessed on 26 August 2021.

Frontline. 2013. 'CIC vs Parties'. 12 June. https://frontline.thehindu.com/the- nation/cic-vs-parties/article4794591.ece. Accessed 7 November 2013/

Gadkari, S. S. 1996. *Electoral Reforms in India.* New Delhi and Allahabad: Wheeler Publishing.

Galvin, Daniel, Ian Shapiro and Stephen Skowronek. 2006. 'Introduction'. In *Rethinking Political Institutions: The Art of the State*, edited by Ian Shapiro, Stephen Skowronek and Daniel Galvin, 1–5. New York and London: New York University Press.

Gandhi, Jennifer, and Lust-Okar, Ellen. 2009. 'Elections under Authoritarianism'. *Annual Review of Political Science* 12(6): 403–22.

Gandhi, Varun. 2017. 'The Right to Recall Legislators'. *The Hindu*, 5 April. http://www.thehindu.com/opinion/op-ed/the-right-to-recall-legislators/article17818590.ece. Accessed on 28 April 2018.

Gargarella, Roberto. 2003. 'The Majoritarian Reading of the Rule of Law'. In *Democracy and the Rule of Law*, edited by Jose Maria Maravall and Adam Przeworski, 147–67. Cambridge, UK: Cambridge University Press.

Garnett, Holly Ann. 2019. 'Evaluating Electoral Management Body Capacity'. *International Political Science Review* 40(3): 335–53. DOI: 10.1177/01925121 19832924.

Gazibo, Mamoudou. 2006. 'The Forging of Institutional Autonomy: A Comparative Study of Electoral Management Commissions in Africa'. *Canadian Journal of Political Science* 39(3): 611–33.

Gehlot, N. S. 1992. 'Electoral Reform in India: A Need for National Action'. In *Electoral Reform in India*, edited by Agarala Easwara Reddi and D. Sundar Ram, 80–92. New Delhi: Uppal Publishing.

Ghatwai, Milind. 2017. 'Politicians, Media and "Paid News": The Case of BJP's Narottam Mishra'. *Indian Express*, 18 July. https://indianexpress.com/article/explained/the-case-of-bjps-narottam-mishra-politicians-media-and-paid-news-4755307. Accessed on 12 June 2021.

Ghosh, Partha S. 1999. 'Whither Indian Polity? (Election 1999)'. *Economic and Political Weekly* 34(48) (27 November): 3340–42.

Ghosh, S. K. 1997. *Indian Democracy Derailed: Politics and Politicians*. New Delhi: APH Publishing Corporation.

Gilmartin, David. 2009. 'One Day's Sultan: T.N. Seshan and Indian Democracy'. *Contributions to Indian Sociology* 43(2): 247–84.

Gilmartin, David, and Robert Moog. 2012. 'Introduction to "Election Law in India"'. *Election Law Journal* 11(2): 136–48.

Godbole, Madhav. 1998. 'Criminalisation of Politics: Empowerment of Voter'. *Economic and Political Weekly* 33(17): 949–50.

Gopakumar, K. C. 2021. 'Paravur Paves the Way for EVMs'. *The Hindu*, 3 March. https://www.thehindu.com/news/national/kerala/paravur-paves-the-way-for-evms/article33981894.ece. Accessed on 16 September 2021.

Gopalaswami, N. 2013. 'NOTA Small Matter, This'. *The Hindu*, 9 October. http://www.thehindu.com/opinion/lead/nota-small-matter-this/article 5214816.ece. Accessed on 16 June 2017.

Government of India (GoI). 1990. *Report of the Committee on Electoral Reforms* (Dinesh Goswami Committee). New Delhi: Ministry of Law and Justice.

http://lawmin.nic.in/ld/erreports/Dinesh%20Goswami%20Report%20 on%20Electoral%20Reforms.pdf. Accessed on 10 November 2016.

———. 2011. *Statistics of Higher and Technical Education: 2007–2008*. New Delhi: Ministry of Human Resource Development. https://www.education.gov. in/sites/upload_files/mhrd/files/statistics-new/Stat-HTE-200708_0.pdf. Accessed on 29 July 2022.

———. 2020. 'All India Survey on Higher Education: 2019–20'. New Delhi: Ministry of Education. https://www.education.gov.in/sites/upload_files/mhrd /files/statistics-new/aishe_eng.pdf. Accessed on 29 July 2022.

Gowda, M. V., and E. Sridharan. 2012. 'Reforming India's Party Financing and Election Expenditure Laws'. *Election Law Journal* 11(2): 226–40.

Grant, Allan. 2005. 'Party and Election Finance in Britain and America: A Comparative Analysis'. *Parliamentary Affairs* 58(1): 71–88.

Guha, Ramachandra. 2008. *India after Gandhi: The History of the World's Largest Democracy*. London: Picador.

Gujral, I. K. 1997. 'Electoral Reforms'. In *Electoral Reforms*, edited by Sharad Dighe and R. B. Sundriyal (Institution of Constitutional and Parliamentary Studies), 1–4. New Delhi: Shree Publishing House.

Hafner-Burton, Emilie M., Susan D. Hyde and Ryan S. Jablonski. 2013. 'When Do Governments Resort to Election Violence?'. *British Journal of Political Science* 44(1): 149–79.

Ham, Carolien van, and Holly Ann Garnett. 2019. 'Building Impartial Electoral Management?: Institutional Design, Independence and Electoral Integrity'. *International Political Science Review* 40(3): 313–34.

Hansen, Thomas B., and Christophe Jaffrelot (eds.). 1999. *The BJP and the Compulsions of Politics in India*. New Delhi: Oxford University Press.

Hasan, Zoya, Eswaran Sridharan and R. Sudarshan (eds.). 2004 (2002). *India's Living Constitution: Ideas, Practices, Controversies*. New Delhi: Permanent Black.

Hazarika, Sanjoy. 1988. 'India's Lower House Passes a Bill Giving the Vote to 18-Year-Olds'. *New York Times*, 16 December. http://www.nytimes.com/ 1988/12/16/world/india-s-lower-house-passes-a-bill-giving-the-vote-to-18- year-olds.html. Accessed on 29 August 2017.

Hindu Business Line. 2013. 'BJP, Govt at Loggerheads over Ordinance to Protect Convicted MPs'. 26 September. http://www.thehindubusinessline. com/news/national/bjp-govt-at-loggerheads-over-ordinance-to-protect- convicted-mps/article5171630.ece. Accessed on 7 June 2017.

Hindustan Times. 2017. 'Why Compulsory Voting in India Is a Bad Idea'. 10 July. http://www.hindustantimes.com/editorials/why-compulsory-voting-in-india-is-a-bad-idea/story-YPjMRRFvnr5GgzlLfxdodM.html. Accessed on 11 October 2017.

———. 2018. 'Election Commission Wants Power to Deregister Political Parties'. 11 February. https://www.hindustantimes.com/india-news/election-commission-wants-power-to-deregister-political-parties/story-XnXfACjlgikmfb2dtqw0xH.html. Accessed on 6 June 2021.

Hoglund, Kristine. 2009. 'Electoral Violence in Conflict-Ridden Societies: Concepts, Causes, and Consequences'. *Terrorism and Political Violence* 21(3): 412–27.

Huntington, Samuel P. 1968. *Political Order in Changing Societies*. New Haven, CT: Yale University Press.

Indian Express. 2013. 'If Political Parties Are Not NGOs, Are They Government?'. https://indianexpress.com/article/news-archive/web/if-political-parties-are-not-ngos-are-they-government/. Accessed 7 November 2013.

———. 2014. 'The EC Touch'. 16 March. http://indianexpress.com/article/opinion/editorials/the-ec-touch. Accessed on 6 October 2017.

———. 2015. 'Gujarat Notifies Compulsory Voting in Local Body Elections'. 28 July. http://indianexpress.com/article/cities/ahmedabad/gujarat-notifies-compulsory-voting-in-local-body-elections. Accessed on 26 October 2017.

———. 2016. 'Ganesh Mandals Urged to Spread Awareness on Electoral Rights in Pune'. 5 September. http://indianexpress.com/article/cities/pune/ganesh-mandals-urged-to-spread-awareness-on-electoral-rights-in-pune-3014002/. Accessed on 6 October 2017.

———. 2017. 'EVM Tampering Issue: A Timeline of Previous Allegations of Voter Fraud'. 9 May. https://indianexpress.com/article/india/evm-tampering-issue-a-timeline-of-previous-allegations-of-voter-fraud-4648045. Accessed on 5 September 2022.

India Today. 1994. '*India Today*–MARG Poll'. 15 July.

———. 2017. 'What Role NOTA Played in Gujarat, Himachal Pradesh Election Results'. 19 December. https://www.indiatoday.in/india/story/nota-vote-share-gujarat-himachal-pradesh-bjp-congress-bsp-aap-1108802-2017-12-19. Accessed on 1 October 2021.

Indo-Asian News Service (IANS). 2018. 'India to Have over 800 Million Smartphone Users by 2022: Cisco Study'. *Economic Times*, 3 December. https://economictimes.indiatimes.com/tech/hardware/india-to-have

-over-800-million-smartphone-users-by-2022-cisco-study/articleshow/ 66917976.cms. Accessed on 24 April 2019.

Ingraham, Christopher. 2017. 'Somebody Just Put a Price Tag on the 2016 Election. It's a Doozy'. *Washington Post*, 14 April. https://www.washingtonpost.com/news/wonk/wp/2017/04/14/somebody-just-put-a-price-tag-on-the-2016-election-its-a-doozy/?utm_term=.5f3dafd069a2. Accessed on 2 February 2018.

International Institute for Democracy and Electoral Assistance (International IDEA). n.d. 'Compulsory Voting'. https://www.idea.int/data-tools/data/ voter-turnout/compulsory-voting. Accessed on 11 October 2017.

Jaffrelot, Christophe, and Gilles Verniers. 2011. 'Re-Nationalization of India's Political Party System or Continued Prevalence of Regionalism and Ethnicity?'. *Asian Survey* 51(6) (November–December): 1090–1112.

———. 2015. 'The Resistance of Regionalism: BJP's Limitations and the Resilience of State Parties'. In *India's 2014 Elections: A Modi-Led BJP Sweep*, edited by Paul Wallace, 28–45. New Delhi: SAGE Publications.

Jain, Bharti. 2017. 'Electoral Bonds Will Rob Poll Funding of Transparency, Fears CEC: Interview with Nasim Zaidi'. *Times of India*, 2 July. https:// timesofindia.indiatimes.com/india/electoral-bonds-will-rob-poll-funding-of-transparency-fears-cec/articleshow/59406789.cms. Accessed on 18 April 2018.

———. 2019. 'EC Wants Print, Social Media under Purview of 48-Hr Ban on Electioneering before Poll'. *Times of India*, 9 February. https://timesofindia. indiatimes.com/india/ec-wants-print-social-media-under-purview-of-48-hr-ban-on-electioneering-before-poll/articleshow/67908929.cms. Accessed on 26 August 2021.

Jain, Subhash C. 2001. 'State Funding of Elections and Political Parties in India'. *Journal of the Indian Law Institute* 43(4) (October–December): 500–11.

James, Toby S. 2018. 'Are UK Elections Conducted with Integrity, with Sufficient Turnout?'. Democratic Audit UK, 15 August. https://www.democraticaudit. com/2018/08/15/audit2018-are-uk-elections-conducted-with-integrity-with-sufficient-turnout. Accessed on 20 January 2021.

James, Toby S., Holly Ann Garnett, Leontine Loeber and Carolien van Ham. 2019. 'Electoral Management and the Organizational Determinants of Electoral Integrity: Introduction'. *International Political Science Review* 40(3): 295–312.

Jansen, Harold. 2020 (2006). 'Political Party Financing in Canada'. *The Canadian Encyclopedia*. https://www.thecanadianencyclopedia.ca/en/article/party-financing. Accessed on 15 November 2021.

Jayaram, Arvind. 2017. 'All You Wanted to Know About: Compulsory Voting'. *Hindu Business Line*, 30 November. https://www.thehindubusinessline.com/opinion/columns/All-you-wanted-to-know-about-Compulsory-voting/article20918448.ece. Accessed on 22 November 2021.

Jebaraj, Priscilla. 2019. 'Political Parties Yet to Comply with RTI Act'. *The Hindu*, 21 March. https://www.thehindu.com/news/national/political-parties-yet-to-comply-with-rti-act/article26601174.ece. Accessed on 29 August 2022.

Jenkins, Rob. 2000. 'Appearance and Reality in Indian Politics: Making Sense of the 1999 General Elections'. *Government and Opposition* 35(1) (Winter): 49–66.

Jinadu, Adele L. 1997. 'Matters Arising: African Elections and The Problem of Electoral Administration'. *African Journal of Political Science* 2(1) (Special Issue: Elections in Africa [June]): 1–11.

Jodhka, Surinder S., and Aseem Prakash. 2016. *The Indian Middle Class*. New Delhi: Oxford University Press.

Joshua, Anita. 2002. 'All-Party Meet Rejects EC Norm on Assets, Antecedents'. *The Hindu*, 9 July. http://www.hindu.com/2002/07/09/stories/2002070905760100.htm. Accessed on 15 October 2013.

J. S. Verma Committee. 2013. *Report of the Committee on Amendments to Criminal Law*. 23 January. http://www.prsindia.org/uploads/media/Justice%20verma%20committee/js%20verma%20committe%20report.pdf. Accessed on 3 June 2017.

Kandeh, Jimmy D. 2003. 'Sierra Lenoe's Post-Conflict Elections of 2002'. *Journal of Modern African Studies* 41(2): 189–216.

Kannaiah, V. 2019. 'How and Why Cash Polls the Votes in Tamil Nadu Elections'. *Indian Express*, 17 April. https://indianexpress.com/article/opinion/how-and-why-cash-polls-the-votes-in-tamil-nadu-elections-5680135. Accessed on 31 May 2021.

Kapur, Devesh, and Pratap Bhanu Mehta (eds.). 2007 (2005). *Public Institutions in India: Performance and Design*. New Delhi: Oxford University Press.

Kapur, Devesh, Pratap Bhanu Mehta and Milan Vaishnav (eds.). 2017. *Rethinking Public Institutions in India*. New Delhi: Oxford University Press.

Kapur, Devesh, and Milan Vaishnav (eds.). 2018. *Costs of Democracy: Political Finance in India*. New Delhi: Oxford University Press.

Karmakar, Rahul. 2018. 'One Dead as Violence Mars Polling in Nagaland (Elections Nagaland 2018)'. *The Hindu*, 27 February. https://www.thehindu.com/elections/nagaland-2018/one-dead-as-violence-mars-polling-in-nagaland/article22865697.ece. Accessed on 19 March 2021.

Karp, Jeffrey, Alessandro Nai, Miguel Angel, Lara Otaola and Pippa Norris. 2017. 'Professional Electoral Management: Building Capacity'. The Electoral Integrity Project, University of Sydney.

Katju, Manjari. 2006. 'Election Commission and Functioning of Democracy'. *Economic and Political Weekly* 41(17): 1635–40.

———. 2009. 'Election Commission and Changing Contours of Politics'. *Economic and Political Weekly* 44(16): 8–12.

———. 2013. 'The None of the Above Option'. *Economic and Political Weekly* 48(42): 10–12.

———. 2016. 'Mass Politics and Institutional Restraint: Political Parties and the Election Commission of India'. *Studies in Indian Politics* 4(1): 77–89.

———. 2019. 'Election Campaigning in a Transformed India'. *India Forum*, 7 May. https://www.theindiaforum.in/article/campaigning-transformed-india. Accessed on 6 March 2023.

Kildea, Paul. 2020. 'The Constitutional Role of Electoral Management Bodies: The Case of the Australian Electoral Commission'. *Federal Law Review* 48(4): 469–82. DOI: 10.1177/0067205X20955097.

Kumar, Arun. 2019. 'Financing Indian Elections: Black All the Way'. *The Hindu*, 16 July. https://www.thehindu.com/opinion/op-ed/financing-indian-elections-black-all-the-way/article28475007.ece. Accessed on 14 June 2021.

Kumar, Ashwani. 2008. *Community Warriors: State, Peasant and Caste Armies in Bihar*. New Delhi, London and New York: Anthem Press.

Kumar, B. Venkatesh. 1999. 'Funding of Elections: Case for Institutionalised Financing'. *Economic and Political Weekly* 34(28): 1884–88.

Kumar, Sanjay. 2002. 'Reforming Indian Electoral Process'. *Economic and Political Weekly* 37(34): 3489–91.

———. 2004. 'Impact of Economic Reforms on Indian Electorate'. *Economic and Political Weekly* 39(16) (17–23 April): 1621–30.

———. 2014. 'The Limits of the Youth Vote in Indian Elections'. Heinrich Boll Stiftung, 19 March. https://www.boell.de/en/2014/03/19/limits-youth-vote-indian-elections. Accessed on 7 November 2017.

Kundapura, Vishwa. 2014. '"SVEEP"ing Moves to Motivate the Voter'. *The Hindu*, 29 March. http://www.thehindu.com/news/national/karnataka/sveeping-moves-to-motivate-the-voter/article5847933.ece. Accessed on 2 October 2017.

Kapoor, M., and S. Ravi. 2014. 'Women Voters in Indian Democracy: A Silent Revolution'. *Economic and Political Weekly* 49(12): 63–67.

Kaur, Sumandeep. 2008. 'Electoral Reforms in India: Proactive Role of the Election Commission'. *Mainstream Weekly* 46(49) (22 November). http://www.mainstreamweekly.net/article1049.html. Accessed on 5 July 2016.

Kaushik, Susheela. 1982. *Elections In India: Its Social Basis*. Calcutta and New Delhi: K. P. Bagchi and Co.

Khare, Harish. 2001. 'Politics of Reordering Chaos'. *Seminar* 497 (January). http://www.india-seminar.com/2001/497/497%20harish%20khare.htm. Accessed on 8 September 2016.

Khanna, H. R. 1997. 'Bane of Money Power'. In *Electoral Reforms*, edited by Sharad Dighe and R. B. Sundriyal (the Institution of Constitutional and Parliamentary Studies), 40–55. New Delhi: Shree Publishing House.

Khanna, Inderjit. 2008. 'Towards a Common Electoral Roll'. *Seminar* 586 (June). http://www.india-seminar.com/2008/586.htm. Accessed on 4 September 2017.

Khera, Reetika. 2004. 'Monitoring Disclosures'. *Seminar* 534 (February). http://www.india-seminar.com/2004/534/534%20reetika%20khera.htm. Accessed on 21 June 2017.

Kirpal, B. N., Ashok Desai, Gopal Subramanium, Rajeev Dhavan and Raju Ramchandran (eds). 2004 (2000). *Supreme but Not Infallible: Essays in Honour of the Supreme Court of India*. New Delhi: Oxford University Press.

Klopp, Jacqueline M., and Elke Zuern. 2007. 'The Politics of Violence in Democratization: Lessons from Kenya and South Africa'. *Comparative Politics* 39(2) (January): 127–46.

Kondepati, Rajendra. 2011. 'Reforming the Campaign Finance Regime in India'. *Economic and Political Weekly* 46(52) (24 December): 70–75.

Krishnaswamy, S. 2001. 'Preparation of Correct Electoral Rolls'. *The Hindu*, 16 October. http://www.thehindu.com/2001/10/16/stories/13160383.htm. Accessed on 23 August 2017.

Kurien, P. J. 1997. 'Electoral Reforms'. In *Electoral Reforms*, edited by Sharad Dighe and R. B. Sundriyal (the Institution of Constitutional and Parliamentary Studies), 18–21. New Delhi: Shree Publishing House.

Laghate, Gaurav. 2016. 'Indian Media and Entertainment Industry to Grow at 10.3% CAGR, to Cross $40 Billion by 2020: PWC Report'. *Economic Times*, 9 June. http://economictimes.indiatimes.com/industry/media/entertainment/media/indian-media-and-entertainment-industry-to-grow-at-10-3-cagr-to-cross-40-billion-by-2020-pwc-report/articleshow/52658169.cms. Accessed on 8 September 2016.

Lakshmi, Rama. 2014. 'India Competes with Election Cycle's Dirty Money Problem'. *Washington Post*, 2 May. https://www.washingtonpost.com/world/ this-is-how-dirty-indias-elections-are-police-seize-cash-in-hearses-on-trains-in-lunchboxes/2014/05/01/68899439-2197-4b77-9215-7bf529d48f42_ story.html?utm_term=.ef35b9e6db03. Accessed on 14 February 2018.

Langa, Mahesh. 2015. 'Gujarat HC Stays Compulsory Voting in Local Polls'. *The Hindu*, 21 August. http://www.thehindu.com/news/national/other-states/gujarat-hc-stays-compulsary-voting/article7565684.ece. Accessed on 11 October 2017.

Law Commission of India. 1999. *170th Report on Reform of the Electoral Law*, May. http://www.lawcommissionofindia.nic.in/lc170.htm. Accessed on 12 September 2016.

———. 2015. *255th Report on Electoral Reforms*, March. http://lawcommissionof india.nic.in/reports/Report255.pdf. Accessed on 5 September 2017.

Lawrence, Thomas B., Monika I. Winn and P. Devereaux Jennings. 2001. 'The Temporal Dynamics of Institutionalization'. *Academy of Management Review* 26(4): 624–44.

Lehoucq, Fabrice. 2003. 'Electoral Fraud: Causes, Types, and Consequences'. *Annual Review of Political Science* 6: 233–56. DOI: 10.1146/annurev.polisci.6 .121901.085655

Lok Sabha Secretariat. 2015. 'Reference Note No. No. 36/RN/Ref./November /2015'. https://164.100.47.193/Refinput/New_Reference_Notes/English/ CompulsoryVoting.pdf. Accessed on 9 September 2021.

Lyngdoh, J. M. 2004. *Chronicle of an Impossible Election: The Election Commission and the 2002 Jammu and Kashmir Assembly Elections*. New Delhi: Viking Press.

Magee, C. 2012. 'The Incumbent Spending Puzzle'. *Social Science Quarterly* 93(4): 932–49.

Mahapatra, Dhananjay. 2013. 'No One Can Contest Elections if Affidavit Silent on Antecedents: SC'. *Times of India*, 14 September 2013. https://timesofindia. indiatimes.com/india/no-one-can-contest-elections-if-affidavit-silent-on-antecedents-sc/articleshow/22567507.cms. Accessed on 1 November 2013.

Malhotra, Sarika. 2014. 'Economy vs Democracy'. *Business Today*, 27 April. http://www.businesstoday.in/magazine/cover-story/lok-sabha-election-2014-campaign-trends-new-govt-challenges/story/204871.html. Accessed on 12 January 2018.

Manor, James. 2005. 'The Presidency'. In *Public Institutions in India: Performance and Design*, edited by Devesh Kapur and Pratap Bhanu Mehta, 105–27. New Delhi: Oxford University Press.

Maravall, Jose Maria, and Adam Przeworski (eds.). 2003. *Democracy and the Rule of Law*. Cambridge (UK) and New York: Cambridge University Press.

March, James G., and Johan P. Olsen. 1984. 'The New Institutionalism: Organizational Factors in Political Life'. *American Political Science Review* 78(3): 734–49.

———. 1989. *Rediscovering Institutions: The Organizational Basis of Politics*. New York: The Free Press.

———. 2005. 'Elaborating the "New Institutionalism"'. Working Paper No. 11, Centre for European Studies, University of Oslo, March. http://www.arena. uio.no. Accessed on 6 December 2020.

Mathew, Liz, and Anuja. 2013. 'MPs, MLAs Must Quit Immediately if Convicted: Supreme Court'. *Mint*, 10 July. http://www.livemint.com/ Politics/R5FCrQyAKYgNtMWlUEHoHI/Convicted-MPs-and-MLAs-have-to-step-down-immediately-says-S.html. Accessed on 7 June 2017.

Mathur, Kuldeep. 2001. 'Strengthening Bureaucracy: State and Development in India'. In *Democratic Governance in India: Challenges of Poverty, Development, and Identity*, edited by Niraja Gopal Jayal and Sudha Pai, 109–31. New Delhi, Thousand Oaks (CA) and London: SAGE Publications.

Mccue, James. 2018. 'Should India, Like Japan, Consider Reducing Its Voter Age?'. *The Print*, 19 July. https://theprint.in/india/governance/should-india-like-japan-consider-reducing-its-voting-age/84977. Accessed on 22 November 2021.

McMillan, Alistair. 2012. 'The Election Commission of India and the Regulation and Administration of Electoral Politics'. *Election Law Journal* 11(2): 187–201.

Mealey, Rachel. 2017. 'Japan Election Campaigns "a Little Bit Old-Fashioned" with Strict Laws and Billboard Bans'. *ABC News*, 14 October. https://www.abc.net.au/news/2017-10-14/election-campaigns-in-japan-an-old-fashioned-affair/9040624. Accessed on 8 September 2021.

Mehra, Ajay, and Gert W. Kueck (eds.). 2003. *The Indian Parliament: A Comparative Perspective*. New Delhi: Konark Publishers.

Mehta, Nalin. 2019. 'Digital Politics in India's 2019 Elections'. *EPW Engage* (Online), *Economic and Political Weekly*. https://www.epw.in/engage/article/ digital-politics-indias-2019-general-elections. Accessed on 8 September 2021.

Mehta, Pratap Bhanu. 2001. 'Reform Political Parties First'. *Seminar* 497 (January). www.india-seminar.com. Accessed on 27 August 2016.

————. 2013. 'Blunt Hammer Syndrome'. *Indian Express*, 4 October. http:// indianexpress.com/article/opinion/columns/blunt-hammer-syndrome. Accessed on 7 June 2017.

Menon, Nivedita, and Aditya Nigam. 2008. *Power and Contestation: Indian since 1989*. Hyderabad: Orient Longman.

Miglani, Sanjeev. 2014. 'Indian Voters Lured by Cash Handouts, Drugs, Bootleg Liquor'. *Reuters*, 15 April. https://www.reuters.com/article/us-india-election -funding/indian-voters-lured-by-cash-handouts-drugs-bootleg-liquor- idUSBREA3E0LQ20140415. Accessed on 14 February 2018.

Milligan, Kevin, and Marie Rekkas. 2008. 'Campaign Spending Limits, Incumbent Spending, and Election Outcomes'. *Canadian Journal of Economics (Revue Canadienne D'Economique)* 41(4): 1351–74.

Mitta, Manoj. 1994. 'T. N. Seshan Reined In'. *India Today*, 30 April.

Mitta, Manoj, Zafar Agha and Yubaraj Ghimre. 1994. 'Electoral Reforms: Zeroing in on Seshan'. *India Today*, 30 June.

Moe, Terry M. 2006. 'Power and Political Institutions'. In *Rethinking Political Institutions: The Art of the State*, edited by Ian Shapiro, Stephen Skowronek and Daniel Galvin, 32–71. New York and London: New York University Press.

Mohanty, Prasanna. 2019. 'Agenda for New Government: A Credible ECI'. *India Today*, 1 June. https://www.indiatoday.in/india/story/agenda-for-next- government-restoring-credibility-of-eci-1539929-2019-06-01. Accessed on 6 September 2021.

Morrow, Paige. 2019. 'UK Election 2019: We Need to Change the Rules on Poll Day Reporting'. Article 19, 11 December. https://www.article19.org/ resources/uk-we-need-to-change-the-rules-on-election-day-reporting. Accessed on 26 August 2022.

Mozaffar, Shaheen, and Andreas Schedler. 2002. 'The Comparative Study of Electoral Governance: Introduction'. *International Political Science Review* 23(1): 5–27.

Mukherjee, Rudrangshu. 2011. *Rajiv Gandhi: Lowering the Voting Age to Eighteen (New Delhi 1988)*. Gurgaon: Penguin Random House.

Muralidharan, Sukumar, and V. Venkatesan. 2000. 'A Presidential Intervention'. *Frontline* 17(3). http://www.hinduonnet.com/fline/fl1703/17030250.htm. Accessed on 3 July 2009. Muralidharan, Sukumar. 1998. 'The Task of Elections'. *Frontline*, 27 December. http://www.frontline.in/static/html/ fl1426/14260040.htm. Accessed 4 February 2017.

Murthy, T. S. Krishna. 2008. *The Miracle of Democracy: India's Amazing Journey.* Noida: HarperCollins Publishers India.

Nadeau, Paul, and Rob Fahey. 2017. 'In Praise of Japan's Election Campaigns'. *TokyoReview*, 24 October. https://www.tokyoreview.net/2017/10/japan-election-campaigns. Accessed on 8 September 2021.

Nagarathinam, Nithya. 2014. 'Criminalisation of Politics'. The Hindu Centre for Politics and Public Policy, 30 April. http://www.thehinducentre.com/verdict/get-the-fact/article5962667.ece. Accessed on 12 July 2017.

Nambiar, Nisha. 2014. 'Special Drive Launched to Spread Voter Awareness, Focus on Low-Polling Areas'. *Indian Express*, 4 October. http://indian express.com/article/cities/pune/special-drive-launched-to-spread-voter-awareness-focus-on-low-polling-areas. Accessed on 6 October 2017.

Nanjappa, Vicky. 2013. 'Survey Shows 1,460 Criminal MPs and MLAs in the Country'. Rediff.com, 10 July. https://www.rediff.com/news/report/survey-shows-1460-criminal-mps-and-mlas-in-the-country/20130710.htm. Accessed on 11 September 2013.

Narayan, Jayaprakash. 2003. 'Elections: Disclosures Are Now Mandatory'. *India Together*, March. https://indiatogether.org/ncerscverd-laws. Accessed on 29 August 2022.

———. 2013. 'Electoral Reforms: How It Can Be Done'. In *Electoral Reforms: Why and How*, edited by K. Raman Pillai, R. K. Suresh Kumar and P. Sukumaran Nair, 311–23. Delhi: Kalpaz Publications.

Narula, Smita. 1999. *Broken People: Caste Violence against India's 'Untouchables'.* New York: Human Rights Watch.

National Commission to Review the Working of the Constitution (NCRWC). 2001. 'A Consultation Paper on *Review of Election Law, Processes and Reform Options*'. https://legalaffairs.gov.in/volume-2-book-1. Accessed on 4 March 2023.

———. 2002a. 'Chapter 4: Electoral Processes and Political Parties'. In *Report*, vol. 1. http://lawmin.nic.in/ncrwc/ncrwcreport.htm. Accessed on 16 January 2018.

———. 2002b. *Report*, vol. 2, book 1, s. no. 6: 'Review of the Working of Political Parties Specially in Relation to Elections and Reform Options (A Consultation Paper, 2001)'. http://lawmin.nic.in/ncrwc/ncrwcreport.htm. accessed on 5 October 2017.

Neumann, S. 1963. 'Toward a Comparative Study of Political Parties'. In *Comparative Politics: A Reader*, edited by H. Eckstein and D. E. Apter, 351–57. New York: Macmillan Publishers.

Nice, David C. 1987. 'Campaign Spending & Presidential Election Results'. *Polity* 19(3): 464–76.

Norris, Pippa. 2014. *Why Electoral Integrity Matters*. New York: Cambridge University Press.

———. 2015. *Why Elections Fail*. New York: Cambridge University Press.

North, Andrew. 2013. 'The Indian Politicians Facing Criminal Charges'. British Broadcasting Corporation (BBC), 15 February. http://www.bbc.com/news/world-asia-india-21469286. Accessed on 3 June 2017.

North, Douglass C. 1991. 'Institutions'. *Journal of Economic Perspectives* 5(1): 97–112.

Odgers, James Rowland. 2016 (1953). 'Chapter 12: Legislation'. In *Odgers' Australian Senate Practice*, edited by Rosemary Laing and revised by Harry Evans, 299–358. Canberra: Department of the Senate, Parliament of Australia.

Offe, Clause. 2006. 'Political Institutions and Social Power: Conceptual Explorations'. In *Rethinking Political Institutions: The Art of the State*, edited by Ian Shapiro, Stephen Skowronek and Daniel Galvin, 9–31. New York and London: New York University Press.

Oliver, Christine. 1992. 'The Antecedents of Deinstitutionalization'. *Organizational Studies* 13(4): 563–88. DOI: 10.1177/017084069201300403.

Onishi, Norimitsu. 2019. 'Who Is Funding the ANC's Election Campaign? South Africans Are in the Dark'. *New York Times*, 9 May. https://www.nytimes.com/2019/05/04/world/africa/south-africa-election-campaign-ramaphosa.html. Accessed on 7 September 2021.

Padmanabhan, Mukund. 2004. 'Bite the Ballot: Post Retirement Posts'. *The Hindu*, 4 April. http://www.thehindu.com/thehindu/mag/2004/04/04/stories/2004040400190300.htm. Accessed on 9 February 2017.

Pai, Sudha. 1996. 'Transformation of the Indian Party System: The 1996 Lok Sabha Elections'. *Asian Survey* 36(12): 1170–83.

———. 1998. 'The Indian Party System under Transformation: Lok Sabha Elections 1998'. *Asian Survey* 38(9): 836–52.

——— (ed.). 2020. *Constitutional and Democratic Institutions in India: A Critical Analysis*. Hyderabad: Orient BlackSwan.

Pallavi. 2019. 'The Many Claims of EVM Tampering in India'. *India Today*, 21 January. https://www.indiatoday.in/elections/story/the-many-claims-of-evm-tampering-in-india-1435638-2019-01-21. Accessed on 7 January 2021.

Palshikar, Suhas. 2013. 'Election Studies'. In *Indian Democracy (ICSSR Research Surveys and Explorations: Political Science)*, vol. 2, edited by K. C. Suri, 161–208. New Delhi: Oxford University Press.

Palshikar, Suhas, and Sanjay Kumar. 2004. 'Participatory Norm: How Broad-Based Is It?'. *Economic and Political Weekly* 39(51) (18 December): 5412–17.

Panchu, Sriram. 2009. 'Free and Fair Election Commissioners?'. *Economic and Political Weekly* 44(9): 10–12.

Pande, Shamni. 2014. 'Just the Right Image'. *Business Today*, 8 June. https://www.businesstoday.in/magazine/case-study/case-study-strategy-tactics-behind-creation-of-brand-narendra-modi/story/206321.html. Accessed on 14 April 2021.

Pandey, Devesh K. 2017. 'Over 5.5 Lakh Voters Went with NOTA'. *The Hindu*, 19 December. https://www.thehindu.com/elections/gujarat-2017/gujarat-second-in-highest-nota-votes/article21938375.ece. Accessed on 1 October 2021.

Parliamentary Education Service. n.d. *Parliament Explained 1: Parliamentary Elections*. https://www.parliament.uk/globalassets/documents/upload/no1 parlyelectionsweb.pdf. Accessed on 1 September 2021.

Pastor, Robert A. 1999. 'The Role of Electoral Administration in Democratic Transitions: Implications for Policy and Research'. *Democratizaton* 6(4): 1–27.

Paul, Samuel. 2003. 'Right to Information on Candidates: How Will the Voters Know?'. *Economic and Political Weekly* 38(15) (12 April): 1447–49.

Peters, B. Guy, and Jon Pierre. 1998. 'Institutions and Time: Problems of Conceptualization and Explanation'. *Journal of Public Administration Research and Theory* 8(4): 565–83.

Peters, B. Guy, Jon Pierre and Desmond S. King. 2005. 'The Politics of Path Dependency: Political Conflict in Historical Institutionalism'. *Journal of Politics* 67(4): 1275–1300.

Peters, B. Guy. 2012. *Institutional Theory in Political Science: The New Institutionalism*. New York: Continuum.

Phillips, Nelson, Thomas B. Lawrence and Cynthia Hardy. 2000. 'Interorganizational Collaboration and the Dynamics of Institutional Fields'. *Journal of Management Studies* 37(1): 23–45.

———. 2004. 'Discourse and Institutions'. *Academy of Management Review* 29(4): 635–52.

Pierson, Paul. 2000. 'Increasing Returns, Path Dependence, and the Study of Politics'. *American Political Science Review* 94(2): 251–67.

Pierson, Paul, and Theda Skocpol. 2002. 'Historical Institutionalism in Contemporary Political Science'. In *Political Science: State of the Discipline*, edited by Ira Katznelson and Helen V. Milner, 693–721. New York: Norton.

Pillai, Ramachandran S. 2002, 'Electoral Reform Measures: CPI(M) Stand on SC Judgement, EC Order'. People's Democracy, 14 July. http://archives. peoplesdemocracy.in/2002/july21/07212002_elc_reforms.htm. Accessed on 21 June 2017.

Press Information Bureau (PIB). 2014. 'SVEEP: For Making Elections Inclusive (Special Feature 4, General Elections 2014)'. 24 February. http://pib.gov.in/ newsite/mbErel.aspx?relid=104195. Accessed on 8 September 2017.

———. 2015. 'Election Commission Launches National Electoral Roll Purification and Authentication Programme (NERPAP) from Today'. 3 March. http://pib.nic.in/newsite/PrintRelease.aspx?relid=116280. Accessed on 1 October 2017.

Press, Jordan, and Joan Bryden. 2016. 'Cash a Factor in 2015 Election Campaign Result'. CBC News, 4 April. https://www.cbc.ca/news/politics/federal-election-finances-campaign-spending-1.3519357. Accessed on 7 September 2021.

Press Trust of India (PTI). 2014a. 'On Women's Day, ECI Holds Special Campaign to Woo Women Voters'. Indian Express, 9 March. http:// indianexpress.com/article/india/india-others/on-womens-day-eci-holds-special-campaign-to-woo-women-voters-2. Accessed on 6 October 2017.

———. 2014b. 'Blackmoney in Polls: Election Commission Creates Multi-Agency Intelligence Grid'. Daily News and Analysis (DNA), 11 March. http://www.dnaindia.com/india/report-blackmoney-in-polls-election-commission-creates-multi-agency-intelligence-grid-1968520. Accessed on 9 June 2014.

———. 2014c. '195 Crore Cash Seized in Poll Season, Andhra Pradesh Tops List'. NDTV, 8 April. http://www.ndtv.com/elections/article/election-2014/195-crore-cash-seized-in-poll-season-andhra-pradesh-tops-list-505725. Accessed on 9 June 2014.

———. 2014d. 'EC Releases Tool to Get Citizen Reports on Illegal Campaigning, Hate Speech during Poll'. Firstpost, 23 April. https://www. firstpost.com/tech/news-analysis/ec-releases-tool-to-get-citizen-reports-on-illegal-campaigning-hate-speech-during-polls-3650543.html. Accessed on 18 September 2022.

———. 2015. 'India Has 1866 Registered Political Parties: Election Commission'. Economic Times, 9 August. https://economictimes.indiatimes.com/news/ politics-and-nation/india-has-1866-registered-political-parties-election-commission/articleshow/48410304.cms?from=mdr. Accessed on 6 June 2021.

———. 2017. 'Major Parties Spent Rs. 5,500 Crore on Uttar Pradesh Poll Campaign: Study'. *Economic Times*, 17 March. https://economictimes. indiatimes.com/news/politics-and-nation/major-parties-spent-rs-5500-crore-on-uttar-pradesh-poll-campaign-study/articleshow/57686403.cms. Accessed on 20 March 2018.

———. 2018. 'NOTA Outperforms Several Political Parties in Five States'. NDTV, 11 December. https://www.ndtv.com/india-news/nota-outperforms-several-political-parties-in-five-states-1961239. Accessed on 1 October 2021.

Proceedings of the Seminar on Electoral Reforms. 1986. *Record of Deliberations, Madras, 1985*. New Delhi: Rajaji International Institute of Public Affairs and Administration.

Public Affairs Centre (PAC). 2006. *Deepening Democracy: A Decade of Electoral Interventions by Civil Society Groups (1996–2006)*. Bangalore: Public Affairs Centre.

Quraishi, S. Y. 2013. 'Pressure of a Button'. *Indian Express*, 3 October. http://www.indianexpress.com/news/pressure-of-a-button/1177434/1. Accessed on 3 October 2013.

———. 2014. *An Undocumented Wonder: The Making of the Great Indian Election*. New Delhi: Rupa Publications.

———. 2015. 'Upholding the Model Code'. *The Tribune*, 12 October. http://www.tribuneindia.com/news/comment/upholding-the-model-code/144770. html. Accessed on 19 January 2017.

——— (ed.). 2019. *The Great March of Democracy: Seven Decades of India's Elections*. New Delhi: Penguin Books.

Rahman, Naziya Alvi. 2015. 'Unable to Trace Them, EC Deletes Names of 12 Lakh Voters from List'. *Daily News and Analysis (DNA)*, 15 October. http://www.dnaindia.com/mumbai/report-unable-to-trace-them-ec-deletes-names-of-12-lakh-voters-from-list-2134981. Accessed on 23 September 2017.

Rai, Praveen. 2009. 'Issues in General Election 2009'. *Economic and Political Weekly* 44(39): 80–82.

Raj, Anand. 2010. 'Revised Rolls Let Voters Down'. *The Telegraph*, 2 November. https://www.telegraphindia.com/1101102/jsp/bihar/story_13126914.jsp. Accessed on 5 October 2017.

Ramakrishnan, T. 2019. 'T. N. Seshan (1932–2019): The Man Who Cleaned Up the Indian Electoral System'. *The Hindu*, 11 November. https://www. thehindu.com/news/national/tn-seshan-obituary-the-man-who-cleaned

-up-the-indian-electoral-system/article29939660.ece. Accessed on 12 October 2020.

Ramon Magsaysay Award Foundation. 1996. 'Seshan, Tirunellai Narayanaiyer, India, 1996'. https://www.rmaward.asia/awardee/seshan-tirunellai-narayan aiyer. Accessed on 12 October 2020.

Rangarajan, Mahesh. 2005. 'Polity in Transition: India after the 2004 General Elections'. *Economic and Political Weekly* 40(32) (6–12 August): 3598–3605.

Ranjan, Sudhanshu. 2012. 'Election Spending and the Law'. *Hindu Business Line*, 30 January. https://www.thehindubusinessline.com/opinion/election-spending-and-the-law/article20390519.ece1. Accessed on 21 March 2018.

Rao, Padmanabha T. 2002. 'Enforcing Hartal by Coercion Illegal, Says SC'. *The Hindu*, 11 May. http://www.thehindu.com/2002/05/11/stories/200205110 2790100.htm. Accessed on 29 March 2017.

Rao, Raghvendra. 2015. 'Error-Free Electoral Rolls Will Be Ready by 2016: Nasim Zaidi'. *Indian Express*, 1 May. http://indianexpress.com/article/india/india-others/error-free-electoral-rolls-will-be-ready-by-2016-nasim-zaidi. Accessed on 19 September 2017.

Rapoport, David C., and Leonard Weinberg. 2000. 'Elections and Violence'. *Terrorism and Political Violence* 12(3–4): 15–50.

Rekkas, Marie. 2007. 'The Impact of Campaign Spending on Votes in Multiparty Elections'. *Review of Economics and Statistics* 89(3) (August): 573–85.

Reddy, Agarala Easwara, and D. Sundar Ram. 1992. 'Democracy and Indian Electoral System: Need for Reforms'. In *Electoral Reforms in India*, edited by Agarala Easwara Reddy and D. Sundar Ram. 14–44. New Delhi: Uppal Publishing House.

Reddy, O. Chinnappa. 2010 (2008). *The Court and the Constitution of India: Summits and Shallows*. New Delhi: Oxford University Press.

Roy, Abhijit. 2018. 'The Middle Class in India: From 1947 to the Present and Beyond'. *Education about Asia* 23(1): 32–37. https://www.asianstudies.org/wp-content/uploads/the-middle-class-in-india-from-1947-to-the-present-and-beyond.pdf. Accessed on 7 February 2023.

Roy, Anupama. 2012. 'Identifying Citizens: Electoral Rolls, the Right to Vote, and the Election Commission of India'. *Election Law Journal: Rules, Politics, and Policy* 11(2): 170–86. DOI: 10.1089/elj.2011.0124.

Roy, Marc-André. 2017. *Criminal Charges and Parliamentarians*. https://lop.parl.ca/sites/PublicWebsite/default/en_CA/ResearchPublications/201728E#a2. Accessed on 17 September 2022.

Roy, Prannoy, and Dorab R. Sopariwala. 2019. *The Verdict: Decoding India's Elections*. Gurgaon: Vintage Books.

Roy, Ranjan. 2007. 'Lawmakers as Law-Breakers'. *Times of India*, 29 April. http://timesofindia.indiatimes.com/home/sunday-times/all-that-matters/Lawmakers-as-law-breakers/articleshow/1974322.cms. Accessed on 4 June 2017.

Rajya Sabha TV. 2015. 'Law Asking "Compulsory Vote" Stayed by Gujarat HC'. 21 August. http://rstv.nic.in/law-asking-compulsory-vote-stayed-gujarat-hc.html. Accessed on 12 October 2017.

Rudolph, Susanne Hoeber, and Lloyd I. Rudolph. 2001. 'Redoing the Constitutional Design: From an Interventionist to a Regulatory State'. In *The Success of India's Democracy*, edited by Atul Kohli, 127–62. Cambridge, UK: Cambridge University Press.

Rukmini, S. 2014. '16th Lok Sabha Will Be Richest, Have Most MPs with Criminal Charges'. *The Hindu*, 18 May. http://www.thehindu.com/news/national/16th-lok-sabha-will-be-richest-have-most-mps-with-criminal-charges/article6022513.ece. Accessed on 17 November 2016.

Salam, Zia Us. 2019. 'Electoral Rolls: Missing Votes'. *Frontline*, 5 July. https://frontline.thehindu.com/cover-story/article24200903.ece. Accessed on 1 July 2019.

Sampat, Kinjal, and Jyoti Mishra. 2014. 'Interest in Politics and Political Participation'. In *Indian Youth and Electoral Politics: An Emerging Engagement*, edited by Sanjay Kumar, 18–46. New Delhi: SAGE Publications.

Sampath, V. S. 2014. 'The Efficacy of Indian Elections Is Time Tested'. Interview with CEC V.S. Sampath. Rediff.com, 2 May. http://www.rediff.com/news/interview/ls-election-exclusive-chief-election-commissioner-v-s-sampath-on-election-2014/20140502.htm. Accessed on 17 December 2016.

Samuel, John, and Jagadananda (eds.). 2003. *Social Watch India: Citizens Report on Governance and Development 2003*. Bhubaneswar and Pune: Centre for Youth and Social Development and National Centre for Advocacy Studies.

Sanchez-Cuenca, Ignacio. 1998. 'Institutional Commitments and Democracy'. *European Journal of Sociology* 39(1): 78–109.

———. 2003. 'Power, Rules, and Compliance'. In *Democracy and the Rule of Law*, edited by Jose Maria Maravall and Adam Przeworski, 62–93. Cambridge (UK) and New York: Cambridge University Press.

Sangita, S. N. 2013. 'Electoral Process and Inclusive Governance'. In *Electoral Reforms: Why and How*, edited by K. Raman Pillai, R. K. Suresh Kumar and P. Sukumaran Nair, 67–88. Delhi: Kalpaz Publications.

Sastry, Trilochan, 2004. 'Electoral Reforms and Citizens' Initiatives: Some Breakthroughs'. *Economic and Political Weekly* 39(13): 1391–97.

———. 2014. 'Towards Decriminalisation of Elections and Politics'. *Economic and Political Weekly* 49(1) (January 4): 34–41.

Sathe, Vasant. 1997. 'Electoral Reforms'. In *Electoral Reforms*, edited by Sharad Dighe and R. B. Sundriyal (the Institution of Constitutional and Parliamentary Studies), 5–9. New Delhi: Shree Publishing House.

Second Administrative Reforms Commission. 2007. *Fourth Report: Ethics in Governance.* http://arc.gov.in/4threport.pdf. Accessed on 16 January 2018.

Sekhar, A. Saye. 2009. 'Fighting Elections: The Unofficial Cost'. *The Hindu*, 6 April. http://www.thehindu.com/todays-paper/tp-national/Fighting-elections -the-unofficial-cost/article16610393.ece. Accessed on 7 February 2018.

Selznick, Philip. 1949. *TVA and the Grass Roots: A Study in the Sociology of Formal Organization.* Berkeley and Los Angeles: University of California Press.

———. 1953. *TVA and the Grass Roots: A Study in the Sociology of Formal Organization.* Berkeley and Los Angeles: University of California Press.

———. 1996. 'Institutionalism "Old" and "New"'. *Administrative Science Quarterly* 41(2): 270–77.

Sen, Ronojoy. 2012. 'Identifying Criminals and Crorepatis in Indian Politics: An Analysis of Two Supreme Court Rulings'. *Election Law Journal* 11(2): 216–25.

Sen, S. R. 1991. 'Electoral System: Urgency of Basic Reforms'. *Economic and Political Weekly* 26(6): 282–83.

Sengupta, Uttam. 2013. 'Ban Cash Spending and Anonymous Donors'. Interview with CEC V. S. Sampath. *Outlook*, 16 December. https://www.outlookindia. com/magazine/story/ban-cash-spending-and-anonymous-donors/288793. Accessed on 14 February 2018.

Sezhiyan, Era. 2006. 'Use Voting Machines against Booth Capturing'. *The Hindu*, 20 October. http://www.thehindu.com/todays-paper/tp-opinion/use -voting-machines-against-booth-capturing/article3063450.ece. Accessed on 29 December 2017.

Shankar, Shylashri. 2009. *Scaling Justice: India's Supreme Court, Anti-Terror Laws, and Social Rights.* New Delhi: Oxford University Press.

Shani, Ornit. 2018. *How India Became Democratic: Citizenship and the Making of the Universal Franchise.* Gurgaon: Penguin Random House India.

Shankar, B. L., and Valerian Rodrigues. 2011. *The Indian Parliament: A Democracy at Work.* New Delhi: Oxford University Press.

Shariff, Abusaleh, and Khalid Saifullah. 2018. 'Electoral Exclusion of Muslims Continues to Plague Indian Democracy'. *EPW Engage* (Online), *Economic and Political Weekly*, 19 May. https://www.epw.in/engage/article/electoral-exclusion-muslims-continues-plague-indian-democracy?0=ip_login_no_cache%3D0d7b78d59fc5d52f1a2914a401eec017. Accessed on 5 June 2021.

Sharma, Mihir. 2017. 'India's Burgeoning Youth Are the World's Future'. *Mint*, 8 September. https://www.livemint.com/Opinion/2WSy5ZGR9ZO3KLD MGiJq2J/Indias-burgeoning-youth-are-the-worlds-future.html. Accessed on 26 April 2019.

Shashidhar, Karthik. 2013. 'How NOTA Worked in the Assembly Elections'. *Mint*, 10 December. http://www.livemint.com/Specials/t5687TxRCE3aKu 4svfHXrK/Assembly-elections-Analysing-NOTA.html. Accessed on 14 June 2017.

Sheth, D. L. 1996. 'The Maturing of a Democracy'. Exclusive ICSSR–CSDS–*India Today* Poll. *India Today*, 31 August.

Sidhu, W. P. S. 1991. 'Chief Election Commissioner Moving On: Seshan to Be Shifted Out'. *India Today*, 15 October.

Sim, Walter. 2017. 'Election Campaign, the Japanese Way'. *Straits Times*, 17 October. https://www.straitstimes.com/asia/east-asia/election-fever-hits-japan. Accessed on 26 August 2021.

Singh, H. Khogen. 2018. 'In the Poll-Bound Nagaland, a Village Flags Down Cash-for-Votes'. *New Indian Express*, 24 February. http://www.newindian express.com/thesundaystandard/2018/feb/24/in-the-poll-bound-nagaland -a-village-flags-down-cash-for-votes-1778487.html. Accessed on 20 March 2018.

Singh, Tanaya. 2015. 'This 66 Year Old Is on a Mission. He Won't Rest till All Electoral Rolls in India Are Error-Free!'. *Better India*, 4 September. https://www.thebetterindia.com/32815/pg-bhat-software-to-find-errors-in-electoral-rolls. Accessed on 24 August 2017.

Singh, Ujjwal Kumar. 2004. *Institutions and Democratic Governance: A Study of the Election Commission and Electoral Governance in India*. NMML Monograph. New Delhi: Nehru Memorial Museum and Library.

———. 2012. 'Between Moral Force and Supplementary Legality: A Model Code of Conduct and the Election Commission of India'. *Election Law Journal* 11(2): 149–69.

Singh, Ujjwal Kumar, and Anupama Roy. 2019. *Election Commission of India: Institutionalising Democratic Uncertainties*. New Delhi: Oxford University Press.

Sirothia, Ankur. 2013. 'Efforts on to Increase Voter Turnout through SVEEP Activities'. *Times of India*, 10 October. https://timesofindia.indiatimes.

com/assembly-elections-2013/madhya-pradesh-assembly-elections/Efforts
-on-to-increase-voter-turnout-through-SVEEP-activities/articleshow/2384
2172.cms. Accessed on 8 November 2017.

Skocpol, Theda. 1992. *Protecting Soldiers and Mothers: The Political Origins of Social Policy in the United States*. Cambridge, UK: Cambridge University Press.

Sreevatsan, Ajai. 2017. 'How Much of India Is Actually Urban?'. *Mint*, 16 September. https://www.livemint.com/Politics/4UjtdRPRikhpo8vAE0V4hK/How-much-of-India-is-actually-urban.html. Accessed on 26 April 2019.

Sridharan, Eswaran. 2010. 'The Party System'. In *The Oxford Companion to Politics in India*, edited by Niraja Gopal Jayal and Pratap Bhanu Mehta, 117–35. New Delhi: Oxford University Press.

———. 2014. 'Class Voting in the 2014 Lok Sabha Elections: The Growing Size and Importance of the Middle Classes'. *Economic and Political Weekly* 49(39) (27 September): 72–76.

Sridharan, Eswaran, and Peter Ronald deSouza (eds.). 2006. 'Introduction: The Evolution of Political Parties in India'. In *India's Political Parties*, edited by Peter Ronald DeSouza and Eswaran Sridharan, 15–36. New Delhi: SAGE Publications.

Sridharan, Eswaran, and Milan Vaishnav. 2016. 'Chapter 4: India'. In *Checkbook Elections?: Political Finance in Comparative Perspective*, edited by Pippa Norris and Andrea Abel Van Es, 64–83. New York: Oxford University Press.

———. 2017. 'Election Commission of India'. In *Rethinking Public Institutions In India*, edited by Devesh Kapur, Pratap Bhanu Mehta and Milan Vaishnav, 417–63. New Delhi: Oxford University Press.

Steele, Abbey. 2011. 'Electing Displacement: Political Cleansing in Apartadó, Colombia'. *Journal of Conflict Resolution* 55(3): 423–45. https://doi.org/10.1177 /0022002711400975. Accessed on 25 February 2023.

Stratmann, Thomas. 2006. 'Contribution Limits and the Effectiveness of Campaign Spending'. *Public Choice* 129(3–4) (December): 461–74.

Sundaresan, Somasekhar. 2018. 'Govt's Electoral Bonds for Political Funding: A Cloak to Hide the Daggers?'. *Business Standard*, 17 January. http://www. business-standard.com/article/opinion/govt-s-electoral-bonds-for-political-funding-a-cloak-to-hide-the-daggers-118011701521_1.html. Accessed on 12 March 2018.

Supreme Court. 2013a. 'Civil Original Jurisdiction Writ Petition (Civil) No. 161 of 2004'. http://www.pucl.org/Topics/Law/2013/vote_none.pdf. Accessed 13 June 2017.

Supreme Court. 2013b. *Resurgence India v. Election Commission of India and Another.* https://indiankanoon.org/doc/77678068/. Accessed on 4 April 2018.

Suri, K. C. 2013. 'Party System and Party Politics in India'. In *Indian Democracy (ICSSR Research Surveys and Explorations: Political Science*, vol. 2, edited by K. C. Suri, 209–52. New Delhi: Oxford University Press.

Syal, Reetika. 2012. 'What Are the Effects of Educational Mobility on Political Interest and Participation in the Indian Electorate?'. *Asian Survey* 52(2) (March–April): 423–39.

Thakkar, Mitul. 2013. 'Chhattisgarh Assembly Elections: NOTA Matches Victory Margin in 45 Seats'. *Economic Times*, 9 December. http://economic times.indiatimes.com/news/politics-and-nation/chhattisgarh-assembly-elections-nota-matches-victory-margin-in-45-seats/articleshow/27104470. cms. Accessed on 14 June 2017.

The Economist. 2014. 'Why American Elections Cost So Much'. 9 February. https://www.economist.com/blogs/economist-explains/2014/02/economist-explains-4. Accessed on 2 February 2018.

The Hindu. 2006. 'Election Commission Needs Reforms'. 31 August.

———. 2008. 'Villagers Find Their Names Missing from Electoral Rolls'. *The Hindu*, 18 November. http://www.thehindu.com/todays-paper/tp-national/ tp-tamilnadu/Villagers-find-their-names-missing-from-electoral-rolls/ article15344141.ece. Accessed on 9 November 2017.

———. 2013a. 'Names Go Missing from Electoral Rolls in Bangalore'. 5 May. http://www.thehindu.com/news/cities/bangalore/names-go-missing-from-electoral-rolls-in-bangalore/article4686157.ece. Accessed on 5 October 2017.

———. 2013b. 'Why Keep Political Parties, Essentially Public Bodies, Out of RTI Ambit?'. https://www.thehindu.com/news/national/why-keep-political-parties-essentially-public-bodies-out-of-rti-ambit/article5011024. ece. Accessed 7 November 2013.

———. 2016. 'Compulsory Voting Is Not Practical in India, Says Zaidi'. 20 October. http://www.thehindu.com/news/national/Compulsory-voting-is -not-practical-in-India-says-Zaidi/article16075931.ece. Accessed on 11 October 2017.

———. 2018. 'Arun Jaitly Bats for Electoral Bond Scheme'. 7 January. http:// www.thehindu.com/news/national/govt-open-to-proposals-to-further-cleanse-political-funding-arun-jaitley/article22391042.ece. Accessed on 18 April 2018.

———. 2019. 'History of EVMs'. 17 March. https://www.thehindu.com/news/cities/Thiruvananthapuram/history-of-evms/article26557304.ece. Accessed on 16 September 2021.

The Telegraph. 2016. 'Glare on EC Reforms Suggestions'. 8 January. https://www.telegraphindia.com/1160108/jsp/nation/story_62760.jsp#.WH8U-NJ96M8. Accessed on 19 January 2017.

———. 2017. 'Compulsory Vote Notice'. 24 January. https://www.telegraphindia.com/1170124/jsp/nation/story_132101.jsp. Accessed on 11 October 2017.

The Tribune. 2002. 'Not in the Right Spirit'. Chandigarh, 9 July. https://www.tribuneindia.com/2002/20020709/edit.htm#top. Accessed on 25 August 2021.

———. 2003. 'Landmark Judgement'. Chandigarh, 14 March. http://www.tribuneindia.com/2003/20030314/edit.htm#top. Accessed on 21 June 2017.

Times of India. 2002. 'Bill to Curb Criminalisation in Politics Passed'. 20 December. https://timesofindia.indiatimes.com/india/bill-to-curb-criminalisation-in-politics-passed/articleshow/31811084.cms. Accessed on 29 August 2022.

———. 2008. 'Names Missing from Electoral Rolls'. 30 November. http://timesofindia.indiatimes.com/home/specials/Names-missing-from-electoral-rolls/articleshow/3775048.cms. Accessed on 23 September 2017.

———. 2018. 'Limit Political Donations by Companies: Ex-Chief of Law Commission'. 31 July. https://timesofindia.indiatimes.com/india/limit-political-donations-by-companies-ex-chief-of-law-commission/articleshow/65205741.cms. Accessed on 26 June 2021.

Tolbert, Pamela S., and Lynne G. Zucker. 1996. 'Institutionalization of Institutional Theory'. In *Handbook of Organizational Studies*, edited by S. Clegg, C. Hardy and W. R. Nord, 175–90. London and Thousand Oaks: SAGE Publications.

Trelles, Alejandro, and Miguel Carreras. 2012. 'Bullets and Votes: Violence and Electoral Participation in Mexico'. *Journal of Politics in Latin America* 4(2): 89–123.

Tushman, Michael L., and Elaine Romanelli. 1985. 'Organizational Evolution: A Metamorphosis Model of Convergence and Reorientation'. In *Research in Organizational Behaviour*, edited by L. L. Cummings and B. M. Staw, 171–222. Greenwich, CT: JAI Press.

Upadhyaya, Anjoo Saran (ed.). 2005. *Electoral Reforms in India.* New Delhi: Concept Publishing Company.

Vaishnav, Milan. 2014. 'The Complicated Rise of India's Regional Parties'. Heinrich Boll Stiftung publication, 6 February. https://in.boell.org /2014/02/06/complicated-rise-indias-regional-parties. Accessed on 12 July 2016.

————. 2017. *When Crime Pays: Money and Muscle in Indian Politics*. Noida: HarperCollins Publishers India.

Varghese, Johnlee. 2014. '186 Members of Parliament Have Criminal Cases Including Murder and Rape'. *International Business Times*, 19 May. http:// www.ibtimes.co.in/186-indian-members-parliament-have-criminal-cases-including-murder-rape-600584. Accessed on 17 November 2016.

Varma, Pavan K. 2014. *The New Indian Middle Class*. Noida: HarperCollins Publishers.

Venkatesan, J. 2006. 'Understanding the Model Code'. *The Hindu*, 9.

————. 2013. 'Poll Papers Liable to Be Rejected for Blank Affidavit: Supreme Court'. *The Hindu*, 14 September. https://www.thehindu.com/news/national /poll-papers-liable-to-be-rejected-for-blank-affidavit-supreme-court/article 5125536.ece. Accessed on 1 November 2013.

Venkatesan, V. 2002a. 'The Voter's Right to Know'. *Frontline*, 8–21 June. http:// www.frontline.in/static/html/fl1912/19120340.htm. Accessed on 23 April 2017.

————. 2002b. 'Fighting Disclosure Norms'. *Frontline*, 20 July–2 August. http://www.frontline.in/navigation/?type=static&page=flonnet&rdurl =fl1915/19150250.htm. Accessed on 31 May 2017.

————. 2002c. 'Election Expenditure: Questions over Electoral Rolls'. *Frontline*, 16 February–1 March. http://www.frontline.in/static/html/fl1904/19040 970.htm. Accessed on 1 October 2017.

————. 2003. 'A Forceful Reiteration'. *Frontline*, 29 March–11 April. http:// www.frontline.in/static/html/fl2007/stories/20030411004203000.htm. Accessed on 21 June 2017.

Venu, M. K. 2013. 'Modi and the Numbers Game'. *The Hindu*, 12 June. https://www.thehindu.com/opinion/lead/modi-and-the-numbers-game/ article4804449.ece. Accessed on 5 November 2021.

Verma, Arvind. 2005. 'Policing Elections in India'. *India Review* 4(3–4) (July–October): 354–76.

Verma, Gyan and Elizabeth Roche. 2014. 'Existing Laws Sufficient to Curb Hate Speech: Supreme Court'. *Mint*, 12 March. https://www.livemint.com/ Politics/j65K3t2agISofDMajWEBbI/SC-asks-Law-Commission-to-look-into-issue-of-hate-speeches.html. Accessed on 25 March 2021.

Verma, S. K., and Kusum (eds.). 2003 (2000). *Fifty Years of the Supreme Court of India: Its Grasp and Reach*. New Delhi: Oxford University Press.

Virmani, Arvind. 2004. 'Election 2004: A Different Explanation'. *Economic and Political Weekly* 39(25) (19 June): 2565–67.

Waghmode, Vishwas. 2017. 'Mumbai University Tells College to Hold Voter Awareness Drive'. *Indian Express*, 5 January. http://indianexpress.com/article/education/mumbai-university-tells-colleges-to-hold-voter-awareness-drive-4459336. Accessed on 6 October 2017.

Weintraub, Ellen L., and Samuel C. Brown. 2012. 'Following the Money: Campaign Finance Disclosure in India and the United States'. *Election Law Journal* 11(2): 241–66.

Wilkinson, Steven I. 2005 (2004). *Votes and Violence: Electoral Competition and Communal Riots in India*. Cambridge, UK: Cambridge University Press.

Witsoe, Jeffrey. 2013. *Democracy against Development: Lower-Caste Politics and Political Modernity in Postcolonial India*. Chicago: University of Chicago Press.

Yadav, Yogendra. 1996. 'Reconfiguration in Indian Politics: State Assembly Elections, 1993–95'. *Economic and Political Weekly* 31(2–3) (13–20 January): 95–104.

———. 1999. 'Electoral Politics in the Time of Change: India's Third Electoral System, 1989–1999'. *Economic and Political Weekly* 34 (34–35) (21–28 August): 2393–99.

———. 2000. 'Understanding the Second Democratic Upsurge: Trends of Bahujan Participation in Electoral Politics in the 1990s'. In *Transforming India: Social and Political Dynamics of Democracy*, edited by Francine R. Frankel, Zoya Hasan, Rajeev Bhargava and Balveer Arora, 120–45. New Delhi: Oxford University Press.

———. 2001. 'A Radical Agenda for Political Reforms'. *Seminar* 506 (October). http://www.india-seminar.com/semframe.html. Accessed on 8 September 2016.

———. 2004. 'The Elusive Mandate of 2004'. *Economic and Political Weekly* 39(51) (18 December): 5383–95.

———. 2005. 'Election Reforms: Beyond Middle Class Fantasies'. In *Electoral Reforms in India*, edited by Anjoo Sharan Upadhyaya, 29–63. New Delhi: Concept Publishing Company.

———. 2015 (2000). 'Understanding the Second Democratic Upsurge: Trends of Bahujan Participation in Electoral Politics in the 1990s'. In *Transforming India: Social and Political Dynamics of Democracy*, edited by Francine R.

Frankel, Zoya Hasan, Rajeeva Bhargava and Balveer Arora, 120–45. Delhi: Oxford University Press.

————. 2017. 'The Devil Is in the Fine Print'. *The Hindu*, 15 February. http://www. thehindu.com/opinion/lead/The-devil-is-in-the-fine-print/article17308089. ece. Accessed on 12 March 2018.

————. 2019. 'This Election, the EC Has Failed the Litmus Test of Appearing to Be Fair: Yogendra Yadav'. *The Print*, 18 April. https://theprint.in/opinion/ this-election-ec-has-failed-the-litmus-test-of-appearing-to-be-fair-yogendra -yadav/223106. Accessed on 9 September 2022.

Yadav, Yogendra, and Suhas Palshikar. 2006. *Party System and Electoral Politics in the Indian States, 1952–2002: From Hegemony to Convergence. In India's Political Parties*, edited by Peter Ronald deSouza and Eswaran Sridharan, 73–115. New Delhi, Thousand Oaks and London: SAGE Publications.

Yuda, Masayuki. 2017. 'How Does Japan Fund Election Campaigns?'. *Nikkei Asia*, 11 October. https://asia.nikkei.com/Business/Finance/How-does-Japan -fund-election-campaigns. Accessed on 8 September 2021.

Zehra, Rosheena. 2017. 'Print Media Is Still Thriving in India and Here Is Why'. *The Quint*, 25 May. https://www.thequint.com/news/india/rise-of-print- media-in-india#read-more. Accessed on 14 September 2022.

Ziegfeld, Adam. 2012. 'Coalition Government and Party System Change: Explaining the Rise of Regional Political Parties in India'. *Comparative Politics* 45(1) (October): 69–87.

————. 2016. *Why Regional Parties? Clientelism, Elites, and the Indian Party System*. New York: Cambridge University Press.

Zucker, Lynne G. 1987. 'Institutional Theories of Organization'. *Annual Review of Sociology* 13(1987): 443–64.

Index